**Annie Rankin** was born in Edinburgh and was educated at Godolphin and Latymer, Hammersmith. She studied English at Manchester College, Oxford, and history of art at the V&A and the Riccardi Institute. Her enthusiasm for travel has frequently taken her abroad, on long trips in Asia and Africa, and visits to Albania, Mexico, Israel, Turkey, Hawaii, and throughout Europe. She has worked at The Daily Telegraph, IPC Magazines and as a freelance feature writer. She currently works for The Sunday Times as a sub-editor.

**Karen Taylor** was born in Epsom and educated at Lady Eleanor Holles, Hampton. She studied French at Lausanne University and later graduated from Manchester College, Oxford with a degree in English. She worked in public relations for three years before becoming a journalist, contributing to various national newspapers and women's magazines. She lived and worked in Geneva and New York, and her travels include visits to India, Africa, the West Indies and throughout Europe. She currently works as a freelance journalist and an outplacement consultant.

# Acknowledgements

Firstly, we greatly appreciated the efficiency, patience and help, from start to finish, of the Barcelona Tourist Board. In particular, we could not have coped without Ramiro Pastor and Mònica Terol.

We are indebted to Michael John Holloway at the British Consulate for sharing his secrets, giving us his time, and for offering us so many contacts. We also thank our friends at TV3, Gil Toll and Jordi Fortuny for responding to ceaseless interrogation. Jorge Marin, Rafael Santos Torroella and Albert Padrol, with their keen insights, all threw fresh light on our research.

Also helpful was the Barcelona Ajuntament, and our thanks go to Montserrat Roig-Serra, Ramon Viladomat and Lluís Hortet. Likewise the Ajuntament of Girona — Francesc Francisco and Miguel Fañanàs — deserve a special mention for a personal guided tour of the city and their entertaining company.

Our understanding of Spanish cooking was enhanced by the boundless hospitality of Porfirio, Pilar and Angelo, not to mention their warm welcome, sense of humour and support. Never to be forgotten are our neighbours Pepe and Domingo who showed us the wilder side of the city; and who, with Esteban, Doci, and all at the Antiquari and Meson del Café, made our time off as informative as it was fun. We also appreciated great tips from Annabel, Mark and Stephen.

Large thank yous go to Cavan and Helen Taylor and Alick Rankin for their crucial support. Further thanks to Charles McGrigor and Sue Rankin for their patience and artistic advice, to Adam Gardner for strategic guidance, and Sean Taylor for his football contribution. Also to Roger Lascelles and Bryn Thomas for taking up the idea, and Marcella Randall for her editing. The Barcelona city map was kindly supplied by the Barcelona Tourist Board. In particular our thanks go to Jordi Baulies and Maria José Ania Lafuente.

Finally, and most emphatically, our thanks go to Emma-Louise Ogilvy for producing the excellent photography in no time at all.

# A Request

The authors and publisher have tried to ensure that this guide is as accurate and up-to-date as possible. Inevitably things change, hotels and restaurants open and close and prices go up and down. If you notice any changes that should be included in the next edition of this book, please write to Annie Rankin and Karen Taylor c/o the publisher (address on title page). A free copy of the new edition will be sent to persons making a significant contribution.

*Lascelles City Guides*

# BARCELONA
## AND BEYOND

Annie Rankin & Karen Taylor

Photographs by
Emma-Louise Ogilvy

**Roger Lascelles,** Cartographic and Travel Publisher
47 York Road, Brentford, Middlesex TW8 0QP.   Tel: 081 847 0935

# Publication Data

| | |
|---|---|
| **Title** | Barcelona and Beyond |
| **Typeface** | Phototypeset in Compugraphic Times |
| **Photographs** | Emma-Louise Ogilvy |
| **Printing** | Kelso Graphics, Kelso, Scotland. |
| **ISBN** | 0 903909 85 5 |
| **Edition** | First Jul 1990, Second Nov 1991 |
| **Publisher** | Roger Lascelles |
| | 47 York Road, Brentford, Middlesex, TW8 0QP. |
| **Copyright** | Annie Rankin and Karen Taylor (Text) |
| | Emma-Louise Ogilvy (Photographs) |

# Distribution

| | | |
|---|---|---|
| **Africa:** | South Africa — | Faradawn, Box 17161, Hillbrow 2038 |
| **Americas:** | Canada — | International Travel Maps & Books, P.O. Box 2290, Vancouver BC V6B 3W5 |
| | U.S.A. — | Available through major booksellers with good foreign travel sections |
| **Asia:** | India — | English Book Store, 17-L Connaught Circus, P.O. Box 328, New Delhi 110 001 |
| **Australasia:** | Australia — | Rex Publications, 15 Huntingdon Street, Crows Nest, N.S.W. |
| **Europe:** | Belgium — | Brussels - Peuples et Continents |
| | Germany — | Available through major booksellers with good foreign travel sections |
| | GB/Ireland — | Available through all booksellers with good foreign travel sections |
| | Italy — | Libreria dell'Automobile, Milano |
| | Netherlands — | Nilsson & Lamm BV, Weesp |
| | Denmark — | Copenhagen - Arnold Busck, G.E.C. Gad, Boghallen |
| | Finland — | Helsinki — Akateeminen Kirjakauppa |
| | Norway — | Oslo - Arne Gimnes/J.G. Tanum |
| | Sweden — | Stockholm/Esselte, Akademi Bokhandel, Fritzes, Hedengrens Gothenburg/Gumperts, Esselte Lund/Gleerupska |
| | Switzerland — | Basel/Bider: Berne/Atlas; Geneve/Artou; Lausanne/Artou; Zurich/Travel Bookshop |

# Contents

## Introduction

## Part I: Background

### 1 Catalunya and the Catalans

## Part II: Preparations

### 2 Planning Your Trip

## Part III: In Barcelona

### 3 Arrival, Departure and Getting Around

### 4 Accommodation

# Part IV: Around Catalunya

# Appendices

# Index

# Introduction

Barcelona is just hitting the Big Time. It may have been a major port since the Romans arrived, but the '80s have seen it emerge as a top travel destination. This is as much due to post-Franco blossoming as to its Olympic nomination. And justifiably so; strikingly diverse, it is beautiful but not prim, exciting yet laid-back. Whether you're seeking beachlife, ancient or modern culture, gluttonous feasts or uninhibited nightlife, it's all within your grasp.

As Catalunya's capital and Spain's second city, Barcelona is at the leading edge of Spanish growth. And with all the advantages of a Mediterranean shore, it has long rivalled Madrid — at least this is what the fervent Catalan nationalists claim. For Catalans speak their own language, and cultivate a personality quite distinct from other Spaniards. And they won't let you forget how they once commanded a Mediterranean empire.

Although inhabiting the hardest working corner of Spain, locals retain an infectious *joie de vivre,* as well as the characteristic Spanish hospitality. Living life to the full, they set greater store by the *fiesta* than the *siesta.* And you'll find spontaneity more prevalent than clockwatching. The climate makes for a bustling streetlife, where pastry smells jostle with the stenches from drains, and a lottery seller hovers on every corner.

The city's core is a muddle of alleys, rich with Gothic monuments and ancient remains, and often enlivened by street musicians. Wide avenues uptown reveal a different aspect — the prosperous commercial centre with its flamboyant architecture and Gaudí's outrageous creations. And many other artists have been inspired by this city, most famously Picasso and Miró.

Even a fleeting visitor's lasting impression must be of an electric city. And this is one which can be enjoyed all year round. What you won't find here is peace, but this can be found just a short distance away in the country villages and mountains.

**Note** You'll find most street names and maps are written in Catalan not Castilian (what most people call Spanish), and we have stuck to this as closely as possible throughout the book.

ONE

# Catalunya and the Catalans

## The People

Strong in the Catalan make-up is an intense national pride which, you are constantly reminded, unites the province, for they believe they are quite distinct from other Spaniards. Catalans are the most pragmatic of Spaniards, with an indomitable spirit which prevails regardless of the central regime. The prosperity of their province has shaped their reputation as an industrious race with a sharp business sense, who are adept at transforming opportunities to gold. And who, compared to their southern counterparts, see money as a burning incentive. It may even be that the lack of political power (for which they have so long fought) has spurred their commercial endeavours and resulting success.

Facing the Mediterranean, in Spain's north-east corner, and open to the rest of Europe, Catalunya is perfectly sited to absorb foreign ideas; and the French influence in particular, continues to creep over the border. The sheer breadth of world suggestion it embraces is apparent everywhere — in the arts, buildings, food and people.

Catalan society puts more emphasis on the intellectual than other Spanish regions. Historically the province has taken its lead not from Spain's capital, but from other European cities — in part the result of Madrid's lack of traditional culture. French culture has had a profound influence, especially in the fields of painting and literature. (And Catalan artists have always swarmed to Paris for their inspiration.)

Catalans welcome progress, and both the industrial and technological revolutions entered Spain via their province. Known as the most European of Spanish cities, Barcelona immediately strikes you as an experimentation ground. It is here that new trends set foot, enjoy a receptive climate and take root. Combine this with a liberated and democratic spirit (unleashed since Franco's grip), and the impression is that anything goes.

On the whole less extrovert than many Spaniards, Catalans can be cool at first; but the old adage of 'once a friend, always a friend', holds true. Altogether more serious, typically a Catalan is less inclined to exaggerate, or is more reticent and dull — depending which way you look at it. This is not to say that he lacks humour or a sense of fun; his lifestyle is lively, and his capital the most gregarious city on the peninsula.

The local character is usually presented as a mixture of two opposing facets: *seny* which roughly translates as a blend of commonsense and determination, and *rauxa,* wild eccentricity with elements of lunacy, flair and spontaneity. (Some would say Miró embodied the former, Dalí and Gaudí the latter.)

Like most southern Europeans, Catalans have a highly developed aesthetic sense. They feel that everything — from themselves and their buildings, to their balconies, gutters and pavements — should appear attractive. Perhaps this goes hand in hand with the Catholics' love of ornament who, unlike many Protestants, do not view decoration as mere indulgence.

One thing you can't miss in Barcelona is sex. Advertised blatantly in the street, on the newstands and even performed on stage, sex is a regular feature of everyday life. That the prostitutes and transvestites should share Barcelona's main street, the Rambles, is symptomatic of this blasé climate. And more surprising than a woman removing her shirt in the Rambles, is that it's hard to find anyone looking shocked.

Yet compare this scene, where topless sunbathing is standard, to the previous one which so recently saw Franco and the Catholic Church hand in hand, and keeping sex down. Just two decades ago holding hands with your lover was considered an outrage, and the censorious Church flinched at any glimpse of naked flesh on film. With the return of democracy, contraception was legalised and Barcelona now very evidently rolls around in her new found freedom.

Feminism appears less advanced than in many European countries. It's rare to see women out for an evening together, while your macho, mustachioed 'Latin lover' still loiters at every bar. Compared to the rest of the country, however, women are better off in Catalunya, and increasingly taking up higher career positions.

Due to ancient land laws, the division of property here has differed from the rest of Spain. The system of primogeniture (leaving land to the first male heir, not repeatedly dividing it) has kept properties intact and farming prosperous. Throughout the province the standard of living is high, and unemployment remains lower than in the rest of Spain. Likewise the quality of life is good, with the sea, mountains, good climate and fertile soil which produces plentiful fresh fruit and vegetables.

It is hardly surprising that so many immigrants flocked to this thriving region in search of a job. The steepest population rises have been this century, a by-product of the rapid industrialisation which has lured workers from throughout Spain. The earliest were mainly Aragonese and Murcians, particularly during the 1920s (when labourers were needed to construct Barcelona's metro and the buildings for the 1929 Universal Exhibition). Since the Civil War vast numbers have come from Andalusia who are not only the most contrasting in temperament but are now by far the biggest group. Less easy to absorb into society than former waves, they are often resented for not only taking local jobs but eroding the culture and language.

---

**Joking Apart**

Jokes are often a sharp indication of local feeling and a popular one goes like this...

Travelling in the same train carriage were a Catalan, an Irishman, a Valèncian and an Andalusian. The Irishman took from his bag a bottle of whisky, gulped back two thirds of it, and threw the rest through the open window. When the Catalan exclaimed at the waste, the Irishman shrugged — "In my country there's no shortage of whisky."

The Valèncian then drew from his case a bag of oranges, which, after sucking at a few and picking the sweetest parts, he chucked through the window. Again the Catalan protested at the waste, and the reply came, "Where I come from there's no shortage of oranges". And so the Catalan solemnly turned to the Andalusian, picked him up and hurled him through the open window.

---

# Geography

Roughly triangular, Catalunya adds up to about 32,000 square kilometres (approximately the same size as Holland or Belgium). The land is divided into four provinces: Barcelona, Girona, Lleida and Tarragona, and each one is further split into *comarques*. These 41 self-contained units are similar to counties and invariably have a deep-rooted sense of individuality, evident in their active customs.

Barcelona is the capital of Catalunya and, after Hong Kong and Bombay, is the world's third most densely populated city. Of this region's six million inhabitants, three and a half million live in Barcelona and its surrounding areas. The lucrative coastline, which extends for about 580 kilometres, is well-trodden, particularly by foreigners. Catalunya's shores, which comprise three costas, are often misnamed: north of Barcelona, the Costa del Maresme runs as far as Blanes; and from here the Costa Brava (wild coast) heads up to France. With Tarragona as its lead city, the Costa Daurada (golden coast) stretches to the south.

For those on a costa beeline, Catalunya's enviable geographical diversity is all too easy to bypass. Here lie four mountain ranges: the Pyrenees, the Transversal, the Prelitoral (which includes Montserrat and Montseny), and the coastal range running south of Tarragona. Although streaked with rivers, there are few lakes; the largest, and an Olympic site, is Lake Banyoles in the province of Girona. Flowing east into the sea are the rivers Ter, Fluvià, Tordera, Besòs, Llobregat, and Francolí while many other tributaries of the Ebre flow west.

The varying altitude naturally dictates climatic differences, but Catalunya generally enjoys gentle Mediterranean weather. Sitting in a basin enclosed by mountains, summer sees the city uncomfortably humid. Although renowned as an active port, there is little evidence of citizens identifying with their coastal location, as, for well over a century, they have turned their backs to the water. There may be a harbour at the bottom of the Rambles, but in many ways the city seems to have sealed itself from the Mediterranean; sea breezes and the sound of gulls are noticeable by their absence. But the redevelopment of the east end will no doubt breathe new life into the metropolis.

# History

Typically a summary of Catalan history from a keen patriot will dwell only on its high points: firstly Catalunya's (especially Tarragona's) Roman greatness, then a long jump to the development of the Catalan Empire around the Mediterranean in the thirteenth and fourteenth centuries. A quantum leap is next made to the Renaixença (Renaissance) in the mid-nineteenth century, when Catalans began to revive their dented morale and dust off their neglected language and culture. Finally, glossing over their repression under Franco, the story will end with their continuing commercial successes, thriving independence and language, and the securing of the Olympic Games.

As much as these peaks, it has been the troughs which have coloured Catalunya's past as it has struggled at various times for survival and national recognition. Located in Spain's north-east corner, shouldering southern France along the Pyrenees, such wide access to the Mediterranean has afforded her numerous opportunities. And it was this position that attracted the Romans, making Catalunya the foremost Roman region of the Iberian peninsula.

Having established themselves at Empúries (the old Greek settlement of Emporion), the Romans spread south to Barcelona and Tarragona. Tarraco (as it was then known) became the golden Roman capital in the second century BC, favoured by the Emperors Hadrian and Augustus. There are endless relics of this era, some marvellously preserved; and throughout the province current archaeological work proves just how rich and diverse Catalan history is.

Catalans are staunchly proud of this ancient heritage, no doubt partly to gloat over their rivals in Madrid — a city created from nothing in the country's barren centre during the eighteenth century. In Barcelona you will sometimes hear Madrid referred to as 'The Doughnut'. This, they explain, is because Spain's centre is nothing but a gaping hole.

After the decline of the Roman Empire, the Visigoths moved in upon Catalunya, establishing a kingdom which lasted until the eighth century. Next came the period of Moorish domination, during which Catalunya was a constant battleground. For although the Arab influence at one time reached beyond the Pyrenees to Poitiers, Charlemagne pushed them back south, relieving the north of Catalunya, and letting their frontier slice through the province. The later Moorish attempt to regain lost land led to the destruction of Barcelona in 985.

Three years later the Count of Barcelona proclaimed Catalunya's

---

### A Gory Story

Four red stripes on a yellow base comprise the Senyera, or Catalan national flag. Officially dating from 1082, and flown at every opportunity, this national symbol is Europe's oldest flag and, indeed, one of the oldest in the world.

One legend tells how its bold design came out of the war wounds of Wilfred the Hairy (the Count who established the House of Barcelona in 878). As Wilfred lay bleeding, after fighting alongside Charles the Bald in Paris, Charles smothered his hands in his ally's blood. And next, as a mark of honour, he smeared his fingers across Wilfred's gold shield, thereby designing the blueprint.

sovereignty, and 988 is now regarded as the moment of the country's political birth. During the next couple of centuries the leading power became the church. This power was centred around the numerous Romanesque monasteries founded after the territory had been won back by the Christians from the Moors. And the nearest Catalunya came to achieving royal status was in 1137 through the marriage of Count Ramon Berenguer IV of Barcelona to Petronila of Aragon, by which stroke the Count took the title of King of Aragon.

Catalunya's heyday as a significant European power arrived with the reign of Jaume or James I (1213-76). Catalan merchants had built up an extensive trade network throughout the Mediterranean to Italy, north Africa and the East, which brought increasing prosperity to the whole country. Gradually this commercial importance led to territorial gains until, at its height in the early fourteenth century, the Catalan-Aragonese Empire spanned the Mediterranean basin to include parts of Greece and Italy, and the islands of Sicily, Corsica, Sardinia and the Balearics. On the mainland her domains crossed the Pyrenees and spread south to incorporate València.

But this glory was shortlived, and Catalunya's field of influence receded sharply. The rot set in with the Black Death in 1348 which killed off one third of the population. Later, this was indirectly assisted by the rise of the Ottoman Empire (Constantinople fell to the Turks in 1453) and, closer to home, by the joining of the crowns of Aragon and Castile with the marriage of Ferdinand and Isabella in 1469. Although at first each kingdom kept its own government, this heralded the start of a united Spain.

The final nail in Catalunya's imperial coffin was Columbus's return in 1492 from discovering the New World (the same year that Granada was won from the Moors by Castile). This shifted the trading focus away from the Mediterranean to the Atlantic, leaving the Catalans out of the many financial rewards reaped by Cádiz, Seville and what would later be Portugal. The loss of the gold trade at this time was a further blow, and from then on Catalunya's independence was slowly strangled, her trading sphere severely limited.

During the next century the absolutist powers of Castile became so demanding on regional troops and revenue, that eventually the Catalans revolted in the War of the Reapers or Segadors (1640-52). Their song *Els Segadors* was later adopted as the national anthem (see box page 105.) They declared Catalunya a republic and asked for the protection of the French King Louis XIII. Yet when

Barcelona was forced into submission in 1652, Castilian deals with the French led to the final loss of the Catalan-speaking regions beyond the Pyrenees (Rosselló and Cerdanya) to the French crown.

This was swiftly followed by the Spanish War of Succession (1700-14) which hinged on who should succeed Charles II. In this the Catalans, like Austria, England and Holland, backed Archduke Charles of Austria against the Spanish and French choice of the Bourbon Philip of Anjou. In 1705 they proclaimed Charles King of the Catalans in Barcelona; and so adamant was their stand that even after Felipe or Philip V had been internationally accepted, the Catalans alone continued to resist him.

Without foreign aid, and outnumbered four to one, they fought valiantly to defend Barcelona. But after laying seige for over a year, Spanish troops stormed the city and forced their surrender on 11 September 1714. (This tragic date is still remembered with a Catalan National holiday.) By this stroke Catalunya lost her sovereignity to the Spanish crown, while her language and laws were banned. And for the next hundred years Catalunya lay low, very much under the domination of the centralist state.

The latter half of the eighteenth century saw a gradual increase in population and prosperity, however, and set the province back on its feet ready to exploit industrialisation. By this time it was said that Catalunya brought in more revenue to the Spanish crown than the whole of the Americas. The textile business, for instance, which for many years was the most important industry in Spain, was concentrated in Catalunya.

Around the mid-nineteenth century the language underwent a revival (see below) which sparked further literary activity, and at the same time the Catalan legal system was given official recognition. The return to prosperity also coincided with the expansion of Barcelona, with its massive new building incentives (see Modernismo, chapter 7). All of these factors came together in what is known as the Renaixença or Renaissance.

This period saw the blossoming of Catalan culture, and Romanticism trickled across the Pyrenees, shown particularly in painting and literature. Catalan soon became the fashionable language to write in, and the traditional literary celebration, the Jocs Florals (Floral Games), was reinstated as an annual event. Poetry grew in popularity, and such writers as Verdaguer and Guimerà became famous beyond Catalunya and had many works translated.

After a brief revolutionary period, the restoration of the Spanish king, Alfonso XII (1874-85) brought peace and industrial success. On the back of an economic boom Barcelona staged the

International Exhibition in 1888 in jubilant mood; Catalunya was riding high.

Crisis in Spain arose just ten years later with the loss of her overseas empire. This turned Spanish focus inwards, and the Catalans began boosting all things Catalan. But it also led to rifts, with many people demanding independence and political freedom. This Catalan Movement split into two divisions: those favouring an independent, cultural Catalunya were spearheaded by Lluís Domènech i Montaner (the famous Modernista architect). The younger, political revolutionary group was led by Francesc Cambó and Enric Prat de la Riba, who founded the first Catalan party in 1901.

Revolutionary agitation and anarchy took root in Barcelona in the early years of this century. This reached a climax of protest in what is known as 'setmana tràgica' (tragic week) in July 1909. Bombs were hurled and churches burned in outrage at conscription for the war in Morocco. Yet this rebellion was confined to a small group, and in the meantime it was a period of great productivity for Modernista architects and artists.

In 1914 political unity established itself in the Mancomunitat, which was the first regional government for two hundred years. Its Presidents, Prat de la Riba and Puig i Cadafalch (another politically active architect), brought Catalunya stability and progress until 1923. And during this time Spain, having kept out of the First World War, took advantage of the situation to boost her exports to the warring countries.

However, a coup in 1923 by General Primo de Rivera brought in a military dictatorship which lasted until 1930. And these years saw a slump in prosperity, with the recovery around 1929's Universal Exhibition being all too fleeting. The following year, municipal elections hounded out Alfonso XIII for his support of Primo's dictatorship. After the King's exile, Francesc Macià proclaimed the Republic of Catalunya. Her political identity was approved in 1932 by the Spanish parliament, and the Catalan government, or Generalitat, was restored.

Hardly had this swung into action, when the Civil War (1936-9) broke out, and in this the vast majority of Catalans supported the Republicans. The whole province fared terribly during this bloody period, and Barcelona in particular suffered great violence. Franco's victory inevitably led to fierce recriminations: Catalan language and culture were severely repressed, local institutions banned, the Generalitat abolished, and its President, Lluís Companys, executed by firing squad.

During the war and the early Franco years, over one hundred thousand Catalans had fled to other countries. Yet Catalunya, as a significant province straining at the leash, was a prime target for Franco's strictures. And he made every effort to limit her individual development, while building up the economic base in Madrid. Writers, actors and artists all suffered strong censorship, even priests speaking Catalan during mass were reported.

Before his death in 1975, Franco cunningly chose his successor — King Juan Carlos I, son of the Count of Barcelona, and grandson of Alfonso XIII. Spain welcomed a return to monarchy, albeit a tamed sovereign, and the transition to democracy has brought with it new hope and a rapid rebuilding of the country.

The charm of old Barcelona; a local collects water from spouting gargoyles.

## Catalunya Today

It appears that Spain has thrived on the continuity of a Socialist national government during the '80s. Nevertheless Catalunya has its own autonomous government which takes a different political standpoint (centre right). This, the Generalitat, has existed as an entity since the Middle Ages.

Headed by the President, the latest agreement, re-established in 1977, allows Catalans a certain amount of self government and responsibility in varying degrees for health and social welfare, the arts, agriculture, transport and tourism. Since so many areas need mutual co-operation, agreements are often difficult to reach. The main power it lacks, and one that is hotly contested due to ambiguous wording in the original charter, is management of the economy.

Occupying little over six per cent of Spanish land, Catalunya is now home to almost 17 per cent of the population of Spain (35 million people). Yet their tremendous level of productivity reaps near one fifth of the gross domestic product. This is the primary sticking point for Catalans, and one that visitors are ceaselessly reminded of. They firmly believe that the rest of Spain drags them back from greater things and feel resentful that this hard earned cash is swiftly whisked away to feed the 'lazy' peasant farmers of the south. They have little conception of patriotism towards Spain, although degrees of Catalan nationalistic fervour vary wildly. Many are becoming inspired by the prospect of 1992, dampening the arguments for independence at a time when Europe is moving towards greater unity.

Barcelona's active port and the accessibility of Europe, Africa and the Near East has made, and continues to make, this a fertile trading ground. Concentrated in Barcelona, but also around Girona and Tarragona, are some of Spain's most intensely industrial zones. Top of the manufacturing league are metals, chemicals, and textiles; among the main exports are cars, books, cement and processed food.

Strong agriculture is promoted by the varied landscape with its core crops of wheat, rice, fodder, vegetables, olives and fruit. Local wines and *cavas* (Catalan champagne) are comparatively cheap, and their heartland lies in the Penedès region south-west of Barcelona. A symptom of this prosperity — Barcelona produces over 40 per cent of Spain's books and almost a quarter of her cars — are the annual trade fairs which bring a regular influx to the city; visitors will feel the impact in higher hotel bills (if they can find a bed).

The other prime source of revenue is tourism which concentrates on the ski slopes and on the beach. One of the most significant international steps taken by Franco's Minister for Tourism in the late '60s was the opening up of Spain to foreigners, by actively inviting tourists and building the national network of *Paradors* (see Part IV). This not only brought incalculable financial rewards, but coincided with the start of her long climb out of the league of 'backward' countries. Catalunya was quick to shake off this image and seize the new opportunity to develop her coastline. Finally Spain joined the European Community in 1986 and into which she will be fully integrated in 1992.

## Jewish Roots

Jews have traditionally had a strong presence in the province, and at times when they were persecuted elsewhere, Catalunya promised a tolerant climate. Traces of close-knit Jewish communities date from the tenth and eleventh centuries, but it was during the mid-twelfth century that they formed an official relationship with Ramon Berenguer IV. After 1149, the settlements in Lleida and Tortosa (and later Barcelona) became known as aljamas, which operated as autonomous units.

From the thirteenth to mid-fourteenth centuries, having been exiled from other parts of Europe, these communities swelled rapidly. And as Jews gathered in all the Catalan towns, their cultural presence grew strong; many were employed as money lenders, doctors and in cottage industries. Although their architectural legacy was slight, they profoundly influenced medicine and boosted the circulation of currency. Soon the smaller communities sought equivalent status to those in the cities, and over 20 *aljamas* were eventually set up. Each had a synagogue, rabbi, cemetery, baker, butcher and ritual bath (mikveh).

With the Black Death and the recession from the mid-fourteenth century, the climate changed and these communities began to wane. In 1391 there were popular outcries against the Jews who were forced to choose between conversion or death. The settlement in Barcelona dissolved and others decreased, and in 1492 all were finally banished by the 'Catholic Kings', Ferdinand and Isabella.

The most important community was in Barcelona, followed by Girona. The former had two sections, the earliest *(Call Major)* existed from the twelfth century until 1391 in the old Roman city. Its major street was Sant Domenec del Call, and in which the synagogue was located at today's number seven. The community stretched around the surrounding streets of Sant Honorat, Arc de Sant Ramon del Call, Sant Sever, Fruita, Marlet. The second, Call Menor, grew from 1257 outside Barcelona's city wall. (See North from Barcelona, Chapter 11).

## The Language

The prime potential difficulty for visitors is being confronted with two quite distinct languages: Catalan and Castilian (otherwise known as Spanish). Since comparatively few foreigners speak Catalan, you are likely to be addressed in Spanish, but the adamant preference for Catalan makes a few key words well advised and guarantees extra respect. In general, the Catalans are gifted at languages, and you'll find many people speak English or French. Everyday areas where you will certainly come across Catalan are on street signs, and often on menus.

Like Spanish, Italian and French, Catalan is a Romance language which evolved from Latin, and the Roman occupation. Aside from Catalunya, it is also spoken in València, the Balearic Islands, Andorra, and in parts of Aragón, southern France and Sardinia. Variations in dialect apart, today it is the language of an estimated six million people.

One of the more revealing insights into the Catalan character is the progress of their language. Sporadically quashed by attempts to destroy Catalunya's individuality, its persistence signifies the quest for a strong national identity. The language matured around the tenth and eleventh centuries, although was no doubt born hundreds of years earlier, since which time it has survived several vicious shots at eradication. Notable attempts include Felipe V's eighteenth-century ploy to make Spanish spoken throughout the Catalan-speaking regions, and equally ferocious suppression under Franco. Its public use was banned, books were burnt and towns re-christened in Castilian.

With the return of democracy, this clandestine language began to revive. Today the Generalitat is determinedly pushing Catalan, particularly in schools, public administration and the media. But the influx of immigrants this century has done much to dilute the language. Recent figures, published by the Information and Documentation Consortium of Catalunya, show that although 90.4 per cent of Catalunya's residents understand Catalan, only 31.5 per cent can write it.

## Fiestas and Festivals

Along with the *siesta,* the Spanish custom of *fiestas* is as well loved as it is well known. With the combination of historical events, traditional holidays, pagan feast days and numerous saints days, Spaniards never lack an excuse for celebration. The manner of revelry may differ around the country, but Catalunya relishes her regional and national festivals. Perhaps surprising to foreigners is the expectation of locals that fiestas are their right, an entertainment which should be freely provided. And indeed most are generously funded by the town council.

Some examples are listed below, but for a full listing see A—Z of Information, chapter 10.

**January 5/6:** On the final night of Epiphany 5th is the **Fiesta del Reis** — a colourful parade around the city centre by night. On the 6th, everything is closed.

**February 12: The Feast of Santa Eulalia** (one of Barcelona's patron saints). Lasting about a week, this is mainly a musical celebration, with many concerts and Gregorian songs.

**February/March: Carnaval** is held the week leading up to Lent, and reaches a climax on the eve of Ash Wednesday. A deep-rooted traditional event in Barcelona, this was forbidden during the Franco regime, and has since been revived with a vengeance. Bedecked in masks and exotic costumes, people overrun the streets, and there is plentiful public entertainment.

More important than in Barcelona are the Carnavals held in Sitges and Vilanova, both of which were so well established that Franco had to allow them. Lavish street parties with abundant food and drink are held, and each town is ablaze with bunting and music. A curious custom in Vilanova is 'the war of sweets'; sherbets and caramels are hurled through the air and the central square becomes ankle-deep in confectionery.

**Easter:** Good Friday is confined to solemn, low key religious celebrations (everything is closed). Throughout Corpus Christi week Barcelona's Cathedral cloister is decorated with broom and cherries. One unusual custom on Easter day is known as *L'Ou com Balla* (Dance of the Egg). Here an empty egg shell is placed in the centre of the font, where it bounces and bobs on the spouting water, often high on the fountain's jet.

The Catalan fondness for sweets is especially evident around Easter when, as well as eggs, elaborate chocolate sculptures, often of famous personalities or politicians are sold all over the city. The Dance of Death is one of the most macabre Holy Week ceremonies and occurs in Verges in Empordà. Dressed as skeletons, people re-enact the fourteenth-century dance of death that was customary during the plague. Its blatant message for spectators is to remember how short life is.

**April 23: Feast of Sant Jordi** (Saint George's Day). You cannot stay in Barcelona long before encountering this legendary figure, and judging by the number of his replicas, it would seem Catalans are almost obsessional about him. Predictably this festival is widely marked, and the exchange of red roses and books, symbolising love and culture, is said to represent the dual aims of the Catalan nation.

**June 23: Verbena de Sant Joan** (Eve of Saint John's Day). This is a big night in Barcelona (and throughout Calatunya) when bonfires are lit in the streets. In the city, the focus is on Montjuïc where a huge fireworks display is held, and musical events keep revellers up most of the night. This is also time to drink *cava* and eat *cocas,* special cakes made to celebrate the event.

---

### Festive Frolics

Spaniards may laugh at the British for going crackers and donning paper hats at Christmas, but they too are a race with curious customs. These telly lovers spend New Year's Eve glued to their screens, for the most terrible luck will befall them should they fail to eat one grape on each stoke of midnight. So revered is this custom that many bars and clubs hand out little bags of twelve grapes to every reveller.

For children, a piece of tree trunk is traditionally kept in the living room, covered with a blanket and regularly fed and watered (with grown ups surreptitiously removing the offerings). On Christmas eve, while the child is beside the tree, singing for its supper — or at least some presents — the family sneak gifts beneath the blanket. After the trunk has been duly tapped, the gifts are magically revealed, and hence the Spanish interpretation of the yule log.

---

**August:** During the third week of August a festival is held in Gràcia and this is a must should you coincide with it. Selected streets are cut off from traffic, variously decorated and dedicated to eating, drinking and dancing. Throughout the week, a riotous atmosphere prevails, created by locals of all ages. It is easy to wander around, as Gràcia is so self-contained, and action naturally leads from one square to the next. A specifically local event, it is followed by similar ones in the other old villages like Sants.

**September 24: The Feast of the Mercé** is strictly a celebration for Barcelona, as the Virgin of Mercé is one of her patron saints. Although by no means the longest standing — it was only instituted at the end of the last century — this has become Barcelona's pirncipal festival. For about four days leading up to the 24th, the city more or less comes to a halt, with street stalls, parties and public celebrations.

Festivities — which in true Catalan style open and close with a booming firework display — are centred around the Gothic quarter; and here every square stages a long programme of theatrical and musical activities. Big name bands usually draw the crowds to Plaça de Catalunya or the open air stadium on Montjuïc, while the old town's squares, like Sant Jaume, Reial and del Rei, offer variously jazz, classical, salsa and local tunes.

Apart from the music there are three key events. Firstly, on the eve of the feast day, is the *'Correfoc'* or procession of dragons. Thanks to Saint George's strong presence, the dragon is an important symbol in Barcelona, and each area of town now has its own special model. This long procession, which takes place after dark, is highly charged and carries an electric atmosphere around town. With the insistent drum beat and smell of fireworks hanging in the air, it is very much an event to be part of. Almost impossible to remain an onlooker, the whole town seems to be out on the street. And the dragons, who spit fireworks from their jaws, are boisterously taunted by members of the crowd who dance ecstatically among the spray.

On the main day come the *'Castellers'* who, by climbing on each others' shoulders form human pyramids or castles. Teams of agile men, women and children from around the province compete to scale the dizziest heights, in what becomes a surprisingly thrilling sight.

This curious Catalan custom of building human castles is a surprisingly gripping spectacle. Tension mounts as the lightest team member scales the top, often crossing himself in case he falls. Learning to take a tumble is all part of the art, however, and *castellers* train to fall inwards on top of each other.

The culmination of this festival is the *'Ball de Gegants'* during which giants, dwarfs and 'bigheads', again representing each district, wend their way through the city. Each area proudly preserves its own pair of giants (traditionally bedecked in medieval costume, although some of the contemporary adaptations are quite hilarious) and they are usually supported by a crew with pipes and drums.

For those inspired by the dragons, one of the most ferocious and best known is the Patum of Berga — the high point in the feast of Corpus Christi. This colourful spectacle includes a dance of devils, a dragon and fireworks.

Comic relief comes bedecked as Bigheads and Dwarfs during the boisterous Mercé fiesta.

# The Olympics and the Future

Barcelona is in a state of flux, and this is one of its most striking impressions. Limbering up in the Olympic limelight, the city is proudly polishing its past; statues are being scrubbed, roads are being built, transport sharpened, technology boosted, and hotels booked.

In October 1986, having persevered since 1920, Barcelona was awarded the '92 Olympic Games. On her side were economic prosperity, geographical diversity, strong industry and modern facilities. Now, the city is very evidently rising to meet the challenge, in particular by reclaiming the stretch of seafront, long lost to industrial activity. The Olympics, which last 16 days, will undoubtedly leave Barcelona a changed place — certainly with thousands of new hotel beds (which many argue will stay empty), and miles of new coast (which probably won't).

Within the city there are four Olympic zones. Foremost (and the best one to visit) is Montjuïc where, among other sites, the main stadium is located. Built in 1929 for the Universal Exhibition, this has been expanded to contain 70,000 spectators and here the opening and closing ceremonies will take place. Close by is the Palau Sant Jordi (a highly innovative construction by Japanese architect Arata Isozaki) and the Picornell swimming pools.

---

### Weathering the Storm

The much heralded inauguration of the Olympic stadium in September 1989 will not be swiftly forgotten. While the rain kept many potential spectators at home, it could not deter a fervent band of Catalan nationalists, who thus appeared greater in number. These, grabbing any public protest opportunity and brandishing banners, booed and hissed at the King.

Yet it was unanimously agreed that the embarrassment of this incident to the majority of Catalans was eclipsed by the arrival of rain. This poured through cracks in the stadium's covered stand, drenching King, President and local dignitaries alike, all of whom had turned out to mark the auspicious occasion.

---

Firmly in the throes of Olympic upheaval is Poblenou. This old quarter, where the Industrial Revolution germinated in the latter part of the nineteenth century, is destined to become Parc de Mar. Here factories have been demolished and a brand new residential area is budding. Set back from the new harbour, where yachting events will be held, lies the Olympic Village, complete with the athletes' apartments and, for the first time, their own private beach.

Uptown, the Diagonal and Vall d'Hebró areas will also be Olympic zones, where existing facilities like the Camp Nou football stadium and Royal Polo Club will become key sites. Further afield, competition venues sprawl to 14 other locations, notably Lake Banyoles in the province of Girona, where rowing events will take place.

Brandished on tee-shirts, badges, and popping up at every opportunity, is COBI the dog, designed by Xavier Mariscal as the Olympic mascot. Although there is some opposition to the Games, evidence of national enthusiasm is the 70,000 volunteers who had signed up even before the event had been secured. With a total investment for the Spanish economy of at least one billion pesetas, the Games will bring employment to some 75,000 people per year between 1989-92. Although it would seem the Olympics have brought Barcelona into the media eye, its nomination is recognition of the city's escalating status in Europe. And, hand in hand with the prices, this will inevitably bring a rise in tourism.

---

### A Dog's Life

One sight that even the swiftest visitors are unlikely to miss is COBI the dog, Barcelona's Olympic mascot and emblazoned on posters and souvenir shops everywhere. This flat-faced yellow hound wearing an inane grin is the creation of Xavier Mariscal, the city's hottest designer. Controversy exploded over the choice of this symbol, and was fanned by Mariscal pointing to similarities between his squat dog and the Generalitat President Jordi Pujol.

Although born in Valencia, Mariscal moved to Barcelona in the early '70s; and despite provocative remarks, such as that Barcelona's biggest problem lay in having too many Catalans, he has been enthusiastically adopted. His output is amazingly varied, largely kitsch and poking fun at the garish, popular costa culture. His cartoons and drawings bedeck anything from fabrics and china to toys, while larger designs run to furniture or the latest night spots.

Hailed as a leader of Spanish design for the last decade, it is COBI which has won him international fame. This loved and hated dog emerged from Mariscal's famous cartoon characters in the 'Garriris' comic strip — three boozing, womanising dogs and their hilarious exploits. And now Mariscal has set up a studio in Poble Nou, close to the Olympic village, from where he can expand his interests and further milk COBI's profile.

Olympic protest is most apparent in Poble Nou, home of the Olympic village. COBI is very much in the doghouse here.

# Catalunya

Viella

FRANCE

ANDORRA

CATALAN PYRENEES

La Seu

Figueres

Cadaqués

Roses

Empurias-brava

Besalú

Ripoll

Empurias

L'Escala

Torelló

GIRONA

La Bisbal

Aiguablava

Vic

Sant Hilari
de Sacalm

Ralafrugell

Viladrau

Palamós

Tossa de Mar

Lloret de Mar

Blanes

Terrassa

Sant Pol

Calella

Sabadell

Mataró

LLEIDA

Montserrat

BARCELONA

Poblet

Santes Creus

Valls

Vilafranca

El Prat (airport)

Reus

Sitges

Castelldefels

Cambrils

TARRAGONA

Salou

Tortosa

L'Ametlla de Mar

Ebra Delta
area

Amposta

Scale 10mm = 15km approx

TWO

# Planning Your Trip

## When To Go

Summer sees tourists swarming to Barcelona and locals fleeing for a month. High season (July and August) is the least comfortable time to visit as the city is hot, sweaty and humid. The August exodus leaves something of a ghost town, and even the hottest night spots cool down. Many shops, restaurants and bars close, and cheaper hotels often have inflated prices for the tourist season.

Although the hazards of a high season visit are the packed beaches and coastal hotels, one great compensation is the abundance of local festivals. Winter temperatures average around ten degrees centigrade, and crisp, sunny days with frosty nights are not uncommon. Weatherwise, the optimum times to visit are late Spring and Autumn, although the Mediterranean climate can be unpredictable.

## How To Get There

Close to the French border and enjoying an enviable geographical location, Barcelona is well served by rail, sea, road and air.

### By Air

British Airways and Iberia run regular scheduled flights from London, a journey of around two hours; British Airways also fly from Birmingham, and Iberia from both Birmingham and Manchester. Flights to Barcelona tend to be slightly cheaper during the week than at weekends; and although prices fluctuate from month to month, expect them to be highest over Easter and from mid July to the end of August. Iberia tickets currently range from £129 to £192.

Many people opt for the cheaper charters which can make good bargains, particularly off-season or last-minute. During summer the bulk of these land at Girona, from where fast trains to Barcelona take just one hour and a quarter. Numerous bucket shop flights are available but, as the best deals change in a flash, the best idea is to scan the newspapers or ask at a local travel agent.

Good agents for discount flights include Trailfinders, 46 Earls Court Road, London W8 (tel: 071 937 5400) and STA Travel, 74 Old Brompton Road, London (tel: 071 581 8233); or try any branch of Thomas Cook, for their head office call 071 499 4000. Anyone with an American Express credit card will find their own travel agency particularly helpful. For courier flights, try Polo Express (tel: 071 759 5383).

## By Sea

Brittany Ferries is the only company operating boats from England to Spain; the crossing takes 24 hours from Plymouth to Santander. The company is represented in Santander by Modesto Piñeiro (tel: (942) 21 45 00), and from where it is about nine hours' drive to Barcelona. It is also possible to reach Barcelona by ferry from the Balearic Islands of Mallorca, Menorca and Ibiza. Alternatively take the hovercraft or ferry across the channel and drive through France, either on the faster, expensive motorways, or the cheaper, scenic roads.

## By Rail

Trains from all parts of Europe connect with Barcelona, although access will be considerably easier by 1992. Look out for the T.G.V. trains (high speed line) which connect direct to the rest of Europe. Currently the entire journey from England takes around 26 hours (although it could be nearer 36 if the connections are poor).

The cheapest way to reach Barcelona by train is via London to Paris, and then to La Tour de Carol near Andorra. From here you buy a ticket to Barcelona. In total, this journey takes 23½ hours. A return ticket from London to La Tour de Carol costs £109 (single £85.70), and you should expect the onward leg to Barcelona to cost around £8.50.

The journey via Portbou takes longer, around 26 hours. It is considerably more expensive if you take a direct train from Paris to Barcelona but it is faster (21 hours). For British Rail Continental enquiries call 071 834 2345. For details of stations within Barcelona and discounts on Spanish trains see Arrival, Departure and Getting Around, chapter 3.

## By Car

Drivers need their driving licence (which must be the pink EC model), a green card which extends their car insurance abroad, and a bail bond which is also obtainable from insurers. (Under Spanish law anyone involved in a traffic incident can be held in jail until their case comes up, and this bond works as an automatic release voucher.) You are supposed to display a GB sticker and headlights should be converted so that they dip to the right hand side (a simple procedure which any garage can do). The law also dictates that you carry a red breakdown triangle and a spare set of light bulbs. (See Motoring section, chapter 10.)

Driving from France, there are three direct routes into Barcelona, which is 149 kilometres from the border. Probably the fastest (and most expensive due to its tolls) is the autopista A7 from Perpignan, which crosses the eastern Pyrenees and Girona. For the two cheaper alternatives, cross the Pyrenees near Andorra on the N20, and take either the N152, which arrives at the north-east end of the city, or the parallel C1411, which reaches the south-west side.

From Madrid (613km) the best route is the N2 highway to Zaragoza, followed by the A2 until it meets the A7 just below Barcelona. If arriving from the car ferry at Santander, first go to Bilbao on the N634 and after, the most direct route is the A68 until you reach Zaragoza. Finally coming up from the south, the best route is the A7 from València.

## By Coach

A number of international companies operate coaches from various parts of Britain to Barcelona, and usually take around 24 hours. The greatest number, however, leave from Victoria Coach station in London. For information on the National Express run Eurolines, which depart from Victoria, call 071 730 0202. These coaches take 24½ hours and return prices start from £99. You shouldn't assume that either the coach or train will be cheaper as, with so many flight discounts, the cheapest method is often by air.

# Money

## Budget

Spanish food, drink and entertainment is still cheap, although as Barcelona enjoys increasing prominence in Europe, prices are creeping up. You can still get by on about £10 a day; a bed in a rock bottom pension costs around £4 a night. Those eligible for youth hostels can find a bed for as little as £2.50.

Cheap set menus of three courses, often including wine, can be found for as little as £3. Metro and bus tickets cost 65 pesetas a ride, while a litre of Super (four star) petrol costs 79 pesetas. A bottle of wine starts at 150 pesetas, while a bottle of beer costs 80 pesetas and a bottle of mineral water, 50 pesetas. Cheap wine is best bought in one-litre bottles, which may well cost little more than 85 pesetas.

### How To Take It

Travellers cheques remain a good bet for security, as do Eurocheques which are now widely accepted; you can also use credit cards in cash dispensers and banks to draw pesetas. All Spanish banks offer the same exchange rates, and in most cases identification is needed. Many hotels and travel agents also change money and accept payment by travellers cheque.

There is no limit to the amount you can bring into Spain. And it is highly advisable to bring some pesetas with you, especially if you are arriving late; the exchange office at Barcelona Airport closes at 23.00 and in Sants Central station at 22.00 (in summer).

# Visas

UK nationals, like most European Community countries, need only a valid passport to enter Spain, although a visa is necessary if you plan to stay longer than 90 days. British Visitor Passports (valid for one year) are not acceptable for visits of over three months' duration. In practice these regulations are hard to enforce, as passports are no longer stamped on arrival.

The Spanish Embassy in Britain is at 24 Belgrave Square, London SW1 8QT (tel: 071 235 5555). The Spanish Tourist Office is at 57 St James's Street, London SW1A 1LD (tel: 071 499 0901).

A visa valid for 90 days can only be obtained in your country of residence, although this can be extended from within Spain twice (giving a total of 270 days). In exceptional circumstances a 90-day visa can be obtained (without having to return to your country of residence) from the Departamento de Extranjeros or Extranjeria in Plaça d'Espanya. Visitors from the USA require a visa for stays of over six months; Australians need to fill out an entry permit on arrival which is only valid for 30 days.

# Insurance

As with any foreign trip, health and travel insurance are desirable. Spain has a reciprocal agreement with the UK by which British citizens are entitled to the same medical treatment as locals. It is not obligatory for UK visitors to have any vaccinations.

It is a sensible precaution to take the DSS form E111 with you (available from post offices in the UK). This is used for reclaiming funds spent on medical care abroad, although it only covers basic emergency care and so is not an adequate substitute for full insurance. It is usually possible to pick up this form on returning home, but this makes the process much slower and more complicated.

# Clothes

Local outfits reflect Barcelona's reputation as the open-minded city of Spain, and anything you pack will go. Coolness is top priority for summer trips and natural fibres remain the best bet. Those planning to explore Catalunya's mountains should expect nights to be quite cool, even in high summer.

Smarter restaurants, and occasionally some bars and clubs, do not allow shorts, but on the whole Barcelona is a relaxed and informal city. Catalans are meticulous dressers, however, and relish the chance to bedeck themselves in their finery. So it is easy to feel shabby in comparison, and should your stay coincide with one of their numerous fiestas, you'll look the part in something flamboyant.

# Travel Checklist

As a sophisticated European city, there is almost nothing you cannot buy here, but the following may be useful: Catalan/Castilian (Spanish) dictionary and Spanish phrasebook, money belt, tampons (these are almost twice the British price), hat, travel adaptor, travel wash and a bath plug. Most types of film are widely available at more or less equivalent prices, but the very fast or slow speed varieties are difficult to buy. The cost of developing film is higher than in the UK, and quality is often less good.

## Suggested Reading

*Homage to Catalonia* by George Orwell (Penguin Books). The most famous novel about the province, this is an astonishing account of Orwell's experiences fighting with the Republicans in the Spanish Civil War.

*The Spaniards* by John Hooper (Penguin Books). An engaging and enlightening survey of contemporary Spain, written after many years as a Spanish correspondent.

*For Whom the Bell Tolls* by Ernest Hemingway (Grafton). Another world famous account of the Civil War.

*Fiesta* by Ernest Hemingway (Grafton). A look at the Spanish customs of the fiesta and bullfighting.

*As I Walked Out One Midsummer Morning* by Laurie Lee (Penguin Books). A lyrical account of a young man's travels through pre-war Spain.

*The Essence of Catalonia* by Alastair Boyd (Andre Deutsch). A comprehensive and penetrating study of the region, its history and its culture.

*In Spain* by Ted Walker (Corgi). A warm, personal tale of experiences travelling in Spain.

*Face of Spain* by Gerald Brenan (Penguin Travel Library). Brenan shares his immense knowledge of Spain in a vivid account of life under Franco in 1949.

*Spain* by Jan Morris (Penguin Travel Library).

*A Visit to Spain* by Hans Christian Andersen (Peter Owen).

For those extending their trip around the country, the Michelin and the Cadogan guides to Spain are both recommended. (See also Bibliography.)

THREE

# Arrival, Departure and Getting Around

## Airports

Barcelona's international airport is at El Prat de Llobregat, 12 kilometres south of the city centre. Rather shabby and littered with long queues, it is undergoing a major Olympic facelift which will almost double present capacity to around eleven million passengers a year.

The best route into Barcelona is the twice-hourly train to Catalunya and Sants stations which costs 150 pesetas and takes around 30 minutes. The last city train leaves the airport at 22.50, or departs from Sants for the airport at 22.20 (time subject to change). Buses are slower, but there is a night service (line EN) which operates every 80 minutes until 02.30 from the airport, or until 03.10 from Plaça d'Espanya.

Taxis to the city centre cost about 1,700 pesetas, although expect to pay more on weekends and holidays. If you are planning any cab journeys around Catalunya (not a recommended option), pick up a free map with approximate prices at the airport taxi centre. El Prat has the usual car-hire firms but only Hertz is currently open 24 hours (except Sunday between 02.00 and 07.00).

Money can be changed at the bank (07.00-23.00 daily) and there are also cash dispensers. There is currently no airport hotel but one is due to open shortly. The Hotel Reservations desk (08.00-22.00 daily) will make bookings for a nominal fee and refundable deposit. The tourist office here operates 09.30-20.00/20.30 Monday-Saturday (depending on the season) and 09.30-15.00 Sunday and holidays.

Apart from the usual national and international flights, there is an hourly shuttle to Madrid from 06.45-23.25. Baggage trolleys are free and porters, recognisable in brown uniforms, charge 55 pesetas per case. For all flight information, call 401 31 31 (or between 23.00 and 07.00 call 401 31 55). (Barcelona's code is 343 from outside Spain, or 93 from another Spanish province.)

Those arriving at **Girona Airport** (which has minimal facilities) will find the bank open 24 hours in summer. There are 24-hour taxis but no buses or trains to the city centre (around 12 kilometres away); a taxi into Girona should cost around 1,600 pesetas. From the city there are five buses a day for Barcelona and frequent trains between 06.00-22.00. The fast ones take about an hour and a quarter. (See chapter 11.)

Airline head offices are mostly centrally located in the Eixample area of Barcelona:
Air France, Passeig de Gràcia,63 (tel: 487 25 26)
British Airways, Passeig de Gràcia,85 (tel: 487 21 12)
Iberia, Passeig de Gràcia,30 (tel: 301 39 93)
TWA, Passeig de Gràcia,55 (tel: 215 81 88)

---

### Suggestions for a Flying Visit

If you have only a weekend in Barcelona, these suggestions will give you an overall picture of the diversity of the city, and make sure you catch the highlights. Kick off with a walk down the Rambles to the port. From here you should wander around the Gothic quarter, taking in the Cathedral and the Picasso Museum.

Stroll up the Passeig de Gràcia to get a glimpse of the new town and its whacky Modernista architecture. From here a trip to Gaudí's amazing church the Sagrada Família should not be missed. And more Gaudí eccentricities are wonderfully displayed within the peaceful Parc Güell.

Another day could be well spent taking the cable car from the pier, over the harbour and up to Montjuïc mountain. From here you can walk round to the Miró gallery or the Olympic stadium. On a fine evening, a great place to soak up the atmosphere is a bar in Plaça Reial, just off the Rambles. And a fish dinner on the beach at Barceloneta will give you a quite different flavour.

---

## Railway Stations

There are five reasonably central stations in Barcelona; look out for the yellow and blue RENFE symbol of the national rail network (tel: 490 02 02). There is also a provincial service, Ferrocarrils de la Generalitat de Catalunya (tel: 205 15 15). This operates within a radius of 50 kilometres on two inland routes: from Plaça de Catalunya to Sant Cugat, Sabadell and Terrassa and from Plaça d'Espanya to Montserrat, Igualada and Manresa. It also runs north of the city to Bonanova, Sarrià and Tibidabo. On the whole this service is cleaner and more reliable.

Sants station, at Plaça dels Països Catalans (tel: 490 02 02) is currently the main terminal for all national and international trains, as well as for those to the airport. França station, on Passeig Nacional, was closed at the time of writing for renovations but is to become the principal station. Sants will still run some lines and many trains will stop at both stations. França was built in 1929 in a Classical style and current plans include an underground art gallery, discotheque and jazz club. Being just five minutes from both the beach and the Gothic quarter, it could make an entertaining place to be delayed.

From Catalunya station, RENFE trains go to the airport, Manresa, Lleida, Vic, Puigcerdà, La Tour de Carol, and north a short distance along the Maresme coast. (For these trains, you should use the entrance near El Corte Inglés rather than at the top of the Rambles.) RENFE trains from Passeig de Gràcia-Aragó run north to Granollers, Girona, Figueres and Portbou-Cerbère.

Reservations are recommended for international trains. You can either make these before the train leaves (allow at least an hour and a half because of the queues) or reserve in advance (either via a travel agent — often reluctant if you haven't bought your ticket from them — or at the station). Even if you reserve in advance, you still have to collect your ticket on the day of departure, suffer the long queues and pay a reservation fee, so again allow plenty of time.

A further complication is the various types of queue, such as one for immediate departure and another for international trains. An alternative system using numbered tickets also operates, but is not necessarily any quicker. This thoroughly infuriating procedure has no simple solution, but if you want to be sure of a seat, it's probably best to reserve your onward journey on arrival. With luck, this tedious situation will be improved when França opens.

The possibilities for discounted rail travel are numerous but tickets have various restrictions; travel agents should have all the details (for agents, see A — Z of Information, chapter 10). RENFE discounts include the Tarjeta Turistica (tourist ticket), valid for eight, 15 or 22 days for free travel on all RENFE trains (except Talgo Paris/Madrid) and Tarjeta Joven which buys half-price travel for those under 26 and which, for a supplement, can be used outside Spain. It's cheaper to buy return tickets than two singles.

For general queries about city transport, there is a public information line (tel: 412 00 00) for advice about metro, bus, train or car. This is available, Monday to Friday 07.30-20.00, Saturday 08.00-14.00, and there are some people who speak English.

### Off the Rails

High season chaos at Sants station left many travellers itching to share their experiences...

A young communist, just back from the Salvador Dalí museum, commented, "I was sent to seven different platforms and encountered the only pedestrian one-way system I have ever come across. Don't trust people in hats — they're not as official as they look. All in all it was much more weird than the museum."

His girlfriend told an equally desperate tale: "I'm an experienced traveller but this station totally confused me — a nightmare. There were hundreds of people looking lost, and we had to walk around in circles to get to the tracks. The few staff on the information desk were surrounded by about 300 people — they've got serious problems."

A housewife and mother of four found the queueing system horribly haphazard. "There I was, English and struggling hard with my few words of Spanish, but no-one seemed prepared to help. And since none of the windows were marked with the destinations, you had to rely on information passed back down the queue, which then proved wrong just as you got to the front — rather like Chinese whispers. And, being August, the place was seething with backpackers who looked so worn out, they were past feeling angry."

Meanwhile growing increasingly frustrated in a ticket queue, was a young woman heading towards a romantic encounter. "I'll be desperate if I miss my boyfriend," she said. "I have already missed several trains just trying to buy a ticket." And usually a safe bet for an optimistic comment, even an anonymous member of the city's PR department could only muster: "Well, I say a prayer for them".

# Ferry Port

Set back from the Passeig de Colom are the International maritime station (Moll Sant Beltràn, tel: 301 25 98) and the Beleares maritime station (Moll de Barcelona, tel: 317 42 62), where boats to the Balearic Islands arrive and depart. Car ferries are operated by the Trasmediterránea Company, and tickets are sold from their office at Vía Laietana,2 (tel: 319 82 12). There are usually two services a day to each island, one around noon and the other overnight. The journey to Palma (Mallorca) takes eight hours, to Mahon (Menorca) nine hours, and to Ibiza nine and a half hours.

An alternative company is CATS LINE S.A., which runs a daily service at 15.00 (except Wednesdays) to Mallorca and Menorca. Their office is at Moll de Barcelona, maritime station 3 (tel: 412 58 56). Currently facilities are limited to a basic cafeteria although this should change as the station is being renovated along with the entire port.

## Coaches

There are three companies which run international coaches: Julia, Est. Autobuses de Sants, beside Sants station (tel: 490 40 40); Via Eurolines, Pau Clarís,117 (tel: 317 33 46/302 58 75); and Iberbus, Paral.lel,116 (tel: 241 64 94/242 33 00).

Provincial buses mostly leave from the Estació del Norte, near Arc de Triomf metro. The only company which serves the Costa Brava is Sarfa, Plaça Duc de Medinaceli,4 (tel: 318 94 34), off Passeig de Colom near the port; all their coaches leave from this address — book early. For their useful recorded information service, which details destinations and times of departure, call 318 93 92.

## City Orientation

### Rambles and Old Town

The prime place from which to start orienting yourself is Plaça de Catalunya, the spacious circus at the heart of the city and head of the Rambles. Slicing through the old quarter, and following the path once carved by a stream, the notoriously fickle **Rambles** shifts character on its way. The top is the preserve of smarter hotels and shops, yet around the port bustles a network of sleazy streets whose neon signs mark out the red light district.

Encapsulating the Catalan spirit, the Rambles accommodates one and all. Despite being the major lure for tourists, its essence survives unaffected; it's still a place enjoyed by strolling Spaniards, and where old men have their shoes shined. Some of its major landmarks are the Liceu Opera House, Boqueria market, Plaça Reial and the Columbus column.

The Rambles divides into five parts, from the top, the first is Rambla de Canaletes, so named after its lucky fountain; those who drink from this are destined to return. Next come Rambla dels Estudis, a favoured student hang-out, Rambla Sant Josep (often called Rambla de los Flors) which is home of the flower sellers and, marked by the Miró mosaic, Rambla dels Caputxins. The final stretch is known as Rambla de Santa Mònica.

The old town contains the remnants of two city walls, near the Cathedral lie relics of the circular Roman fortifications, while the line of the later city wall is marked out by today's Rondas (Sant Pau, Sant Antoni, Universitat and Sant Pere). The area within these divides into distinct sections known as *barris* or *barrios*. Foremost

A maze of narrow alleys make up Barcelona's old town.

is the **Barri Gòtic** (Gothic Quarter) where the Roman city was founded in 270 BC, and which is still the political centre. This has three proud squares, Plaça de Sant Jaume, Plaça del Rei and Pla de la Seu in front of the Cathedral, while its upper side streets are crammed with boutiques and pensions.

This was only separated from its neighbouring Barri Ribera by the ugly, nineteenth-century thoroughfare, Vía Laietana. Less of a tourist zone, despite the Picasso museum and some great bars, this has rickety, overhanging houses which leave its tight alleyways dank even on a hot day. During the Middle Ages, this was a prestigious area, home to the nobles, merchants and sailors.

To the right of the Rambles as you face the port, lies the **Barri Xines.** This is considered the city's most dangerous ground, where plentiful prostitution and drug dealing attract trouble. It supports the firmly local bars, seedier pensions (some desperately dismal) and the most active streetlife. Not to be ignored if you want to make some interesting discoveries.

---

**Neighbourhood Watch**

It's easy to be oblivious to some of Barcelona's more obscure regulations. A stroll around the Barri Ribera and Barri Gòtic would suggest the former sheltered a cleaner community. For while Ribera balconies are unabashedly draped in washing, in the Gothic quarter there's never a knicker in sight. Acutely aware of the value of tourism and striving to keep their city's core aesthetically pleasing, the authorities have banned the hanging out of washing.

But this is only one of many odd rules. Consideration for passing pedestrians has prohibited watering window boxes before ten at night. And washing your car in these narrow streets, also illegal, is bound to bring out the *barrio* in protest.

---

### Eixample

Immediately above Plaça de Catalunya, and forming the bulk of the city, is Eixample (a term which literally means extension). This vast, symmetrical nineteenth-century addition was built during the economic boom which demanded the destruction of the last, old, restricting city walls. The inspiration of architect Cerdà, it forms a grid divided by a long diagonal highway (Diagonal) stretching right across town.

Its ample avenues stand in sharp contrast to the narrow lanes of the older quarters; the two grandest being Rambla de Catalunya and Passeig de Gràcia, home of the smarter hotels, shops and restaurants. The latter is graced with elaborate street lamps, and even the steely-blue pavement and the municipal benches are Gaudí's responsibility.

As the nucleus of Catalan Modernismo, it is packed with such famous sights as Gaudí's Casa Batlló, the Pedrera and the Sagrada Família; other creations include works by Domènech i Montaner and Puig i Cadafalch. But aside from these mansions, the area reveals a remarkable attention to detail seen through doorways or on the façades of small shops; look out for the characteristic coloured glass, wrought iron and ceramic decorations.

## Gràcia

At the top of Passeig de Gràcia above Diagonal lies Gràcia, once a separate medieval village which was later linked to the city by Eixample. This self-contained residential area has attracted the young and hip, around whom bars, restaurants and nightclubs have recently shot up. Today, its narrow streets and lovely squares retain a bohemian but civilized feel, quite different to the sharper edge of the Gothic quarter. Like many of the old villages, Gràcia's character and customs (which include several annual fiestas) remain undiluted. Notable sights include Gaudí's Parc Güell which lies on the outskirts and one of his early works, Casa Viçens.

## Zona Alta

This peaceful and wealthy residential zone, situated above Diagonal and bordered by Vía Augusta (to the top left on any city map) incorporates the former towns of Sarrià and Sant Gervasi as well as the modern conurbation of Pedralbes. Apart from the large University campus and private sports clubs, it is an important business area with several high class hotels, banks, commercial buildings and night clubs. Notable sights include the Royal Palace and Monastery of Pedrables but it's the famous Camp Nou (FC Barcelona) football stadium which pulls in the crowds.

## Port and Barceloneta

Barcelona's seafront is responsible for its significant maritime past, as well as much of the commercial standing it enjoys today. From the port, at the bottom of the Rambles, the coast curves around Barceloneta, a triangular area once inhabited by the sea-faring community, and still an active fishing port. This was created in the seventeenth century after sand gathered here when the port was constructed. Today it has a holiday feel celebrated in the mass of fish restaurants as well as on its beaches. The Olympics has been a catalyst for milking more from the coastline, for which miles of new

Dawn scene at the quay is well worth catching. Although fishing has traditionally been central to city life, pollution and the influx of Atlantic fish have assisted its recent decline, and fish is no longer cheap in Barcelona.

beaches are being opened up north-east to Poblenou.

Unlike the docks in so many large cities, Barcelona's harbour is still a bustling trade centre — indeed third in the Mediterranean for traffic volume. Major alterations are underway to redesign and expand the port, not only for the Olympics but to cope with the ever-increasing commercial activity.

Aptly sited, the Columbus monument (with an interior lift to the upper platform) guards the harbour. But the best way to view the port and marina is to take the cable car, either from the pier or from Barceloneta, up to Montjuïc hill.

### From Poble Sec to Sants

The thoroughfare Paral.lel carries constant traffic from the port to Plaça d'Espanya — a major roundabout and the exit for short distances south. A little further uptown in the west of the city lies Sants station (in an area which was originally a separate village). Much of this area has industrial origins and the port end has a seedy, downbeat feel perpetuated by the thriving sex clubs. Although scattered with bars, there are few good restaurants, but several bawdy music halls cheer up the otherwise uninspiring Paral.lel.

### Montjuïc

In the south of the city overlooking the port looms Montjuïc mountain. Historically, this strategic location dictated a military role, and its peak cradles a fortress, originally a prison and now the military museum. Its name derives from the Jews who once lived outside the city walls around the hill. On the far side of Montjuïc is a cemetery, which was first reserved for this community until it later became a municipal burial ground.

In 1929 Montjuïc hosted the Universal Exhibition whose facilities have since been adapted for the Olympic Games. The base of the mountain is skirted by exhibition halls which house the annual *ferias* (trade fairs). And at the foot of the stairway leading to the Palau Nacional are the luminous fountains which are often ablaze with coloured lights and music.

Montjuïc's abundant attractions (which far outweigh those of Tibidabo) include an amusement park, botanic garden, many important museums, theatres and sports facilities. There's a free bus from Plaça d'Espanya part way up the slope (see Bus, below) and a good reason for a trip to the top is just the cooler, fresher air.

### Tibidabo

Towering over the city and commanding spectacular views is Tibidabo, the wooded peak of the Collserola hills. The summit is reached by an old fashioned tram and a funicular railway. Interrupting the skyline is the monumental Sagrat Cor church and an amusement park. Tibidabo also has a museum and some excellent restaurants and bars up the side of the hill.

# City Transport

### Metro

A pleasant change from many cities, Barcelona's metro is cheap, efficient, safe and simple. (A slight drawback is its hours which don't mirror the late-night life.) It operates between 05.00-23.00 Monday-Thursday, 05.00-01.00 Friday, Saturday and eve of holidays, 06.00-24.00 Sunday and holidays. On the whole, carriages are clean, air conditioned and have foolproof, flashing diagrams which indicate the approaching station. Surprisingly, the modern trains are also free from advertising.

A single trip is 75 pesetas on weekdays or 90 pesetas at weekends and holidays, but a better bet are the various *tarjetas,* valid for ten rides. Buy either Tarjeta T-1 (425 pesetas) good for bus, metro,

Tramvía Blau (Generalitat's provincial rail service and Montjuïc cable car); or T-2 (400 pesetas) which excludes the bus. Another option in summer are passes of varying duration which allow free use of all public transport.

Pick up a map at the tourist office as they're not always available at stations. There are four metro lines (although these may be extended) and the map also shows overland trains, Tramvía Blau (to Tibidabo) and funicular trains.

### Bus

There is a dense network of buses crossing the city, most of which operate from 06.30-22.00. A few lines continue well into the early hours, and occasionally round the clock. There is a separate night service which runs from 22.00-04.00 along the main routes. Bus tickets (the same as those for the metro) cost 70 pesetas (90 pesetas weekends and holidays). These can be purchased on the bus, in metro stations and at certain banks.

Bus maps and timetables are available from the tourist offices. There are four types of bus, colour-coded as follows: main ones for the city centre are red; yellow ones largely serve the city outskirts, though sometimes pass through the centre; blue indicates the night buses; and green marks the peripheral lines. A simple rule to remember is that the red ones always stop at the three central squares (Catalunya, Universitat and Urquinaona), and those coded blue always stop near Plaça de Catalunya.

There is a free bus which runs from Plaça d'Espanya to Poble Espanyol on Montjuïc. This leaves every half hour between 10.00 and 15.00, 16.00-21.00, 22.00-24.00. A good way to orientate yourself is the 100 bus, which tours a wide circle of all the major sights; for a single fare, you're free to get on and off as you please. (For more details see Sports and Activities, chapter 8.)

### Taxi

Barcelona's abundant black and yellow taxis operate all hours and are cheap by international standards; the tariff starts at 225 pesetas. Within the city is all one taxi zone, but the zones (and therefore the price) change at its edges, clearly signposted as you drive out on any of the highways.

A green light on top indicates availability, and a placard inside the windscreen saying *Lluire* or *Libre* (free). There are three price bands, calculated by the number of passengers, luggage and day of the week: the number 1, 2 or 3 on top will be lit accordingly (1 being the most expensive).

If a driver ignores you, it may be his day off, indicated by a code letter displayed in the window or on the side. (These correspond to the days of the week in Spanish (see Appendix) except X which signifies Wednesday.) Another option is Teletaxi, available 24 hours daily (tel: 212 22 22). Alternatively you can call for a taxi on 357 77 55/358 11 11/490 22 22/433 10 20.

---

### Linguists in the Driving Seat

Preparations for the Olympic Games have been permeating almost every aspect of life in Barcelona. The Ajuntament are even taking public relations to grass roots level by introducing — and funding — English language lessons for their taxi drivers. For those enterprising enough to take up the offer (some scorn it as subjugating themselves and the Catalan language) a couple of hours a week for a school year are provided free of charge.

The carrot at the end of the course is a five day trip to London or New York, with family, to extend their horizons and consolidate their learning. Summer 1988 saw over three hundred *taxistas* and their spouses descend on the Charing Cross Hotel in London for a taste of the city's black cabs and British cooking.

---

## Car

Having your own car affords greater flexibility, and the major roads in Spain are generally good, the autopistas excellent, if costly. There are, however, a number of disadvantages to bringing a car, and public transport is considerably more economical. Petrol is barely any cheaper than in Britain, and garages are few and far between. There is also a chronic shortage of parking space all over the city. Barcelona accommodates over two million cars a day and, aside from perilous effects on the environment (visible as a great yellow cloud hovering overhead) there are few safe places to leave a car.

An active clamping unit operates throughout the city, as well as many removal vans. If your car vanishes, look for a small yellow triangular sticker on the ground which states the address of the police pound and expect to pay a hefty fine. It is common to see the pavements peppered with stickers — an indication of this department's zeal.

Foreign number plates promise rich pickings, and it is inadvisable to leave anything inside the car; windscreens have been smashed for as little as a road map or tee-shirt. The only secure option is an underground car park, absurdly expensive if you are staying any length of time. (For more information on motoring and petrol stations, see A — Z of Information, Chapter 10.)

## Car Hire

Hiring is a reasonable alternative for trips outside the city. Try Vanguard at Londres,31 (tel: 439 38 80) which also rents motorcycles; Budget, Avinguda Roma,15 (tel: 322 90 12); Rental Auto, Avinguda Sarrià,32 (tel: 230 90 71); Godfrey Davis, Viladomat,214 (tel: 439 84 01); Atesa, Balmes,141 (tel: 237 81 40); and Avis, Casanova,209 (tel: 209 95 33). The last two have airport branches: Atesa (tel: 302 28 32), Avis (379 40 26).

## Bicycle Hire

Bikes can be hired from Bicitram at Avinguda Marquès d'Argentera, in front of França station (tel: 792 28 41); Los Filicletos, Passeig de Picasso,38 (tel: 319 78 11); Biciclot, Sant Joan de Malta,1 (tel: 307 74 75).

No self respecting townhouse could be seen without its iron balcony.

Be it a dragon or monster, bandit or creepy-crawly — Gaudí's shimmering Casa Battló invites extravagant living images. This is the jewel of a staggering group of buildings known as the 'manzana de discordia' in Passeig de Gràcia.

FOUR

# Accommodation

Hotels and hostels are classified by the familiar star system, although Spanish stars are awarded generously and more often for facilities than overall quality or cleanliness. In general, the city has relatively few luxury hotels, but offers great variety and value in the middle bracket. Not surprisingly, numerous hotels are springing up for the Olympics. In the business-class hotels, demand and prices escalate dramatically during the *'ferias'* (the 34 annual trade fairs). The same is true of high season (July and August), and at both these times it's advisable to book early.

Places to stay are predictably scattered throughout the city, but certain areas have more potential for chance finds. In general, most of the pensions and cheaper hostels can be found in the Old Quarters, particularly the Barri Gòtic, which, as the heart of the city, is the best area to stay. The more upmarket and business hotels are mainly located around Plaça de Catalunya, throughout Eixample and Zona Alta.

In Spain, accommodation is divided into confusing categories which are defined below. However, recent legislation requires the hostels to become either hotels or pensions; and this mixed group is now in the process of deciding either way. Prices quoted are for a double room with en-suite bath or shower (D). Unless otherwise stated, all prices exclude tax which is either six or 12 per cent depending on the hotel price. These prices are intended *only* as a guideline and are subject to regular increases. Telephone and fax numbers are listed without the province code which is 93 from within Spain, or 010 343 if dialing from Great Britain. The code is 011 343 from the USA, and 0011 343 from Australia. For the most up to date list of accommodation, contact the tourist office.

## Hotels

Payment can usually be made by travellers cheque, Eurocheque or credit card (the most widely accepted being Visa, MasterCard, American Express and Diners). All rooms must have an en-suite shower or bath. Expect the top hotels to have air-conditioned rooms with telephone, TV, video and mini bar; 24-hour room service, laundry and babysitting are also standard. Many offer full conference facilities and parking, but swimming pools and health clubs are relatively rare.

Breakfast is almost always an additional charge across the range. The cheaper hotels generally provide breakfast, may serve other meals, and usually have a communal TV room. HA means Hotel Apartamento which always have self catering facilities; these can be better value for families, groups or long-term rent. Most have communal facilities which may include a restaurant, swimming pool or parking.

## Hostels

These are graded one to three stars and span the broadest range. Some are indistinguishable from basic pensions and others are like quality hotels, although often cheaper. Breakfast is usually available for an extra charge.

## Pensions and Guest Houses

Cash is generally the only way to pay, and tax (if not overlooked) is usually included in the quoted price. Where there is no shower or bath in the room, the prices given are for a double room; there is sometimes a charge for the communal shower. Some have a TV room and, very occasionally, a bar.

## Youth Hostels

Expect youth hostels to cost around 600 pesetas per night, and some may require you to show a youth hostel card. Unlike most hotels and hostels, these don't always have a 24-hour reception. The Youth Hostels Association's London branch is at 14 Southampton Street, WC2, (tel: 071-836 1036) anyone can obtain a membership card here, regardless of age or nationality. Or contact Direcció General de Joventut, Generalitat de Catalunya, Vildomat, 319, 08029, (tel: 322 90 61). Open 09.00-14.00, 15.00-19.00.

## Camping

Catalunya is a camper's delight which boasts around three hundred options. Sleeping on the beach is not allowed. For more details about the region's sites, pick up the 'Catalunya-Campings' brochure from the tourist office at Gran Vía de les Corts Catalanes, 658, and most tourist offices around the province. A selection of campsites close to Barcelona is listed at the end of this chapter.

## Paradors

Paradors are national hotels, usually contained in spectacular old buildings. (For more information about selected Paradors see Part IV Around Catalunya, Introduction to the Region.)

*Note:* Accommodation is divided broadly by area and borderline establishments appear in the most logical section.

This is a city which demands an eye for detail. Elaborate street lamps are among the most memorable ornaments.

# Rambles and Old Town

### Hotels

★ ★ ★ ★ ★ Ramada Renaissance, Rambla,111. 08002. Tel: 318 62 00/Tx: 54634/ Fax: 301 77 76. Metro Liceu/Catalunya. D 21,250. Perfect for business trips, its many facilities include transforming your room into an office with a personal computer and fax. Spacious, modern and upmarket, it's overflowing with staff. Ask for a room with a Rambles view.

★ ★ ★ ★ Colón, Avinguda Catedral,7, 08002. Tel: 301 14 04/Tx: 52654/Fax: 317 29 15. Metro Jaume 1/Urquinaona. D 11,600. Ask for a room opposite the spectacular Cathedral façade. This tasteful and comfortable hotel has wide corridors and attractive rooms furnished in subtle pastels. Good value and highly recommended, this is one of the best in its bracket.

★ ★ ★ ★ Rivoli Rambles, Rambla,128, 08002. Tel: 302 66 43/Tx: 99222 RIVO-E/Fax: 317 50 53. Metro Catalunya. D 14,900. Recently opened, this has good facilities including a fitness centre. Decorated with attractive murals, it has a prime position on the Rambles.

★ ★ ★ ★ Royal, Rambla,117-119, 08002. Tel: 301 94 00/Tx: 97565 RYAL-E/Fax: 317 31 79. Metro Catalunya. D 13,600. With a modern glass and concrete exterior, its rooms are decent and comfortable, but you could do better for the price.

★ ★ ★ Fornos, Rambla,44, 08002. Tel: 318 20 16/Fax: 302 00 28. Metro Liceu. D 5,830 (tax included). Average and functional.

★ ★ ★ Gaudí, Nou de la Rambla,12, 08001. Tel: 317 90 32/Tx:98974 HOGA. Metro Liceu. D 6,600. Sited opposite Gaudí's Palau Güell, bedrooms are much better than the mediocre reception promises. The small suites are exceptional value and overall this hotel is civilised and homely.

★ ★ ★ Gótico, Jaume 1,14, 08002. Tel: 315 22 11/Tx 97206/Fax: 315 38 19. Metro Jaume 1. D 8,450. Well located, with helpful management and pleasant rooms.

★ ★ ★ Metropol, Ample,31, 08002. Tel: 315 40 11/Fax: 319 12 76. Metro Drassanes. D 6,100. This well kept hotel has an attractive modern interior with a bright breakfast room overlooking a pink courtyard. Good value and recommended.

★ ★ ★ Moderno, Hospital,11, 08001. Tel: 301 41 54/Tx: 98215. Metro Liceu. D 6,800 (cheaper in winter). Pleasant with plain rooms.

★ ★ ★ Montecarlo, Rambla,124, 08002. Tel: 317 58 00/Tx: 93345 SRMS E/Fax: 317 57 50. Metro Liceu. D 7,000. Modern with good facilities.

★ ★ ★ Oriente, Rambla,45-47, 08002. Tel: 302 25 58/Tx: 54134 LIHO/Fax: 318 34 33. Metro Liceu. D 8,200. Popular for 150 years, this has interesting features, particularly the dining room with its round, central well and glass roof. Bright corridors and good, spacious rooms, some with Rambles views.

★ ★ ★ Regencia Colón, Sagristáns,13-17, 08002. Tel: 318 98 58/Tx: 98175 HRCO/Fax: 317 28 22. Metro Urquinaona. D 8,400. With attractive floral rooms, this hotel has a cosy, discreet feel.

★ ★ ★ Rialto, Ferràn,40-42, 08002. Tel: 318 52 12/Tx: 97206/Fax: 315 38 19. Metro Liceu. D 8,875. A modern interior with plain, pleasant rooms.

★ ★ ★ HA Ronda, Sant Erasme,19, 08001. Tel: 329 00 04/Tx: 97206/Fax: 315 38 19. Metro Universitat. D 8,450. In rather a backwater, this is dreary but sufficient, and includes some self-catering apartments.

★ ★ ★ Suizo, Plaça de l'Àngel, 12, 08002. Tel: 315 41 11/Tx: 97206 HSUI-E/Fax: 315 38 19. Metro Jaume 1. D 8,450. Reasonably comfortable with simple rooms.

★ ★ ★ Turin, Pintor Fortuny,9, 08001. Tel: 302 48 12/Fax: 302 10 05. Metro Liceu. D 6,550. Adequate but quite cramped and not special.

★ ★ ★ Villa Madrid, Plaça de Villa Madrid,3, 08002. Tel: 317 49 16. Metro Catalunya/Liceu. No credit cards. Although well located in a quiet square, this is tacky and unappealing with clashing furnishings.

★ ★ Cortés, Santa Anna,25, 08002. Tel: 317 91 12/Tx: 98215 MGG. Metro Catalunya. D 4,800 (cheaper in winter). Located in a lively shopping street, this has an average, rather drab communal area.

★ ★ España, Sant Pau,9, 08001. Tel: 318 17 58/Tx: 50574. Metro Liceu. D 4,470. This has an attractive interior with a Modernista dining room; with its good value set menu, the restaurant is a popular haunt with Catalans at lunch. Some of the beds are terrible, however, and watch out for extortionate telephone surcharges.

★ ★ Flor Parks, Rambla,57, 08002. Tel: 318 13 24/Tx: 50092 SUN-E/Fax: 301 55 44. Metro Liceu. D 5,400 (only American Express). Sufficient and reasonable value, but rather dingy communal areas.

★ ★ HA Mur-Mar, Rambla, 34, 08002. Tel: 318 27 62. Metro Liceu. D 5,400. Spacious but with drab furnishings. Some rooms have balconies overlooking the Ramblas which offer better views but less peace.

★ ★ Principal, Junta de Comerç,8, 08001. Tel: 318 89 70/Tx: 98655 HLPL-E/Fax: 412 08 19. Metro Liceu. D 5,800. This appealing establishment has a friendly atmosphere and plenty of individuality, with ornate painted bedroom furniture.

★ Apolo, Rambla,33, 08002. Tel: 301 57 00/Tx: KUKA 99245/Fax: 241 22 04. Metro Liceu/Drassanes. D 5,000. Noisy, rather dirty location; this is being refurbished, and will move up to the two or three star bracket with equivalent price rises.

★ Cosmos, Escudellers,19, 08002. Tel: 317 18 74. Metro Liceu/Drassanes. D 3,286 (tax included). In the heart of the red light district, this has surprisingly clean, white-tiled rooms. Quite good value.

★ Inglés, Boqueria,17, 08001. Tel: 317 37 70/Tx: 98215 MGG. Metro Liceu. D 3,700. Plain, fairly decent rooms, if a little airless.

★ Internacional, Rambla,78-80, 08002. Tel: 302 25 66/Tx: 54134 LIHO-E/Fax: 318 21 72. Metro Liceu. D 5,650. An adequate hotel in a prime site on the Rambles, but not ideal for the disabled as there's no lift to the reception.

★ Lloret, Rambla,125, 08002. Tel: 317 33 66. Metro Catalunya. D 4,950 (cash only). A very pleasant hotel which has airy bedrooms, tiny balconies and good bathrooms.

★ Nouvel, Santa Anna,18-20, 08002. Tel: 301 82 74. Metro Catalunya. D 4,520 (cash only). Stylish, with charm and character, this is attractively furnished, particularly the breakfast room.

★ Toledano, Rambla,138, 08002. Tel: 301 08 72. Metro Catalunya. D 3,200. This has a faintly gypsyish feel with its lace bedspreads, ornate lamps and welcoming atmosphere. Pleasant rooms.

## Hostels

★ ★ ★ El Casal, Tapinería,10, 08002. Tel: 319 78 00. Metro Jaume 1. D 4,875 (tax included). Situated right beside the Cathedral, this is fairly standard and functional.

★ ★ ★ Continental, Rambla,138, 08002. Tel: 301 25 70/Fax: 302 73 60. Metro Catalunya. D 6,500. The pretty floral rooms have style and charm, some overlooking the Rambles. All with unusually tall beds (apparently ideal for packing cases). This has plenty of character and is excellent value. Helpful management and highly recommended.

★ ★ ★ Cuatro Naciones, Rambla,40, 08002. Tel: 317 36 24/Tx: 99256 HCN-E/Fax: 302 69 85. Metro Liceu. D 5,618 (tax included).

The comparatively enticing entrance hides a dreary, tasteless interior with adequate facilities.

★ ★ ★ Park, Avinguda Marquès de l'Argentera,11, 08003. Tel: 319 60 00/Tx: 99883 PARH-E. Metro Barceloneta. Recently renovated and elevated from one to three star status with equivalent price rise. Handy for França station when it re-opens.

★ ★ Condal, Boqueria,23, 08002. Tel: 318 18 82. Metro Liceu. D 3,180 (includes tax). Light and clean, its quite basic rooms surround a whitewashed inner courtyard.

★ ★ Dali, Boqueria,12, 08002. Tel: 318 55 80. Metro Liceu. D 2,000 (cash only). A pretty standard hostel like so many others in Boqueria, the favourite street for budget travellers.

★ ★ Europa, Boqueria,18, 08002. Tel: 318 76 20. Metro Liceu. D 2,800 (cash only but planning to take credit cards soon). Average rooms, most of which have balconies, but not inspiring.

★ ★ Jardí, Plaça de Sant Josep Oriol,1, 08002. Tel: 301 59 00. D 3,100 (tax included). A justifiably popular place with budget travellers. Well sited, with communal rooms overlooking two attractive squares, it has a friendly, airy and well-scrubbed feel.

★ ★ Roma, Plaça Reial,11, 08002. Tel: 302 03 66. Metro Liceu. D 2,800 (tax included, cash only). Bright, clean rooms in Barcelona's most notorious square.

★ ★ Rey Don Jaime 1, Jaume 1, 11,08002. Tel: 315 41 61. Metro Jaume 1. D 2,800 (cash or travellers cheque). Housed in what was once a Marquess' mansion, the building is 350 years old and retains some original features. Rooms are simple, often with balconies and some with good sized baths. Overall it's rather individual and has helpful management.

★ Campi, Canuda,4, 08002. Tel: 301 35 45. Metro Catalunya. D 2,500. Claiming to be suitable for nuns and Catholic families, this is quaint and cosy with ample rooms and old fashioned furniture.

★ Capitol, Rambla,138, 08002. Tel: 302 51 32. Metro Catalunya. D 2,200. This has a dingy entrance, but rooms are quite bright and all have balconies.

★ Layetana, Plaça de Ramón Berenguer el Gran,2, 08002. Tel: 319 20 12. Metro Jaume 1. D 1,700 (tax included, cash only). Communal shower. Right beside the Cathedral, this good value hostel is bright and airy.

★ Monegal, Pelai,62, 08001. Tel: 302 65 66. Metro Catalunya. D 6,100. Sighted right on Plaça de Catalunya, and with its entrance through a jewellery shop, this is not the most peaceful place. The better rooms have great views over the square, but the smaller ones are airless and poor value.

★ Noya, Rambla,133, 08002. Tel: 301 48 31. Metro Catalunya. D 1,800. Communal shower. Clean, airy and a good bet for the budget traveller.

★ Opera, Sant Pau,20, 08001. Tel: 318 82 01. Metro Liceu. D 2,500 (tax included). Basic, slightly scruffy rooms.

★ Peninsular, Sant Pau,34-36, 08001. Tel: 302 31 38/Fax: 301 08 85. Metro Liceu. D 4,135 (tax included). Originally an Augustinian monastery, the highlight is an elegant inner courtyard with hanging plants encircled by balconies. Arched doors open onto a stunning tiled seating area. The owner takes obvious pride in his hotel. Highly recommended, this is a great find and certainly the best value in this area (although Sant Pau is not its most salubrious by night).

## Pensions and Guest Houses

— Aneto, Carme,38, 08001. Tel: 318 40 83. Metro Liceu. D 2,000. Communal shower. Slightly cramped but light and decent; one of the better pensions in this vicinity.

— Bahía, Canuda,2, 08002. Tel: 302 61 53. Metro Catalunya D 3,000 (cash only). Communal shower. With modern, spotless rooms (which all have balconies), this is a pleasant and wholesome place to stay.

— Bienestar, Quintana,3, 08002. Tel: 318 72 83. Metro Liceu. D 1,600 (cash only). Communal shower. Shabby entrance and stairway, but run by a friendly lady, and the rooms are scrubbed and fair-sized.

— Canaletas, Rambla,133, 08002. Tel: 301 56 60. Metro Catalunya. D 2,200 (cash only). Prime location with good beds, but at the top of steep stairs (no lift), and it can get hot and airless in summer.

— Colon-3, Colón, entrance in Plaça Reial, 08002. Tel: 318 06 31. Metro Liceu. D 3,000 (tax included, cash only). Light rooms with bright bedspreads and modern paintings. Laundry possible, which is unusual in a pension. Ask for a room overlooking the magnificent, bustling Plaça Reial. This is one of the most appealing and best located in its bracket. Above is a hostel with shared rooms for 600 pesetas. No need for a YMCA card but you must be under 35.

— Fernando, Volta del Remei,4, 08002. Tel: 301 79 93. Metro Liceu. D 2,000 (cash only). Communal bath. Small but adequate rooms overlooking a rather seedy passageway.

— Fina, Portaferrisa,11, 08002. Tel: 317 97 87. Metro Catalunya/ Liceu. D 1,900 (cash only). Communal shower. Simple, modern and good value. One of the better pensions around and all rooms have balconies.

— Marítima, Rambla,4, 08001. Tel: 302 31 52. Metro Drassanes. D 2,000 (tax included, cash only). Communal shower. Sufficient, often with three or four beds per room, but only two communal showers. No seating area but the washing machine is a rare bonus.

— Palermo, Boqueria,21, 08002. Tel: 302 40 02. Metro Liceu. D 2,000 (cash only). Nice big beds but this hostel is functional and not especially clean.

— Santa Ana, Santa Anna,23, 08002. Tel: 301 22 46. Metro Catalunya. D 2,000 (tax included, cash only). Communal shower. Adequate, and popular in summer due to its prime location; only one shower per floor, however, and its frequent use is not encouraged!

— Torán, Banys Nous,5, 08002. Tel: E/Fax: 302 46 93. Metro Liceu. D 1,200 (cash only). Communal shower. One of the cheapest places around but dark and fairly dingy.

### Youth Hostels

— Hostal de Joves, Passeig de Pujades,29, 08018. Tel: 300 31 04. Metro Arc de Tromf/Bogatell. 460 pesetas per night.

— Kabul, Plaça Reial,17, 08002. Tel: 318 51 90. Metro Liceu. 725 pesetas per night.

---

**Local Tribute**

A comprehensive world atlas will list around 15 places named Barcelona, reaching as far afield as the Philippines. Yet few British people have heard about the village of Barcelona in Cornwall, around which a poignant tale hangs. During the War of Spanish Succession (1700-14), the British, like the Catalans, Dutch and Genoese, were keen to curb the French influence, and hence backed the Austrian Hapsburgs against the Bourbon claim.

One of the British soldiers who went to lend his support to the Catalans was the son of a renowned Cornish family, the Trelawnes. On his return voyage in 1714 his ship tragically sank near the Scilly Isles and, in memory of his worthy cause, his father rechristened a tiny village in the area.

---

# Eixample

### Hotels

★ ★ ★ ★ ★ Avenida Palace, Gran Vía de les Corts Catalanes,605, 08007. Tel: 301 96 00/Tx: 54734 APTEL-E/Fax: 318 12 34. Metro Catalunya. D 19,600. Originally a cinema, this building has a grand, gilded interior, with old fashioned wooden panelling and period furniture. Bedrooms are spacious and comfortable but not outstanding. Facilities include a health club and beauty parlour. Helpful management, and highly recommended.

★ ★ ★ ★ ★ Diplomatic, Pau Claris, 122, 08009. Tel: 317 31 00/Tx: 54701 DIPLOH E/Fax: 318 65 31. Metro Passeig de Gràcia. D 19,000. Comfortable with good facilities which include a pool, but dark corridors lead to tasteless rooms decorated with clashing fabrics and swirly carpets that leave you cross-eyed.

★ ★ ★ ★ ★ Meliá Barcelona-Sarrià, Avinguda Sarrià,50, 08029. Tel: 410 60 60/Tx: 51033 HMBS E/Fax: 321 51 79. Metro Hospital Clínic. D 23,520 (tax included). Modern, comfortable and flashy with good facilities, but lacking character.

★ ★ ★ ★ ★ Presidente, Diagonal,570, 08021. Tel: 200 21 11/Tx: 52180/Fax: 200 22 66. Metro Diagonal/Hospital Clínic. D 19,100. An unremarkable building both inside and out, but with excellent views up Diagonal, especially from the higher rooms. A standard double is not particularly spacious and has no seating area, but the bathrooms are luxurious, and overall comfort is top priority.

★ ★ ★ ★ ★ Ritz, Gran Vía de les Corts Catalanes,668, 08010. Tel: 318 52 00/Tx: 52739/Fax: 318 01 48. Metro Catalunya/Urquinaona. D 35,500. With an old fashioned, grand and opulent interior, this has spacious rooms and fantastic views. The bathrooms are sumptuous, especially those with sunken mosaic 'Roman baths'. Certainly the most tasteful luxury hotel in the city but not the best value, especially as there is no swimming pool.

★ ★ ★ ★ Alexandra, Mallorca,251, 08008. Tel: 215 30 52/Tx: 81107 ALXDR-E/Fax:216 06 06. Metro Passeig de Gràcia. D 16,900. This is a low-key, modern hotel, has a circular marble staircase, and is air conditioned to the point of freezing. Pleasant rooms and recommended for business visitors.

★ ★ ★ ★ Barcelona, Casp,1-13, 08010. Tel: 302 58 58/Tx:54990/Fax: 301 86 74. Metro Catalunya. D 12,000. Frequented by business people and centrally located, this has a rather tasteless decor and lacks character.

★ ★ ★ ★ Calderon, Rambla de Catalunya,26, 08007. Tel: 301 00 00/Tx: 51549 HOCA-E/Fax: 317 31 57. Metro Catalunya. D 15,300. Thoroughly modern with excellent facilities, including a swimming pool and sports club. International business style with cool marble interior and low ceilings; the restaurant is decorated with bedouin-style drapes. Makes up in comfort what it lacks in character.

★ ★ ★ ★ Condes de Barcelona, Passeig de Gràcia,75, 08008. Tel: 487 37 37/Tx: 51531 ECBR-E/Fax: 216 08 35. Metro Passeig de Gràcia. D 16,900. A spectacular building with a tasteful interior and friendly atmosphere. Catering mainly for business clients, this is well-appointed and comfortable.

★ ★ ★ ★ Cristal, Diputació,257, 08007. Tel: 301 66 00/Tx: 54560 HOCRI-E/Fax: 317 59 79. Metro Catalunya. D 13,125. A modern business-class hotel with a black, chrome and smoked glass decor. Adequate facilities but short on character.

★ ★ ★ ★ Dante, Mallorca,181, 08036. Tel: 323 22 54/Tx: 52588 DANTE-E/Fax: 323 74 72. Metro Hospital Clínic/Diagonal. D 10,500. This is adequate, but not notable for its comfort or style, and the restaurant is only available for groups or functions.

★ ★ ★ ★ Derby, Loreto,21-25, 08029. Tel: 322 32 15/Tx: 97429 DEHO-E/Fax: 410 08 62. Metro Hospital Clínic. D 12,900. Opposite its sister the Gran Derby, and similar in style, the rooms are spotless, modern and tasteful.

★ ★ ★ ★ Ducs de Bergara, Bergara,11, 08002. Tel: 301 51 51/Tx: 81257 HOTDB/Fax: 317 34 42. Metro Catalunya. D 16,500. This has a fine old entrance and a tasteful, understated interior. Rooms are featureless but have good facilities. One of the better hotels in this range.

★ ★ ★ ★ Euro Park, D'Aragó,325, 08009. Tel: 257 92 05. Metro Girona. D 9500. In a scruffy part of town, this seems to have been given rather a generous star rating. The gloomy rooms are on the small side and have no desks.

★ ★ ★ ★ HA Gran Derby, Loreto,28, 08029. Tel: 322 20 62/Tx: 97429 DEHO-E/Fax: 410 08 62. Metro Hospital Clínic. D 16,500. Stylishly designed, modern interior with immaculate tiled floors. All are suites and the spacious duplex apartments are well furnished, each with a spiral staircase and plentiful cushions. Recommended.

★ ★ ★ ★ Gran Hotel Cristina, Diagonal,458, 08006. Tel: 217 68 00/Tx: 54328/Fax: 205 65 06. Metro Diagonal. D 10,500. Modern with good facilities, and standard rooms with pretty bathrooms.

★ ★ ★ ★ Majestic, Passeig de Gràcia,70-72, 08008. Tel: 215 45 12/Tx: 52211 EISSA. Metro Passeig de Gràcia. D 17,000. A well equipped hotel, and one of few with an outdoor pool, but the interior is rather tasteless.

★ ★ ★ ★ Master, València,105, 08011. Tel: 323 62 15/Tx: 81258 NHMST/Fax: 323 43 89. Metro Hospital Clínic. D 13,600. Tasteful, international-style business hotel, with well equipped rooms.

★ ★ ★ ★ Nuñez Urgel, Urgell,232-34, 08036. Tel: 322 41 53. Metro Hospital Clínic. D 12,000. Sufficiently clean and comfortable, but slightly tacky and there are better bargains to be found elsewhere.
★ ★ ★ ★ Regente, Rambla de Catalunya,76, 08008. Tel: 215 25 70/Tx: 51939/Fax: 487 32 27. Metro Passeig de Gràcia. D 12,650. Standard business hotel with a solarium and a tiny, roof-top pool. Otherwise little to recommend it, having a dingy restaurant and unattractive lounge.

★ ★ ★ Aragon, Aragó,569-571, 08026. Tel: 245 89 05/Tx: 98718 APHO-E/Fax: 418 51 57. Metro Clot. D 7,900. A pleasant hotel but out on a limb, on a noisy thoroughfare.
★ ★ ★ Astoria, París 203, 08036. Tel: 209 83 11/Tx: 81129 ASTEL/Fax: 202 30 08. Metro Diagonal. D 9,500. Comfortable, with more atmosphere and character than most business hotels; it has quite a grand salon, but no restaurant.
★ ★ ★ Atenas, Avinguda Meridiana,151, 08026. Tel: 232 20 11/Tx: 98718 APHOH E/Fax: 232 09 10. Metro Clot. D 7,700. Situated on the depressing highway out of town, the hotel has pleasant, modern rooms and a roof-top pool.
★ ★ ★ Condado, Aribau,201, 08021. Tel: 200 23 11/Tx: 54546/Fax: 200 25 86. Metro Diagonal/Hospital Clínic. D 9,500. A decent, homely and unflashy business hotel, but only mediocre rooms.
★ ★ ★ Covadonga, Diagonal,596, 08021. Tel: 209 55 11/Tx: 93394 CVHT-E/Fax: 209 58 33. Metro Hospital Clínic. D 8,400. Largely for business clients, this is adequate and reasonable value, some rooms with a tiny balcony overlooking Diagonal.
★ ★ ★ Ficus, Mallorca,163, 08036. Tel: 253 35 00/Tx: 98203/Fax: 205 65 06. Metro Diagonal/Hospital Clínic. D 8,500. Standard, comfortable business hotel, currently being refurbished.
★ ★ ★ Granvia, Gran Vía de les Corts Catalanes,642, 08007. Tel: 318 19 00. Metro Catalunya. D 7,100 (cheaper in winter). Grand, comfortable and highly recommended, this has plenty of character and is the best value in this bracket. It has a spacious terrace and magnificent airy salon ornately furnished with gilded mirrors and chandeliers.
★ ★ ★ Gravina, Gravina,12, 08001. Tel: 301 68 68/Tx: 99370. Metro Catalunya/Universitat. D 9,900. Modern convenient business hotel which is sufficiently comfortable but not special.
★ ★ ★ Regina, Bergara,4, 08002. Tel: 301 32 32/Tx: 59380 HREG-E/Fax: 318 23 26. Metro Catalunya. D 9,680. In a good location with decent but unremarkable rooms.

★★★ Taber, Aragó,256, 08007. Tel: 318 70 50/Tx: 93452 HTBRH E. Metro Passeig de Gràcia. D 7,900. A moderate business hotel, in which some rooms have a small separate seating area; but the tasteless decor even runs to a tartan bar.

★★★ Wilson, Diagonal,568, 08021. Tel: 209 25 11/Tx: 52180/Fax: 200 83 70. Metro Diagonal/Hospital Clínic. D 9,800. Uninspiring mustard-coloured furnishings, the rooms are comfortable with great bathrooms.

★★ Antibes, Diputació,394, 08013. Tel: 232 62 11. Metro Sagrada Família. D 4,500. Limited facilities and no restaurant; the rooms are cool but fairly basic.

★★ Lleó, Pelai,24, 08001. Tel: 318 13 12/Tx: 98338-E. Metro Catalunya. D 6,000. Currently being refurbished, this has adequate, modern rooms but the street is noisy.

**Hostels**

★★★ Paseo de Gràcia, Passeig de Gràcia,102, 08008. Tel: 215 58 24. Metro Diagonal. D 4,717. Shabby with an uncomfortable mix of old and new furnishings.

★★★ Urbis, Passeig de Gràcia,23, 08007. Tel: 317 27 66/Fax: 447 37 42. Metro Catalunya/Passeig de Gràcia. D 5,790. This Modernista building of faded grandeur has interesting features and peeling walls. Although not the cheapest, this hostel is well located and unusual.

★★ Cisneros, Aribau,54, 08011. Tel 254 18 00. Metro Universitat/Passeig de Gràcia. D 3,021 (cash only, tax included). Run as a boarding house, this is popular with students and long-term budget visitors, although short stays are possible. Basic and noisy with a functional cafeteria.

★★ Condestable, Ronda Universitat,1, 08007. Tel: 318 62 68. Metro Universitat. D 4,000. Plain, cramped, whitewashed rooms, with no communal room. Not the best value, but in a prime location.

★★ Din, València,191, 08011. Tel: 254 12 00. Metro Universitat/Passeig de Gràcia. D 4,930 (cash only, tax included). Large and airy but slightly overpriced.

★★ Lider and Vicenta, Rambla de Catalunya,84, 08008. Tel: 215 19 23. Metro Passeig de Gràcia. D 3,000 (cash only, tax included). These two hostels are run jointly by one owner; both are quite basic and cramped but clean enough.

Towering achievement: Barcelona's prosperous port with the Christopher Columbus Column and the Santa Maria, a reproduction of the vessel in which he discovered the New World.

★★ Montserrat, Passeig de Gràcia,114, 08008. Tel: 217 27 00. Metro Diagonal. D 2,800 (cash only). Dingy and lacking atmosphere, there are better bets elsewhere.

★★ Neutral, Rambla de Catalunya,42, 08007. Tel: 318 73 70. Metro Catalunya/Passeig de Gràcia. D 2,550. Comfortable in a basic way, and good value. Most rooms have sofas and some also have street balconies.

★★ Palacios, Gran Vía de les Corts Catalanes,629, 08010. Tel: 301 37 92. Metro Passeig de Gràcia. D 2,950. Simple, whitewashed rooms, but no lift and two flights of stairs. One of few places to allow pets.

★★ Windsor, Rambla de Catalunya,84, 08008. Tel: 215 11 98. Metro Passeig de Gràcia. D 4,100 (cash only). A bright and smartened up hostel; it has rather odd furniture, but is nice enough and reasonable value.

★ Ciudad Condal, Mallorca,255, 08008. Tel: 215 10 40. Metro Passeig de Gràcia/Diagonal. D 3,700 (cash only). Bright, cheery, and one of the best hostels of its type.

★ Goya, Pau Claris,74, 08010. Tel: 302 25 65. Metro Urquinaona. D 2,770 (cash only). A typical and sufficient pension.

★ Oliva, Passeig de Gràcia,32, 08007. Tel: 317 50 87. Metro Passeig de Gràcia. D 3,500 (cash only). At the top of an attractive oval stairwell, this is cool, airy and tasteful. With good rooms, it is one of the best in its bracket.

★ Rosa, Pelai,14, 08001. Tel: 301 08 42. Metro Catalunya/ Universitat. D 2,200. Basic facilities with no seating area, but rooms are large, light and reasonable value.

# Gràcia

### Hotels

★★★★ Condor, Vía Augusta,127, 08006. Tel: 209 45 11/Tx: 52925 HOCON/Fax: 202 27 13. Metro Plaça Molina/Muntaner train station. D 12,000. On the outskirts of Gràcia, this is an average but pleasant business hotel.

★★★★ Park Putxet, Putget,68-74, 08023. Tel: 212 51 58/Tx: 98718 APHO-E/Fax: 418 51 57. Metro Lesseps/ El Putget train station. D 9,900. On the outskirts of Gràcia, this is decent and sufficiently comfortable with a roof-top conservatory restaurant.

★ ★ ★ HA Augusta, Lincoln,32-34, 08006. Tel: 218 33 55/Tx: 98820 HGPL-E. Metro Plaça Molina. D 10,600 (tax included). Fully equipped, but modern and characterless; some of the apartments have large terraces. Better value for families or groups.

★ ★ ★ Belagua, Vía Augusta,89-91, 08006. Tel: 237 39 40/Tx: 99643 NHVAG-E/Fax: 415 30 62. Metro Fontana. D 10,300. A modern, comfortable if rather bland business hotel.

★ ★ ★ HA Gala Placidia, Vía Augusta,112, 08006. Tel: 217 82 00/Tx: 98820 HGPL-E. Metro Plaça Molina. D 9,000 (tax included). A modern, tacky interior but rooms are well equipped, each with a private lounge.

★ ★ ★ HA Silver, Bretón de los Herreros,26-30, 08012. Tel: 218 91 00. Metro Fontana. D 5,200 (tax included). Good value apartments for families and longer stays, but nothing special.

### Hostels
— La Cartuja, Tordera,43, 08012. Tel: 213 33 12. Metro Joanic. D 4,000 (cash only). Good value, pleasant and simple, this is well located for enjoying Gràcia.

### Pensions and Guest Houses
— Norma, Gran de Gràcia, 87, 08012. Tel: 237 44 78. Metro Fontana. D 2,000 (tax included, cash only). Communal shower. At the top of a challenging staircase, this is well-kept and pleasant.
— San Medín, Gran de Gràcia, 125, 08012. Tel: 217 30 68. Metro Fontana. D 2,000 (tax included, cash only). Communal shower. A dingy staircase reveals a surprisingly bright, well-kept pension, with quaint and cosy rooms. Good value.

### Youth Hostel
Verge de Montserrat, Passeig de la Mare de Déu del Coll, 41-45, 08023. Tel: 213 86 33. Metro Vallcarca. Youth hostel membership card needed. 650 pesetas per night.

(**Opposite**) Seen from the cable car on the pier, the shady Rambles snakes away from the port following the path once carved by a stream.

(**Overleaf**) Playing with fire — one of a train of dragons taunted by daredevil revellers at the Marcé fiesta.

# Zona Alta

## Hotels

★ ★ ★ ★ ★ Princesa Sofía, Plaça Pius X11, 08028. Tel: 330 71 11/Tx: 51032 SOFI-E/Fax: 330 76 21. Metro Maria Cristina. D 20,650. Popular with business people and probably the best-known hotel in Barcelona. Unbeatable facilities include several restaurants, a large swimming pool and conference rooms, but it's not for those in search of local character.

★ ★ ★ ★ ★ Suite Hotel, Muntaner,505, 08022. Tel: 212 80 12/Tx: 99077 APHM/Fax: 211 23 17. El Putget train station. D 19,900. Good value, as every room is a suite; these are peaceful, generously designed, and have an outside terrace. There is a pleasant atmosphere and a cool fountain restaurant in the basement.

★ ★ ★ ★ Arenas, Capità Arenas,20, 08034. Tel: 204 03 00/Tx: 54990/Fax: 205 65 06. Metro Maria Cristina. D 12,500. Good facilities and pleasant rooms.

★ ★ ★ ★ Hesperia, Dels Vergós,20, 08017. Tel: 204 55 51/Tx:98403 PVIA-E/Fax: 204 43 92. Les Tres Torres train station. D 12,200. A quiet, modern business hotel with standard comforts. No restaurant, only a functional cafeteria, and it is a long distance from the city centre.

★ ★ ★ ★ Rekor'd, Muntaner,352, 08021. Tel: 200 19 53. Muntaner train station. D 11,000. Not luxurious but comfortable, homely suites which have only single beds, no doubles.

★ ★ ★ ★ HA Victoria, Avinguda Pedralbes,16, 08034. Tel: 204 27 54/Tx: 98302 LIHV-E/Fax: 204 27 66. Metro Maria Cristina. D 13,500. Attractively furnished, spacious apartments, all with terraces. The communal facilities include a swimming pool and restaurant; these are good value and certainly the most appealing of the apartment hotels.

★ ★ ★ Castellnou, Castellnou,61, 08017. Tel: 203 05 50/Tx: 98718 APHOH E/Fax: 205 60 14. Les Tres Torres train station. D 8,800. Modern and comfortable, this is attractively decorated and has a wholesome feel.

★ ★ ★ Les Corts, Travessera de les Corts,292, 08014. Tel: 322 08 11/Tx: 59001 BRRS-E. Metro Les Corts. D 10,300. A reasonable, tasteful and modern business hotel, which is a long way from the centre of town.

★ ★ ★ Mikado, Passeig de la Bonanova,58, 08017. Tel: 211 41 66/Tx: 97636/Fax: 211 42 10. Sarrià train station. D 10,500.

Reasonable facilities but slightly cramped, characterless, and far from the centre.

★ ★ ★ Mitre, Bertran,9-15, 08023. Tel: 212 11 04/Tx: 54990/Fax: 418 94 81. Padua train station. D 9,500. A run-of-the-mill, adequate business hotel; no restaurant and poorly located.

★ ★ ★ Pedralbes, Fontcuberta,4, 08034. Tel:203 71 12/Tx: 99850 NHSHP-E/Fax: 205 70 65. Sarrià train station. D 10,000. Pleasant, modern, international-style business hotel in a residential area.

★ ★ ★ Rallye, Travessera de les Corts,150, 08028. Tel: 339 90 50/Fax: 411 07 90. Metro Les Corts. D 8,250. Situated on the edge of town, close to Barcelona's football club, this may be handy for fans, but not for anyone else. Unremarkable rooms, but one of the few hotels with a roof-top pool and a panoramic city view.

★ ★ ★ Residencia, Passeig de la Bonanova,47, 08017. Tel: 211 50 22. Sarria train station. D 7,845 (cash only, including tax). Attached to a medical college, it is mainly for medical students and their families, but occasionally other visitors are accepted. Short on space and facilities, however, and not recommended.

★ ★ ★ Tres Torres, Calatrava,32, 08017. Tel: 417 73 00/Tx: 54990/Fax: 418 98 34. Tres Torres train station. D 9,500. Recently modernised, it has standard comforts but is very bland.

★ ★ ★ Zenit, Santaló,8, 08021. Tel: 209 89 11/Tx: 54990/Fax: 205 65 06. Muntaner train station. D 8,500. Decent rooms with white tiling, but only breakfast is available.

★ ★ Bonanova Park, Capità Arenas,51, 08034. Tel: 204 09 00/Tx: 54990/Fax: 204 50 14. Metro Maria Cristina. D 7,000. Pleasant, tasteful, clean and modern.

★ ★ L'Alguer, Passeig Pere Rodríguez,20, 08028. Tel: 334 60 50. Metro Collblanc. D 5,000. A rather depressing hotel with next to no facilities. Sited on the outskirts of town, it is handy for nothing but the football stadium.

### Youth Hostel
Pere Tarrés, Numància, 149-151, 08029. Tel: 410 23 09. Metro Les Corts/Maria Cristina. 650 pesetas if you're under 26 and show a membership card (more without a card).

# Barceloneta

### Hotels
★ Santa Marta, General Castaños,14, 08003. Tel: 319 44 27/Tx:

97206 ATT.STA.MARTA/Fax: 315 38 19. Metro Barceloneta. D 3,600. Dreary and unappealing.

### Hostels

★ ★ La Hipica, General Castaños,2, 08003. Tel: 315 13 92. Metro Barceloneta. D 2,350 (lower in winter, cash only). Pleasant, clean rooms.

★ ★ Del Mar, Plaça del Palau,19, 08003. Tel: 319 33 02/Tx: 97206/Fax: 315 38 19. Metro Barceloneta. D 4,137 (tax included). Good access for the beach, but this hotel is shabby, poorly lit, and has tasteless furnishings.

★ El Oasis 11, Plaça del Palau,17, 08003. Tel: 319 43 96. Metro Barceloneta. D 3,710 (visa or cash only, extra in summer). Pretty basic and dingy, but not bad for the budget-conscious who want to be near the beach.

## From Poble Sec to Sants

### Hotels

★ ★ ★ Expo, Mallorca,1-23, 08014. Tel: 325 12 12/Tx: 54147 EXHO E/Fax: 325 11 44. Metro Sants. D 8,800. Surprisingly there are few hotels around Sants station. Expo is modern and ugly with tasteless furnishings (although renovations are in progress); the roof-top pool is a bonus.

★ ★ ★ Terminal, Provença,1, 08029. Tel: 321 53 50/Tx: 98213/Fax: 419 25 29. Metro Sants. Standard rooms, and overall sufficient with reasonable facilities, if rather drab.

★ ★ Auto-Hogar, Avinguda Paral.lel,64, 08001. Tel: 241 84 00/Fax: 241 11 33. Metro Paral.lel. D 5,300. Overpriced and dingy with a drab interior. Some rooms have balconies but Paral.lel, an arterial road, is not a sought-after view.

★ Climent, Gran Vía de les Corts Catalanes,304, 08004. Tel: 223 98 07. Metro Espanya. D 4,700 (visa or cash only, tax included). The rooms are basic and unattractive, some with no wardrobe or carpet.

★ Coronado, Nou de La Rambla,134, 08004. Tel: 242 34 48/Tx: KUKA 99245. Metro Paral.lel. D 5,000. Sufficient but overpriced and seedy area.

★ Sans, Antoni de Campany,82, 08014. Tel: 331 37 00. Metro

Sants. D 3,200 (tax included, Visa and MasterCard only). Functional, unattractive and convenient for little other than Sants station.

★ Transit, Rector Triadó,82, 08014. Tel: 424 60 13. Metro Sants. D 5,100. Modern, appealing rooms, and overall, this is much better than the area promises.

## Hostels

★ ★ Abrevadero, Vilà i Vilà 77, 08004. Tel: 241 22 05/Tx: KUKA 99245/Fax: 241 22 04. Metro Paral.lel. D 3,900. Dingy with standard rooms and basic furniture; poorly located, there's better value elsewhere.

★ Rio, Sant Pau,119, 08001. Tel: 241 06 51. Metro Paral.lel. D 1,550 (cash only). Cheap with average rooms, but at the wrong end of Sant Pau for centrality and safety.

## Camping

— Cala Gogó, Carretera del la Platja, 08820, El Prat. Tel: 379 46 00. Nine kilometres south of the city, this is a first class camping with 1,500 sites.

— Estrella de Mar, Carretera C-246, km 16,7, 08860 Castelldefels. Tel: 665 32 67. Around 17 kilometres south of Barcelona, this is a second class camping with 550 sites.

— Hispano, Carretera N-11, Km 641, 08320 Masnou. Tel: 555 08 75. Sixteen kilometres north, it is a first class camping with 120 sites.

— Don Quijote, Carretera. N-11 Km. 639,08390 Montgat. Tel: 389 10 16. Thirteen kilometres north of Barcelona, this is a second class camping with 140 sites.

A bird's eye view: the whole of life can be spied from Barcelona's balconies. Neighbourhood watch comes naturally in the close quarters of the Gothic area.

FIVE

# Food, Drink and Restaurants

## Catalan Cuisine

Meat, olive oil and garlic are still the main players in Spanish kitchens. And Catalan cuisine, which is becoming better known beyond its home is bold and hearty. Typical dishes combine strong tastes, frequently meat with fruit or seafood: duck with pears or prunes, or chicken and king prawns are classic examples. Grilled meat (often with chips) is common, and the typical menu lists beef, veal, rabbit, pork, lamb, goat, kid and chicken.

Pig is the key animal, and smoked, cured or cooked, Spaniards relish every last part. Trotters crop up on many a menu, as do snouts and ears on the tapas counter. Medallions of pork with mushrooms, prunes and pine nuts *(llomillets al bolet)* is a wholly Catalan speciality. *Butifarra amb mongetes* (pallid slices of steamed sausage mixed with white beans) is a staple regional dish. And it is normal to find pork lard replacing butter or olive oil in Catalan recipes.

Rabbit *(conill)* makes a cheap and tasty main course, often combined with *"all i oli"* — a strong, garlic mayonnaise. Widely seen as a delicacy, game of all sorts appears regularly, especially around the province. Partridge, pheasant, hare and wild boar all excite the local palate. Look out for *perdiu a la vinaigreta* (partridge baked in a sharp vinegar gravy). And both this and chicken *(pollastre)* are tasty when cooked *a la caçadora,* in a tomato and red pepper sauce. Offal is always popular and tripe in tomato sauce has a strong presence.

Despite being a seaport, much of the fish consumed in Barcelona is imported from other parts of Spain or Europe; and many of the larger shellfish are Atlantic creatures, hailing straight from Scotland and northern climes. As a result, fish is neither cheap nor a regular feature in budget restaurants. Frequently found, however, are the Mediterranean varieties — sea bass *(lubina),* red bream *(besugo),* angler fish *(rape),* hake *(merluza)* and turbot *(rodaballo).*

Cod is also abundant, both fresh and salted; and one common regional dish is *esqueixada,* a cold cod salad with onion, pepper and olives. *Suquet* is the most typical Catalan stew made from fish with dense flesh, like sea bass, monkfish and rockfish. And keep an eye out for the superb, wholesome fish casseroles, *zarzuela* and (its more fashionable rival) *cazuela.* These combine two or more varieties of soft white fish with a hard boiled egg and thick, rich sauce.

Available all over Spain, but of Valèncian origin, are gigantic seafood paellas; Catalan paellas often contain meat, especially rabbit. A more regional and strange-looking rice dish is *arroz negro,* tinted black by the ink of squid. (A great place specialising in rice dishes is Elche at Vilà i Vilà,71, tel: 241 30 89). And anchovies (the best of which come from L'Escala) are used to perk up many dishes.

Never shy of rich additions and erring towards a sweet tooth, chocolate may be slipped into a savoury dish, such as squid in chocolate sauce *(calamars xocolata).* Likewise cava sauces are used to dress up fish, chicken and shellfish. And in Mediterranean style, a garlic and tomato sauce can smother almost anything.

Cheap and remarkably tasty, is the Catalan mainstay of *pa amb tomàquet* — a large slice of white bread smeared with tomato, olive oil and garlic. Sometimes eaten alone, this is commonly topped with *pernil serrà* or *jamón serrano* (serrano ham), or anything you fancy, after which it becomes a *tostada.* Occasionally you'll be presented with the ingredients and left to concoct your own.

With the odd exception of boiled potatoes, it's rare to find vegetables served with a main dish. Even accompanying salads tend to be an unimaginative mix of tomato, onion and olives. And surprising, given the availability of fresh local produce, is the frequency with which tinned vegetables crop up. Catalan salad *(amanida Catalana)* is a basic salad mixed with slices of cold meat.

Popular vegetable dishes, often served as a starter, include *espinacs a la Catalana* (spinach with raisins and pine nuts) and *espinacs a la crema* — a rich, creamed variety. *Escalivada,* a cold, oily mixture of skinned aubergines and red peppers is a frequent starter and something of an acquired taste. Another regular is a plain plate of boiled beans and potatoes.

Recipes for garlic soup *(sopa d'all)* seem to call for an entire garlic (although the roughly chopped cloves are mild and chewy after simmering); into this eggs and bread are usually steeped. Another provincial broth is *escudella* made from ham or beef bone stock and which appears to be a mixture of leftovers, typically pasta, potato, chickpeas and vegetables; when scraps of mince are included it is known as *carn d'olla.* And the Andalusian *gazpacho* (chilled tomato and vegetable soup) is also widespread.

Unmistakably the prime pudding is *crema Catalana,* a rich, eggy custard with a burnt sugar coat; while *flan,* the Spanish equivalent of crème caramel, is its main contender. Cakes and ice creams which contain *músic* (dried fruit and nuts) are always popular. *Músic* can be served alone as a dessert, often with the sweet wine Moscatel; it can also be added to *mel i mató,* the mild, white cheese eaten with honey. The almond fudge *turrón* comes in several guises within pastries and ice creams. Especially juicy is the Galician speciality, *tarta de Santiago.* This moist almond sponge is dusted with icing sugar and served with pudding wine (Mistela, or in smarter venues Els Meus Amors) — best poured on top.

*Chocolate con churros* is a special treat all over Spain and, eaten on high days and holidays, these twisted fritters are dipped into a thick, hot chocolate. Other *postres* (desserts) are frozen versions of *crema Catalana* using rich vanilla ice cream, or fruit ices in frosted shells like coconut, lemon and melon.

There are plenty of alternatives to the local cuisine, however, as most nationalities are represented in Barcelona (see International Cooking section below). Probably as a result of the tapas culture, and the customary lingering over lunch, fast food is less prevalent here than in some countries. (McDonalds has few high street slots, expect to translate your chicken McNuggets to a McPollo.)

Indulgence is the first ingredient of Spanish cooking, with health as low priority. This is gradually changing, however, as seen in the growing number of vegetarian restaurants. On the whole, Spanish plates are dished up without fussy decoration, but the more delicate French influence is apparent here in the smarter restaurants.

Cooking from different Spanish regions can all be sampled in Barcelona. Catalan cooking is considered number two, led by the Basques, whose cooking is legendary as much for its mammoth portions as it is for its fabulous fish dishes. If you have the chance both this and Galician cuisine are well worth trying.

# Wine

Catalunya is primarily remembered for its *cava* (sparkling white wine) which is mostly excellent, and means champagne is not just the preserve of special occasions. An international success, *cava* has been marketed as a great value sparkling wine, never attempting to rival the labels of northern France (though Catalans frequently refer to it as *xampan*). The smartest establishments still offer French champagne (as much for its snob appeal as its higher quality), but *cava* is found everywhere.

Sant Sadurní d'Anoia, an area within the Penedès region, is the heartland of the *cava* industry, and it is well worth visiting one of the *cava* houses (see South and Inland from Barcelona, chapter 12). The two most famous are Freixenet and Cordoniú, both major worldwide exporters. Particularly worth sampling is a small label, Segura Viudas, which is now owned by Freixenet.

Catalunya's plentiful vineyards keep local table wines comparatively cheap. Penedès is the foremost region, although closely followed by the wines from Emporda. Rosés *(rosados)* are widely appreciated, especially chilled in summer; keep an eye out for Conde de Caralt and René Barbier (a light, fruity variety) which are both commonly served with fish. All colours of these two lables are worth testing, and particularly special, although expensive, is the Cabernet Sauvignon from René Barbier.

Masia Bach is a well known make with a good rich *tinto* (red) and dry *rosado*. Wines from Lleida have an increasing reputation, in particular the Raimat label have some outstanding brands — try Clos Abadia, a full bodied, soft red made from Cabernet Sauvignon grapes. Gran Corona and Sangre de Toro are both respected local *tintos*.

**Sangria** is the Spanish punch, made with young red wine or cheap *cava,* a splash of Cointreau, gin and brandy, orange and lemon slices, sugar and ice. This can be delicious as a sunny daytime drink, but beware of watery versions passed off as the real thing in tourist haunts. There are, of course, abundant sherries *(jerez),* the most regularly found being the dry Tio Pepe or Fino Laina.

Fruit liqueurs or schnappes are enjoying a recent boom, especially *melocotón* (peach), *manzana* (apple), and *melón*. Particularly fashionable among Barcelona's yuppies, these can be an apperatif, an after dinner *digestivo,* or drunk as a cocktail with a fruit mixer.

Brandy comes close to many a Spanish heart, and the likes of Veterano, Soberano and Fundador are popular high street brands. Cardenal Mendoza and Gran Duc D'Alba are both expensive, top quality labels. Torres Diez (10) has a rich, ruby colour, a distinct fruity taste, enjoys a great following and a lethal reputation.

# Soft Drinks

Coffee in Catalunya is fresh, strong and as integral a part of daily life as sleeping; but Spaniards are very particular about this ritual: the short sharp shock, *café solo,* for instance, must always be topped with a thin layer of froth *(crema);* anyone finding this an insufficient jolt should ask for a *doble.* Also small but served in a short glass with a dash of milk is a *cortado.*

*Café con leche* comes in a large cup and saucer and should be made with hot milk. Regular black coffees of this size, regarded by locals as an odd tourist habit, are known as *café Americano.* Occasionally the more international places serve an Italian-style cappuccino.

The cold varieties include *café con hielo* — a *café solo* which you pour over a separate glass of ice, or a *granizada de café* — sweetened black coffee with crushed ice. A *biberón* is a sickly option, where a glass with a thick layer of cold condensed milk is topped with hot coffee.

Almost any type of spirit is splashed into coffee, though mostly brandy *(coñac): trifásico* — milky coffee with a dash of brandy, *carajillo* — half black, half brandy, or *café caliente (de carretero)* — black with heated brandy, sugar and a slice of lemon. Due to the powerful smell of a *carajillo* made with anis, this is occasionally referred to as a *perfumado. Café Irlandés* (Irish coffee) served in a stemmed glass is also prevalent.

A decaffeinated *(descafeinado)* powdered option, though rarely advertised, is sometimes available, but expect some jokes about wimpish behaviour. Tea *(té),* especially drunk with milk, is a relative rarity in Spain, but infusions are on the increase; most widely available are *poleo-menta* (peppermint), *manzanilla* (camomile) and *tila* (limeflowers). Since these are seldom strong enough to disguise the taste of the tap water, ask for it made with *agua mineral.*

Main local soft drinks are *granizadas,* tall glasses of crushed ice, and sweetened fruit juice (usually lemon) or cold coffee. Another favourite is *horchata,* a sweet drink of milky consistency made from water and crushed earth almonds. This can be fairly insipid, particularly when made with tap water. (For the best *horchata* in town, go to the café Lluís Sirvent, Ronda de Sant Pau,3.)

*Note:* All soft drinks are given in Spanish.

# Restaurants

Unlike so many other countries, Spain still promises many good value, basic restaurants which dish up high quality food. The Rambles, Gothic quarter and Gràcia are where you're likely to chance upon discoveries of all types. Alternatively Eixample and the neighbouring Zona Alta hold the more upmarket establishments. Since their wide streets and huge buildings are not conducive to aimless wandering, it's best to have an end in mind. (Aribau and València offer the greatest selection.) Barceloneta remains the place for fish.

As a rule of thumb, restaurants in Barcelona are open between 13.00 and 16.30 hours and 20.30 until 24.00 hours. Unless specified those below open daily although hours and days may well change. (For the latest information see the *Guía del Ocio*.) August is traditionally the month for locals to leave the city and consequently many restaurants close.

Most restaurants in the medium and top brackets accept major credit cards and sometimes Eurocheques. As in other parts of the world, the cost of the house wine rises in relation to the overall price of the establishment, although even in upmarket places this tends to be comparatively cheap.

Wine, water and bread are usually included in the price of the daily set menu (obligatory by law) which can be an exceptional bargain. These are generally only available at lunchtime, except in the cheaper restaurants. The broad price categories are for one full meal and intended only as an indication: **Top** costing over 3,000 pesetas, **Medium** costing between 1,000 and 3,000 pesetas and **Budget** costing up to 1,000 pesetas. Listed below are some recommendations in each area.

## Rambles and Old Town

### Top
**Agut,** Gignàs,16. Tel: 315 17 09. Metro Jaume I/Drassanes. (Closed Sunday night, Monday and July.) A fashionable place with locals, there are often queues and it's best to book at weekends. Sophisticated, well presented dishes with some typical Catalan specialities and good value house wine. The atmosphere is informal and vibrant — highly recommended.
**La Bona Cuina,** Pietat,12. Tel: 315 41 56. Metro Jaume I. (Closed Tuesday.) Adjacent to the Cathedral, this caters mainly for tourists

with elaborate, grandiose decoration and Modernismo-style furniture. It serves top quality cuisine with Catalan specialities, such as duck with pears or *zarzuela;* and offers an excellent wine list, with good house wine from Tarragona. (Its sister restaurant **La Cuineta** is close by at Paradís,4.)

**Los Caracoles,** Escudellers,14. Tel: 302 31 85. Metro Liceu. In the thick of the red light area, this riotous and typically Spanish restaurant has been going non-stop since 1835. Its walls are alive with bright tiles and celebrity photographs, while dexterous waiters dispatch hearty Catalan dishes. Popular with locals and tourists alike, this is highly atmospheric and recognisable by its sizzling, open stove.

**El Gran Cafè,** Avinyó,9. Tel: 318 79 86. Metro Liceu. (Closed Saturday lunch and Sunday.) A surprisingly sumptuous find in a seedy street, this is popular with politicians and business people for lunch, but becomes more romantic in the evening. It serves nouvelle cuisine French and Catalan dishes, with fish specialities like ravioli with langoustines and unusual cold soups.

**Quo Vadis,** Carmen,7. Tel: 302 40 72. Metro Liceu. (Closed Sunday and August.) This upmarket, uptight establishment caters mainly for business clients, especially at lunchtime. Serving excellent Catalan and international dishes, their specialities include fighting-bull steak, game and exotic varieties of mushroom.

**Senyor Parellada,** L'Argentería,37. Tel: 315 40 10. Metro Jaume I. (Closed Sunday, festivals and August.) The extensive menu of delicious Catalan and traditional Spanish recipes is accompanied by reasonably priced wines. This is the place for politicians to lunch and writers and artists to dine; at all hours it resounds with animated conversation. The airy, arched room has attractive paintings, plants and split cane blinds.

**Siete Puertes,** Passeig d'Isabel II,14. Tel: 319 44 62. Metro Barceloneta. (Meals served continuously from 13.00-00.30.) Large and bustling, this is definitely an institution. Over the years it has attracted so many famous clients that tiny plaques pepper the wooden panels indicating where Picasso or Lorca once sat. Enjoying a wide reputation and a constant stream of diners, surprisingly this is only just in the top price bracket. The cooking is excellent, the service attentive, not fussy. House specialities are fish grills and paella, and they have a rice dish for each day of the week.

### Medium
**Al Primer Crit,** Banys Vells,2. Tel: 319 10 97. Metro Jaume I.

(Closed Monday night and August.) This unobtrusive restaurant, with balcony tables, was originally an oil shop. The atmosphere is peaceful and the food a mix of reasonable value Spanish dishes.

**Agüir,** Riereta,8. Tel: 329 95 55. Metro Liceu/Paral.lel. (Closed midday Sunday, midday Monday and August.) A surprisingly sophisticated find for such a dingy part of the old town. This restaurant serves small, tasty portions of rich food with a varied Catalan menu. The modern black and white interior glows with warm red and green lights. Excellent value and recommended.

**Can Lluís,** Cera,49. Tel: 241 11 87. Metro Paral.lel. (Closed Sunday and festivals.) One of the best value restaurants in this section. A small, civilised and homely place which offers a wide range of well cooked Catalan dishes; try their garlic mushrooms or baked partridge *(perdiu a la vinaigreta).* Full of atmosphere, there are bound to be queues at weekends, but it's worth waiting.

**Culleretes,** Quintana,5. Tel: 317 30 22. Metro Liceu. (Closed Sunday night, Monday and most of July.) An unpromising exterior hides a large, vibrant and genuinely Spanish restaurant which was founded in 1786. It has bright, tiled walls and stained glass windows, and is a popular place with local families, especially for Sunday lunch. Wholesome cooking at a reasonable price.

**Egipte,** Jerusalem, 3. Tel: 317 74 80. Metro Liceu. (Closed Sunday.) Just behind the Boqueria market, and one of Barcelona's most popular restaurants — especially with arty and media types — this stays open late on opera and theatre nights. Filled with antique furnishings, it occupies four floors with numerous balconies, alcoves and private rooms; the atmosphere is electric. High quality Catalan and international dishes include a five-layer savoury *tortilla* cake or chicken and king prawn casserole. Excellent value, particularly at lunchtime when it has a cheap set menu, but best to book at weekends. One of its sister restaurants is almost opposite in Jerusalem, and another, **Egipte Rambla,** at Rambla,79.

**La Cua Curta,** Carassa. Tel: 315 30 02. Metro Jaume I. (Evenings only, closed Sunday and Monday.) More or less limited to pâté, cheese and wine this has a respectable, wine bar atmosphere and cavernous interior. A good place for a light meal but not the best value. Worth a visit for the cheese fondue.

**La Morera,** Plaça Sant Agusti,1. Tel: 318 75 55. Metro Liceu. (Closed Sundays, festivals and August.) This is frequented for its tasty, reasonably priced Spanish and international cuisine. A popular place for younger Catalans and parties, it promises a lively atmosphere.

**La Rioja,** Durán i Bas,5. Tel: 301 22 98. Metro Catalunya/Jaume

I. (Closed Sunday, Saturday night in summer.) Specialising in Riojan dishes, this restaurant has a bright interior and family feel.

**La Vinateria Del Call,** Sant Domènech del Call,9. Tel: 302 60 92. Metro Liceu/Jaume 1. (Nightly except Sunday.) This informal, authentic Catalan bar is tucked into a tiny back street off the well-trodden tourist track. Decorated with the ubiquitous hanging hams, it has low lights and a vibrant atmosphere which draws the locals. Cold tapas includes pâté, cheese, ham and *tortilla;* wines come from all over Spain but specialities are Riojan.

**Pizza Nostra,** Montcada. Tel: 319 90 58. Metro Jaume I. (Closed Monday.) Just beside the Picasso museum, this offers crispy, American-style pizzas with generous toppings, imaginative salads and wicked-looking desserts.

**Pla de la Garsa,** Assaonadors,13. Tel: 315 24 13. Metro Jaume I (Evenings only until around 02.00.) Full of character, the beamed interior has rickety nooks and crannies, especially up the spiral staircase. A relaxed place which specialises in cured meats, smoked fish, pâté and cheese.

**Recó d'Aragó,** Carmen,28. Tel: 302 67 89. Metro Liceu. (Closed Tuesday.) One of few Aragonese restaurants in the city, this offers a cheap set menu. It has a dull interior, and serves regional specialities using lamb, rabbit and kid.

### Budget

**Amaya,** La Rambla, 20-24. Tel: 302 10 37. Metro Liceu/Drassanes. This large, civilized restaurant opens out behind a greasy tapas bar. With Basque specialities, it has particularly good looking seafood and puddings. The prevalence of locals and bustling feel bode well. This only makes the budget bracket if you have the set menu.

**Casa José,** Plaça de Sant Josep Oriol,10. Tel: 302 40 20. Metro Liceu. (Closed Sunday.) One of the most popular haunts with budget tourists, this is a busy and down-to-earth place. Generous portions of plain Spanish cooking which, at 350 pesetas for the two-course set menu, is excellent value.

**Compostelà,** Ferràn,30. Tel: 318 23 17. Metro Liceu. (Closed Tuesday.) Just off the Rambles, this unpretentious restaurant serves typical plain but tasty Spanish fare. With a basic interior, it's not an obvious choice and is frequented mainly by local families. Reasonably priced with particularly good seafood.

**L'Encanteri,** Dagueria,13. Tel: 319 65 02. Metro Jaume 1. (Closed Sunday.) This describes itself as a typical tavern and champagne house *(xampanyería),* but is most recommended for its simple Catalan food and good value set menu. Run by a charming family, it is rather quaint, full of character and a relaxed place for a drink or snack. Open until 02.00, it even serves fried eggs and bacon.

**La Garduña,** Morera,17-19. Tel: 302 43 23. Metro Liceu. (Closed Sunday.) Inside the back of the Boqueria market, here you find cheap dishes using fresh local produce. Genuine and wholesome, their specialities include ham hock and *zarzuela.*

**Guixot,** Riereta,8. Tel: 329 95 53. Metro Paral.lel. (Until 01.00 daily.) A busy place whose tasty bar snacks include sandwiches, savoury or sweet crêpes and salads.

**La Rivolta,** Hospital,116. Metro Liceu. Reputedly Barcelona's only anarchist pizzeria, this place has a friendly atmosphere which pulls a young crowd and some interesting haircuts. To the tune of radical Catalan music, you can drink at the bar or eat well (tasty, fresh food served quickly) for under 500 pesetas.

**Portalon,** Banys Nous,20. Metro Liceu. (Closed Sunday.) Once a stable, now serving great tapas, this restaurant is one of the cheapest around. The tone is rough and ready, and it has a raw, earthy feel and musty, alcoholic smell. With old casks and bottles kicking around, this successfully uses ordinary surroundings to create an atmosphere.

---

### Divine Cooking

Those with a sweet tooth will have no trouble satisfying their cravings in Barcelona; here no street is complete without a *pastelería.* And local bakers put the competition to shame with their creamy tarts, iced biscuits, big buns and multi-coloured meringues.

Not only do many villages push their own local pastry but saints days, far from being abstemious occasions, are celebrated with a dedicated cake. For All Saints Day (1 November), shop fronts are packed with *panellets;* concocted in various colours, these are mainly soft, marzipan balls rolled in pine nuts. Similarly, San Juan (24 June) is honoured with a *coca,* a long, thin cake which contains fruit or nuts.

To ward off ill luck, you must eat *turrón* after Christmas dinner, but Easter Monday boasts the best cooked-up trickery. Traditionally godparents give their godchildren a *tortell* — a doughnut which sports a paper crown. Deep inside lurks either a charm or a bean; if you uncover a gift you are proclaimed King of the day, but discover a bean and the price you must pay.

# Eixample

## Top

**Chicoa,** Aribau,73. Tel: 253 11 23. Metro Passeig de Gràcia. (Closed Saturday, Sunday and August.) This charming place serves top quality Catalan and Spanish cuisine. Its typically Spanish interior and discreet service attracts both business people and romantic couples.

**Gran Colmado,** Consell de Cent,318. Tel: 318 85 77. Metro Passeig de Gràcia. (Closed Sunday and holidays.) This original delicatessen serves exquisite tapas at the bar or full meals at tables in the back. Once a textile factory, its narrow, fridge-lined interior is brightly lit and displays produce by country of origin. The icy-coloured turquoise and chrome decor makes shopping an unusually cool and enjoyable experience. A great place for gifts, particularly wines, liqueurs, preserves and teas.

**La Mercantil Peixatera,** Aribau,117. Tel: 253 35 99. (Last orders 01.30, closed Monday lunch.) Here a constant hum of animated conversation enlivens the airy, modern brasserie look. It so effectively combines simplicity and sophistication that, despite the bright lights, this is even romantic. The superb quality cuisine of exquisite fish dishes, is based on a blend of French and Catalan recipes. The best find in the area.

**O'Nabo de Lugo,** Pau Claris,169. Tel: 215 30 47. Metro Passeig de Gràcia. (Closed Sunday and most of August). This Galician outfit has a tapas bar downstairs (open from 08.00), and a quality restaurant upstairs. The plain interior sports regional clogs and Galician bagpipes, and offers an above average menu.

**La Punyalada,** Passeig de Gràcia,104. Tel: 218 83 44. Metro Passeig de Gràcia. It would be easy to overlook this excellent restaurant which has an unremarkable, brightly lit interior. But, founded in 1900, it has a catching atmosphere and high quality cooking which bring people back. The varied menu includes fillet steak in whisky and flamboyantly tossed *flambée* specialities. The chef enjoys playing with contrasts — hot, wild strawberries in Cointreau and pepper with ice cream went down well.

**Reno,** Tuset,27. Tel: 200 91 29. Gràcia train station. Widely considered one of the leading restaurants in Barcelona, this serves beautiful Catalan and French cuisine.

**Sibarit,** Aribau,65. Tel: 253 93 03. Metro Passeig de Gràcia. Aimed mainly at business people, this serves good international cuisine in luxurious surroundings. Attentive service, but rather hushed and short on atmosphere.

## Medium

**Els Balcons,** Provença,203. Tel: 254 60 83. Provença train station. (Closed Saturday lunch, Sunday night and August.) This has a reasonable value, genuinely Catalan menu. Try the rich scallops *au gratin* in cava; or one for the brave is *calamars xocolata* — elastic squid strips in chocolate sauce.

**Cala y Kima,** Aragó,40. Tel: 426 35 03. Metro Rocafort. (Closed Tuesday and Sunday midday.) This pocket-sized café is chirpy, unpretentious and serves a great cheese fondue. Pavement seating is popular, although Aragó, a major thoroughfare, has its fair share of juggernauts.

**Campechano Merendero,** València,286. Tel: 215 62 33. Metro Passeig de Gràcia. This original restaurant serves up grilled meats in a cheerful, easy-going way. Flying flags, checked cloths and a thatched bar colour the simple Catalan fare; and the barbecue theme is accentuated by the life-sized stuffed boar installed in his very own pine forest.

**El Corte Inglés,** Plaça de Catalunya. Metro Catalunya. (Lunch only, closed Sunday.) This circular cafeteria, notable for its view of the city, can be found on the top floor of Barcelona's leading department store. You pay a set price for unlimited plates from the extensive hot and cold buffet. Good food, but it's not cheap unless you can eat your money's worth.

**Gran Bodega,** València,193. Metro Passeig de Gràcia. (Nightly until 01.00.) A testament to the archetypal tapas bar, this is larger than life. Sit out on the pavement or inside where tables, though numerous, are always at a premium. A heart-warming array of tapas has overtaken the bar and the kitchen emits an endless stream of delicacies. The decor is strictly typical — tiles, bottles, barrels and hanging hams — the diners largely local.

**Madrid-Barcelona,** Aragó,282. Tel: 215 70 26. Metro Passeig de Gràcia. (Closed Saturday night, Sunday and August.) This combines well-dressed waiters and tables with an old-fashioned interior and a pleasant café atmosphere. Here the emphasis is strongly on Catalan cooking, with *esquixada* and *escalivada,* garlic liver and stuffed peppers all making an appearance. Try the delicious fish terrine and their rusty house white wine from Penedès. Good value, especially the lunchtime set menu. This is highly recommended.

# Gràcia

## Top

**Botafumeiro,** Gran de Gràcia,81. Tel: 218 42 30. Metro Fontana. (Open 13.00-01.00, closed Sunday night and Monday.) An unbeatable place for fish, particularly shellfish, where the quality and presentation are excellent. And, with a superfluity of waiters, the price is extremely high. The interior is comfortable though fairly tasteless, but this is recommended for its superb cuisine. Popular with business people, it is one of few smart restaurants to offer full meals all day.

**El Galliner,** Martínez de la Rosa,71. Tel: 218 53 27. Metro Fontana. (Closed Tuesday and August.) A great discovery, this restaurant is tucked into three narrow rooms and has a superb menu. Cod dominates, and this basic fish is cleverly transformed by an unlikely choice of sauces (even honey or orange). A pale pink colour scheme, masks and tiny paintings complete the bohemian interior. Comfort is top priority, and you sit at low tables in cushioned cane armchairs.

**Roig Robí,** Sèneca,20. Tel: 218 92 22. Metro Diagonal. (Closed Sunday and festivals.) One of few central restaurants with outdoor seating in a beautiful, leafy courtyard. The tone is quiet and romantic, and the nouvelle cuisine includes carefully prepared Catalan and French dishes.

## Medium

**Los Asadores,** Avinguda Príncep d'Astúries,4. Tel: 237 89 07. Metro Fontana. Busy and bustling, here the emphasis is squarely on meat: *carns a la brasa* is the speciality, and cow hides are hung as partitions. Mammoth steaks are brought on wooden boards, although a few lighter options are available.

**Atzavara,** Francesc Giner,50. Tel: 237 50 98. Metro Diagonal. (Closed Wednesday.) This serves a broad range of dishes, from tortillas, salads and pastas to snack-size portions. Small, modern, and easy going, this is a great place for a light bite. Try some of the tasty varieties of goat's cheese.

**Bar Restaurant del Teatre,** Montseny,47. Tel: 218 67 38. Metro Fontana. (Closed Sunday and Monday.) Part of the Lluire theatre, the hall is also the theatre bar and is plastered with actors' photographs. Attracting arty types, here the genuinely Catalan menu is exceptional value. You eat on a raised platform with wooden floors, low slung lights and cane blinds. A discreet place which is barely obvious from the street. (Best mid-week, however, as choice diminishes when supplies run down at the end of the week.)

**Figaro,** Ros d'Olano, 4. Tel: 238 19 22. Metro Fontana. (Closed Sunday.) An Italian bar serving good, reasonably priced meals. It offers pasta and an excellent *carpaccio* (thin slivers of raw beef), all served up under dim lights in a modern interior.

**Flash Flash,** Granada del Penedès,25. Tel: 237 09 90. Metro Diagonal. This is frequented for its vast array of tortillas served up (all too hastily) in a '70s-style interior with white leather sofas. Despite its novelty, the food is unremarkable and it seems this place has seen better days.

**Tastavins,** Ramón i Cajal,12. Tel: 213 60 31. Metro Fontana. (Closed Sunday and most of September.) This straightforward Catalan restaurant is in the budget end of this category. Here the cooking is homely and genuine, with a strong emphasis on meat — such as their *Bistec Cabrales* (in a blue cheese sauce) or shoulder of lamb. There is also a good wine list; try the sharp and fruity Malón de Echaide. Easy going and recommended.

**Taverna El Nou Glop,** Montmay,49, Gràcia. Tel: 219 70 59. Metro Joanic/Fontana. (Evenings only except Sunday and festivals, closed Tuesday.) This serves good-value, plain Catalan food with specialities of grilled meat and *tostadas*. It has a simple whitewashed interior, bustling atmosphere and fast turnover.

### Budget

**Ca l'Agusti,** Verdi,28. Tel: 218 53 96. Metro Fontana. (Closed Wednesday.) Jolly and unpretentious, this is particularly recommended for lunch, with a set meal for 600 pesetas. The alternative menu includes tapas, cheese, *tostadas* and a wider than usual range of salads. The best in this section.

**Los Amigos,** Martínez de la Rosa. Metro Diagonal. This offers absurdly cheap local fare with a daily set menu for 450 pesetas; here a litre of wine and coffee will only bring the bill up to 520 pesetas.

**L'Olla del Torrent,** Torrent de l'Olla,106. Tel: 210 49 01. Metro Fontana/Diagonal. (Open 16.00-01.00, closed Wednesday). This small, boring café interior has a great menu and staff who take trouble. Specialising in crêpes, both savoury and sweet, they also serve *tostadas, tortillas,* and a glut of gooey *postres.*

**Mesón El Rebost,** Verdi,19. Tel: 217 86 01. Metro Fontana. Cheap and cheerful with checked table cloths and friendly service, this has a contrived rural decor. Mediocre, and rather insubstantial snacks, include pâté, cheese and salad. More filling is the rich choice of elaborate puddings.

**Taverna la Llesca,** Terol,6. Metro Fontana. (Open until 01.00, closed Monday and August.) This is a simple, easy-going place where *tostadas* rule, whether topped with cheese, ham, tuna, garlic or pâté. Other specialities include grilled and skewered meats. All good value and served up in an airy, non-gimmicky interior.

# Zona Alta

### Top

**El Asador de Aranda,** Avinguda Tibidabo,31. Tel: 417 01 15. Avinguda Tibidabo train station. Inside this palacial Modernista mansion there is something of a banquet atmosphere. The richly decorative interior was created by a disciple of Gaudí, and despite numerous dining rooms, it is inevitably full. It specialises in grilled lamb, served at the table over mini glowing coals. It usually operates a set menu, which includes an original mixed starter and a fruity *digestivo* served with aniseed biscuits. Vital to book at weekends.

**El Café de la Republica,** Avinguda República Argentina,83. Tel: 210 23 03. Metro Vallcarca/Lesseps. (Open evenings until 02.30/03.00 Friday and Saturday, closed Sunday and festivals.) The house specialises in meat fondue and cheese *raclette,* with a broad choice of other dishes such as roast beef in orange. An inviting place where you'll be well looked after; this attracts young professionals and models for cocktails and predictions — palmists and tarot readers operate by night.

**Celler d'en Joe,** Teodara La Madrid,32. Tel: 417 88 57. El Putxet train station. Entering this original restaurant is like visiting someone's home, whose mish-mash of sentimental clutter has a well travelled feel. Somewhat shabby around the edges, the ambience is laid-back. Like the surroundings, the imaginative menu is an odd mix with a few Polynesian specialities. This joint rings of affluent hippies; the owner (who operates flexible hours and menu) describes his customers as friends. Don't miss the whisky-soaked prunes.

**La Venta,** Plaça Doctor Andreu. Tel: 212 64 55. Avinguda Tibidabo and the Tramvía Blau. (Closed Sunday.) Near the top of Tibidabo, this combines an enviably fresh location with exquisite dishes. It is a glamorous place where fine nouvelle cuisine is served discreetly. On summer evenings tables on the pretty terrace are at a premium and it's best to book at weekends. Stop for a pre-dinner drink in Merbeye, their bar next door, which exhibits some of the latest design ideas; look out for the cut off columns.

**Medium**

**Can Massana,** Plaça del Camp,6. Tel: 417 06 74. Putxet train station. (Closed Wednesday and Sunday night.) This bright, refined restaurant is family-run and friendly. Excellent cooking at a reasonable price, which includes Catalan specialities like chicken and prunes. Good atmosphere and worth the journey, but don't try and eat too late (the kitchen closes at 23.00).

# Barceloneta

Starting at Barceloneta metro the broad Passeig Nacional stretches down to the sea. Here almost every inch of pavement is monopolised by someone eating seafood. There are some good restaurants along this street (see below) but, for greatest flavour, it's worth continuing seawards to Platja de Sant Miquel (round to the left at the bottom).

This cramped back street has a distinct holiday feel. Side by side are a hoard of restaurants which sprawl onto the sand and lure sunbathers. Stationed outside each, and supported by a glossy display of wet fish, stands a salesman poised to ensnare you. But more persuasive are the open kitchens whose cooks compete in a dexterous performance of fish chopping and simmering.

Prices vary considerably; you'll spot the cheaper, more chaotic places by their lack of candles and wobbly tables. But specialities all along the sand are invariably mixed fish grills and seafood paellas. For maximum atmosphere head for the tables nearest the tide, where wandering musicians cash in. Firmly in the **Top** bracket and both highly recommended are **El Salmonette** and **Can Gato Negro,** next door to each other on Platja Sant Miquel.

**Medium**

**Cafe Puda Manel,** Passeig Nacional,60-61. Tel: 319 30 13. Metro Barceloneta. (Closed Monday.) Opened in 1870, and one of the best along the road, this is still run by the same family. Deceptively ordinary with basic checked table cloths, it serves fantastic seafood. Succulent mixed fish grill with baby squid, mussels and *pescaditos*.

**El Rey de la Gamba,** Passeig Nacional, 46-48-53. Tel: 319 30 14. Metro Barceloneta. This vast, successful restaurant spreads over three consecutive venues. As its name suggests, the speciality is prawns, or equally popular (and dripping from the ceiling) is *jamon serrano,* served with vast *tostados.* Frantic and fun with Formica tables on the pavement, this is something of a local institution.

# Poble Sec

## Top

**Casa Nostra,** Parlament,1. Tel: 325 27 30. Metro Poble Sec. (Closed Sunday evening and Tuesday.) Undoubtedly the best restaurant in this area, it is well worth a detour from the usual tourist zones. Nothing is too much trouble for the charming owners, Pilar, Porfirio and Angelo, who is also the superb and dedicated chef. Casa Nostra serves immaculately presented international cuisine, with dishes from all over Spain which are conscientiously updated. Ask for *suquillo* (delicious casserole of cod), their *cabrito* (kid marinated in spices) or the cured salmon with sweet mustard and dill sauce, among Angelo's delectable secret recipes. The house *rosado* is excellent value, and don't miss their famous truffles and cream.

# Poblenou

## Top

**Els Pescadors,** Plaça Prim, Metro Poblenou. Hiding in an area currently unadulterated but on the brink of an Olympic transformation, this lovely restaurant spills onto a pretty square. It does a thriving trade — their successful formula relies on delicious fish dishes presented with an absence of fuss — and merits a special journey to this part of town. Best to book.

# International Cooking

**Bunga Raya,** Assaonadors,7. Tel: 319 31 69. Metro Jaume I. (Closed Monday.) Describing itself as a casa satay, it serves Malaysian and Indonesian dishes and halal meat. This mellow little restaurant has an authentic, if a little limited, menu. Dishes are well prepared and superb value, expect to pay less than 1,000 pesetas. Don't miss the *roti,* soft holey pancakes.

**Cantina Mexicana,** Encarnació,51. Tel: 210 68 05. Metro Fontana/Joanic. (Closed festivals.) This serves medium-priced Mexican snacks or full meals in easy-going surroundings. Cocktails, such as tequila slammers or marguritas, are downed in the courtyard at the back.

**Govinda,** Plaça Vila de Madrid,4-5. Tel: 318 77 29. Metro Catalunya/Liceu. (Closed Sunday and August.) This claims to be the only Indian vegetarian restaurant in Spain. It has a peaceful, welcoming atmosphere with quality ingredients, service and presentation. The imaginative dishes include thalis and rice with cherries and watermelon. There's no alcohol, but try one of their lassies (even mango or mint) or rarities like fresh apple juice, rose and lemon drink and Indian teas. Highly recommended and popular with discerning locals.

**Jardn Chino,** Tordera,52. Tel: 258 57 69. Metro Joanic. A fairly cheap little place which serves authentic Chinese meals. Relaxed and friendly, if a touch haphazard.

**Kiyokata,** Muntaner, 231. Tel: 200 51 26. Metro Hospital Clínic. (Closed Sunday and festivals.) Exceptional Japanese food served in a stark, black and white interior. This has a vibrant atmosphere and, favoured for business lunches, it's best to book.

**Nuevo Seul,** d'Enric Granados,89. Tel: 253 11 63. Provença train station. Korean specialities.

**Pekin,** Rosselló,202. Tel: 215 01 77. Provença train station. (Closed Sunday.) This swish, expensive Chinese restaurant serves excellent food with attentive service — don't expect to lift a finger. Black plates and bronze-panelled walls contribute to the western, highly designed interior.

**A Los Ponchos,** València,196. Tel: 254 06 67. Metro Passeig de Gràcia. A fashionable Argentinian and Chilean restaurant.

**Rajah Restaurant,** Sant Pau,39. Tel: 329 23 03. Metro Liceu. (Closed Thursday.) Recently opened, this cheap and casual restaurant serves great Asian and tandoori cuisine. Hectic and popular (particularly with locals) turnover is fast. Run by the same family is the basic Pakistani restaurant **Shalimar** at Carme,71.

**Taj Mahal,** Londres,89. Tel: 322 32 33. Metro Hospital Clínic. This upmarket Indian restaurant serves good quality curries, watered down to suit the western palate.

**Tokyo,** Comtal,20. Tel: 317 61 80. Metro Catalunya. (Closed Sundays and festivals.) This quality Japanese restaurant has a simple, partitioned interior. Cheap by international prices, it still falls in the top price bracket, and reservations are advised at weekends.

**Tut Ankh Amon,** Rauric,18. Tel: 412 52 01. Metro Liceu. This family-run Egyptian restaurant offers six bargain set menus. Their speciality, a secret recipe, is the crisp and spicy *falafel*. Table cloths feature pharaohs while the golden columns are painted with hieroglyphics. Excellent value.

**Zurracapote,** Arístides Maillol,21. Tel: 334 29 30. Metro Palau Reial. Cuban specialities.

# Vegetarian

**Biocenter,** Pintor Fortuny,24. Tel: 302 35 67. Metro Liceu/ Catalunya. (Lunch only, closed Sunday and festivals.) This doubles up as a restaurant and shop selling health foods and cosmetics. The three-course set menu is good value; try the crisp, colourful self-service salad bar or the mixed plate of rice, vegetables and seaweed. Take-aways are also available.

**Les Corts Catalanes,** Gran Vía de les Corts Catalanes,603. Tel: 301 03 76. Metro Catalunya. A more upmarket, mainstream restaurant with salad bar, take-aways and health food shop. The menu includes soup, salad, pizza, pasta and hot vegetable dishes. Alcoholic drinks are a surprising addition to the customary range of juices, ginseng and herbal teas.

**Illa de Gràcia,** Sant Domènech,19. Tel 238 02 29. Metro Diagonal/Fontana. (Open lunch and dinner, closed Monday and second half of August.) Trying to shake off the hippie, healthy image of vegetarianism, this has a cool interior brightened by modern artworks, and a less obviously 'wholefoody' menu than others. Well cooked and presented, crêpes, pastas, soups, salads and mousses are served in their own good time.

**L'Hortet,** Pintor Fortuny, 32. Tel: 317 61 89. Metro Liceu/Catalunya. (Lunch only, closed Sunday and festivals.) This only operates a three course set menu which is excellent value at 450 pesetas. Peaceful and local, it serves a wholesome, filling and healthy meal; dishes include vegetable purée and an excellent *gazpacho*. The interior is simple, and it's worth waiting for a table as turnover is fast.

**Macrobiotica Zen,** Muntaner,12. Tel: 254 60 23. Metro Universitat. (Weekday lunches only, closed August.) Probably Barcelona's best vegetarian restaurant, this serves a slim choice of dishes, all of which are faultlessly wholesome. Try the excellent plate of the day, a heap of rice and vegetables or their tempting and far from abstemious puddings. It's good value and doubles up as a health food shop.

**Self Naturista,** Santa Anna,13. Metro Catalunya. (Open until 22.00, except Sunday.) Although the least appealing of Barcelona's vegetarian restaurants, this self-service cafeteria produces a wide range of fast food dishes. Don't be put off by long lunchtime queues which shrink rapidly as there's plenty of seating. Much quieter in the evening, but by this time the salads are invariably limp.

A city of music, where every square lends itself gracefully to an impromptu concert.

By day or night, Plaça del Sol is the very pulse of Gràcia — drawing out the whole community and inevitably their dogs.

SIX

# Bars, Nightlife and Entertainment

Wild, sleazy or sophisticated, Barcelona's nightlife is never shy. With something for everyone, a night out might mean music hall, opera, disco, cabaret, bowling or bingo. The Catalan tendency to seize new ideas is illuminated by night — be it fox-trotting or wife-swapping — anything goes without a second glance.

Most clubs are uptown and hardened clubbers do a circuit, knowing precisely which place peaks at what time (and if you happen to be on the track the wrong way, you may leave a trail of deserted hot spots behind). When entrance is free, you are liable to make up for this in expensive drinks, although a good night out is still more affordable here than in many European cities.

Since most Spaniards work until 20.00 — and after which it is not unusual to pursue another activity or night class — evenings get off to a slow start. Few people dine before 22.00 (in the family home it's often nearer 23.00), so entertainment seldom begins before midnight, and clubs don't limber up before at least 02.00. Recent attempts to clip the city's night wings mean many bars now close at 02.30 or 03.00. There is still ample action around the clock, but it is less easy to stumble upon.

Naturally Thursday, Friday and Saturday are the big nights, and many clubs, bars and restaurants operate extended hours at weekends. But a surprising addition is the late afternoon gambit, which is typically a feature of Sundays and festivals. Sometimes this is the preserve of teenagers, but it is quite feasible to go disco or ballroom dancing before tea of a Sunday.

Cultural nightlife is rich, and especially in summer when Grec, the annual arts festival, takes place. Named after the Grec (Greek style) amphitheatre on Montjuïc, in which the festival was initially contained, events have since spread around the city. This is funded by the town hall with the support of commercial sponsors, and for six weeks (last week of June to the first week of August) Barcelona is awash with music — classical, jazz, folk, rock and pop concerts — as well as theatre and dance shows. Tickets are obtainable in advance (from May by writing to La Palau de la Virreina, Rambla,99, Barcelona 08002, tel: 301 77 75). For most events it is possible to buy tickets on the door, or a few days before from the box office at the above address (open 10.00-19.00).

Outdoor nightlife has much to recommend it, particularly through the long summer. For non-stop entertainment, you can't beat a chair on the Rambles, or better still sample a fiesta; and there's a fair chance of coinciding with one since most segments of the city have their own celebrations. Along with their individual traditions, music is the normal form of revelry; and it is common to find every square in the area buzzing well into the early hours. (See Catalunya and the Catalans, Chapter 1).

Hand in glove with its seafaring roots comes the predictable quota of overt prostitution. This is mostly concentrated (day and night) in the red light district which sprawls all over the port end of the Rambles. Another major hang out, close to the smartest part of town, and leading away from the top business hotel (Princesa Sofía) is along Avinguda de Joan XXIII. This, free from protesting residents, uses its very isolation to support a brisk and blatant trade.

Although times and closures of venues are listed below, these are liable to change frequently. Clubs officially close at 03.30, but the reality can be quite different. Likewise many bars stay open long after their designated closing time (usually 02.30 or 03.00), and it's possible to find yourself continuing well into the morning behind closed shutters. For the latest information, consult the *Guía del Ocio,* a weekly entertainment guide available from newsstands and published every Friday, or the Guía del Pais.

# Cafés

Café lingering, a somewhat Latin pastime, is as evident in Barcelona as elsewhere in Spain, but certain squares have a monopoly on the action.

**Plaça Reial** (Metro Liceu.) Just off the Rambles, a visit to this loved and hated haunt is a must. Once the site of a Capuchin convent, this arcaded, neo-Classical square is now graced by Gaudí's wrought iron lamp-posts, tall palms and a central fountain. A schizophrenic place, this at times appears beautiful, and at others, seedy, littered and stinking of urine. Host to both the weekly stamp collectors' meeting (Sunday mornings) and nightly drug deals, its numerous bars are always packed, though loyalties shift around the square's sides with the sun. A gripping vantage point for getting beneath the city's skin, it has an air of defiance and attracts characters from all walks of life; junkies, tramps, animals, pigeons and children mill around its benches and bars. The token addition of a permanent police vigil has done little to curb the action. A good bet for late night drinks, its inimitable atmosphere compensates for the invariably surly service. And when the bars close Karma nightclub carries on (see below).

**Plaça del Sol** (Metro Fontana.) First timers to Gràcia should go for the jugular by heading directly to this attractive square. Gràcia may have been enveloped by the gargantuan Barcelona, but its distinct village character has not been devoured. Here, as in so many *plaças,* one sees Spaniards doing what they most enjoy — passing the time of day, either in gentle stroll or peacefully seated. And as the nucleus of the community, it draws out elderly residents, families, kids and dogs alike.

Dusk sees the pace quickening and the ringside bars taking on a more fashionable aspect. A magnet for the young and arty who have recently moved in on the village, it bristles with activity. Café del Sol has a loyal following, while the best local tapas can be found opposite in Taberna Marcelino, and the nightclub El Dorado next door rakes in the dancers after 02.00. This is an ideal site from which to spiral off through the surrounding network of alleys, and unearth its many bars, clubs and restaurants.

**Bar del Pí** (Metro Catalunya) Plaça de Sant Josep Oriol. (Daily until 22.30.) Overlooked by one of the best budget pensions, this is a daytime haunt for backpackers, hippies and buskers. A delightful, mellow place which seems to lure the more talented street musicians, this lone café has good tapas and seats in one of the prettiest squares in the old town.

**Drugstore,** Passeig de Gràcia,71. (Open 24 hours daily.) The only place to drink around the clock, this has a bar, restaurant, billiards room and shops, including a newsagent and supermarket. Popular for breakfast before dawn, it's fun, tacky and not cheap.

**Gelateria Italiana Pagliotta,** Jaume I,15. Run by an amusing Italian and his team, this is the best ice-cream bar in town and uses genuine Italian recipes. It also serves great milk and natural fruit shakes.

**Meson del Café,** Llibreteria,16. (Open 07.00-24.00, closed Sunday and festivals.) One of few authentic coffee shops left in the area, this is now something of a local institution. It was founded in 1909, and the original coffee machine is displayed above the bar. With its own rituals and names for every variety, coffee is served by entertaining characters who juggle constant orders with precision.

There are a few seats, but the initiated take their drinks standing. Brave the breakfast crush for the best *ensaimades* in town.

**Café de l'Opera,** Rambla,74. (Daily until 03.00.) Directly opposite the opera house, this Italian-style café is the best on the Rambles, and as such, a prime spot for bag snatchers. This is a great place to linger, where tables, inside or out, are hot property.

**The Times,** Loreto,21. (Daily until 24.00.) This modern coffee shop forming part of the Derby Hotel, provides good snacks and copies of the *Financial Times*.

**Viena,** La Rambla,115. (Daily 09.00-01.00.) Good for late snacks, this serves tasty fast food like frankfurters and filled mini croissants, sometimes to the accompaniment of a piano. Best to overlook the cherubs floating on the ceiling and waiters in eidelweiss waistcoats.

**Café Zurich,** Plaça de Catalunya,1. (Daily until 00.30, 22.30 on Sunday.) Right on Plaça de Catalunya, this classic meeting place is a special favourite with foreigners.

# Tapas Bars

You can find tapas wherever you turn but some of the best bars are hoarded in the backstreets around the port. Of mixed origin and good value, this riotous collection are packed in along Ample and Mercé, and their proximity to the post office has dubbed them *"tascas de correos"*. Give those on the port a wide berth; in comparison, these places are lifeless and expensive.

**Bodega la Plata,** Mercé,28. (Open 10.30-22.30, closed Sunday, festivals and August.) This pint-sized bar only offers superb *pescaditos fritos* (tiny fried fish), tomato salad and Vilafrancan wine straight from the barrel.

**Can Ganassa,** Plaça de la Barceloneta. (Open until 02.00, closed Wednesday.) A popular tapas bar which is set back from the main thoroughfare of Barceloneta in a quiet square. It is a good place for a drink before dinner on the beach; or for tasty snacks, try the mussels and shellfish.

**Casa El Agüelo,** Avinyó,37. (Evenings until 01.00, or 03.00 on Saturday.) This basic, rustic bar is often crowded and has a scruffy feel with benched seating, low beams and a littered floor. The small selection of average tapas includes ham, salami and cheese. A drinking hole with good atmosphere, but gruff service and certainly not a bargain.

---

**Tasty Tips**

Although most suited to the hotter southern climate, tapas can be found throughout Spain. The word literally means cover, because the early tapa was a free slice of smoked ham or chorizo salami placed over every glass like a lid — some say to keep out the flies. Now, far from a mere mouthful and often a meal in itself, around this have shot up a diverse range of establishments, and an increasingly lucrative industry.

Still, the regulars at most bars haven't changed: roasted almonds, anchovy-stuffed olives, garlic mushrooms, artichoke hearts, slices of tortilla, russian salad, squid, clams, prawn croquettes, smoked ham, meat balls and cheese cubes crop up on most trays. Other more challenging tapas include crispy, chewy pigs' ears and even their snouts.

---

**Bar Celta,** Mercé,16. (08.00-01.00 daily.) Satisfying all one's expectations of real tapas, this backstreet Galician bar serves the best seafood in the area. Better than the basic tables at the back is the bustling, magnet-shaped bar which, packed with fresh and tempting tapas, pulls a rowdy crowd. Choose their musty Galician wine served in traditional shallow bowls and don't miss the deliciously moist Santiago cake.

**José Luis,** Diagonal,520. (Daily 08.00-01.00.) An upmarket, pricey tapas bar serving beautifully presented, unusual hot or cold snacks. Good for a late night bite, its only drawback is the bright lights.

**La Socarrena,** Mercé,21. (Open until 00.30 or weekends until 02.00, closed August.) Drop into this small, Asturian bar for its specialities of *queso de cabrales* (a sweet, piquant blue cheese made from a mixture of cow, goat and sheep's milk) and chilled, still Asturian cider. This is given extra fizz by the barman who, in contorted pose, rains cider from behind his head into an almost horizontal glass. Deceptively difficult, beginners may waste most of this strong brew in imitation.

**Tasca "La Musiqueta",** Avinyó,31. (Evenings until 02.00, closed Tuesday and winter.) This cheap and cheerful bar offers a slim selection of tasty tapas and machine games. Popular with young people, its walls brandish postcards and posters while tables are decorated with cigarette burns.

**El Xampanyet,** Montcada,22. (Open 12.00-16.00 and 18.30-24.00, closed Sunday night, Monday and August.) Always full and always fun, this has a special atmosphere; the mixed crowd are attracted by the delicious homemade *cava,* the fresh cider and superb tapas (notably the anchovies). Its friendly characters and typically

Spanish, tiled interior with ancient rows of bottles, beer kegs and *porróns,* make this one of the best finds in town.

## Bars

Bars form the mainstay of Barcelona's nightlife. An extension of their daytime café life, lingering over a *copa* is an integral part of the Spanish approach to relaxation. By British standards drinks are cheap, except in the more elite spots, and measures dangerously generous.

For design, Barcelona is one of Europe's leading cities and this reverence for the aesthetic is apparent in the recent crop of high design bars. Discerning drinkers are spoilt for choice, and tremendous ingenuity goes into creating each venue. Here you will find every conceivable type of style, gimmick or entertainment — from the hi-tech interiors, to the old and fraying. Squash into a dodgem car, have your palm read, go bowling, or don a *sombrero* and strum a guitar.

The stylish *'bar musical'* — usually offering live music — has recently been encroaching on the nightclubs' territory; these are the places to go during those hours post dinner, but while clubs are still deserted. Likewise *'cafés-concert',* which usually hold some show or cabaret are on the increase.

**Andy Capp,** Bonavista,13. (Nightly until 02.00.) This vibrant, scruffy bar has brilliant grafitti murals and attracts a hip crowd; where loud rock, reggae or ska music add to the generally loose feel.
**L'Antiquari B'Art,** Veguer,13. (Nightly until 03.00.) Once an antique shop, this sits in the oldest part of the city and its musty cellar still contains an ancient wine press. One of the later openers of the area, this only hots up around midnight, when it attracts the wilder members of the *barrio.* Atmospheric and deceptively lively, this is recommended for its great music, pool table and entertaining barmen, Domingo and Esteban.
**El Ascensor,** Bellafila,3. (Nightly until 02.00.) This small, old-fashioned bar is entered through the door of an antique lift. Cheerful and unassuming, it is popular with young Catalans and one of the least touristy bars in the Gothic quarter.
**Berimbau,** Passeig del Born,17. (Nightly until 03.00.) This small, dusky bar plays good music, and has a relaxed, intimate atmosphere. It specialises in strong Brazilian cocktails — try their *caipirinia* — and while not the cheapest, like the other bars in this

street, it certainly warrants a detour.

**Berlin,** Grunyí. (Open 24.00 until 03.00, closed Tuesday.) Dimly lit and smoky, this has a small pool room and a clandestine feel. Tucked into one of the passages of the old town (Barri Ribera), this cellar-like dive attracts an alternative bunch of locals.

**Boadas,** Tallers,1. (Daily 12.00-02.00, closed Sunday from June to September.) Founded in 1933, it is the oldest cocktail bar in the city and claims a star-studded list of past clients, including Joan Miró. This small bar has sophisticated pretentions, an over active air-conditioning machine, and mixes delicious, lethal cocktails.

**Boliche,** Diagonal,510. (Nightly until 03.00, Friday and Saturday until 03.30.) Another in the long string of yuppie design bars, this has a warmer atmosphere than some, and is recommended for its bowling alley (open until 02.45) at the back.

**El Born,** Passeig del Born,26. (Evenings until 03.00, closed Sunday.) Once a cod store, this tiny bar has a homely feel encouraged by its spread of books and newspapers. It has a comfortable interior with a beamed ceiling and a bar made of old marble fish basins. A spiral staircase leads up to a restaurant which serves light snacks of ham, pâté and cheese.

**El Café,** Torrent de L'Olla,48, Gràcia. This late-night French café is rowdy and fun.

**Casa Quimet,** Rambla del Prat,9, Gràcia. (Evenings until 02.30, closed Monday and August.) Also known as Bar de las Guitarras, guitars of every shape and sound are strung from a peeling ceiling. Open for 50 years, this is an old hippie's paradise, where you are given a hat as you enter, and can try your hand at any guitar. This easy-going, scruffy place has walls papered with layers of old drawings and great '60s photographs around the door.

**Elephas,** Gran Vía de les Corts Catalanes,649. (Nightly until 02.30.) Bulging with antiques, and named after the elephant who dominates their sixteenth-century Flemish tapestry, this bar has a sumptuous, Baroque feel. China, candlesticks, crimson walls and low lights form a sultry backdrop for smoochy couples settled in deep sofas, arranged in intimate nooks. The leather studded bar, supported by naked female torsos, completes the sensuous theme.

**Estebar,** Consell de Cent,257. This popular gay bar between Muntaner and Aribau is crowded well into the early hours.

**La Fira,** Provença,171. (Monday-Thursday until 03.00, Friday/ Saturday until 04.00, and 24.00 on Sunday.) Unique and fun, the theme is fairground, the interior crammed with a fantastic collection of gruesome paraphernalia of which a museum would be proud. A novel place, where in circus style, drinks are dispensed beneath a giant, striped awning. Participation is the rule; sip drinks in swinging seats, dodgem cars, or gaudy carriages, and snacks, such as popcorn, are strictly suitable. One of the best finds in town.

**Les Gens Que J'Aime,** València,286. (Nightly until 02.30). The stops have been pulled out to give this basement bar an atmosphere at once intimate and mysterious. Dark and brooding, here palmists and tarot readers ply their trade among well-heeled drinkers. The emphasis is on comfort, and the relaxing interior has soft seats, low lights and an eclectic mix of objets d'art.

**Local Bar,** Fossar de les Moreres. (All day until 03.00.) In the newly created *plaça* beside Santa Maria del Mar, this bar also has a sneaky back entrance off Passeig del Born. Minimalist and short on comfort, customers perch on stools.

**London Bar,** Nou de la Rambla,34. (Closed Tuesday.) With recently changed management, this bar is now one of the funkiest in the old town, playing jazz and spontaneous live music every night. A collection of music lovers lounge around the dimly-lit, Modernista interior. The atmosphere is laid-back and fortune tellers occasionally operate here.

**Mabana,** Riera Baixa,12. This small, scruffy African bar is linked to Spain's only centre for the promotion of African culture (around the corner in Hospital,107).

**Mirablau,** Final Avinguda Tibidabo. (Open 12.00-05.00, Monday from 17.00.) A chic bar at the top of the blue tramline to Tibidabo, this is fashionable for its city vistas. Pay for the pleasure of drinking, poised literally over the parapet, where open sides leave just a ledge between you and the edge. Especially popular in summer, the bar musical downstairs hots up in the late evening.

**Miramelindo,** Passeig del Born,15. (Nightly until 00.30/01.30, weekends until 03.15.) Yet another great bar in this old fashioned little Rambla. Listen to jazz, sipping inventive cocktails amid colonial-style decoration. Try their Cuban *mojito* (made with fresh mint), the cava concoction, or their non-alcoholic speciality. Snacks are limited to cheese and pâté.

**Nick Havanna,** Roselló,208. (Nightly until 04.00.) Describing itself as the ultimate bar, it never lacks custom and the crowd here forms early. Interesting for its innovative design, it consists of a huge room with cement floor and columns, and an empty centre around which yuppies sip cocktails. By late evening, however, the extensive spotlights and occasional live music warm up this rather too cool joint.

**(Opposite)** Colourful iron balconies ensure that home life spills out into the open in the narrow alleys of the Gothic quarter.

**El Nostre Raco,** Aribau,103. (Nightly until 00.30.) Although not worth a detour, this is handy, being near good clubs and restaurants. The curious mix of decoration is aiming for a bohemian look, and the house gimmick is a strong cava punch. (This *tisana* is served in a tilted carafe, horribly reminiscent of a specimen bottle.)

**El Nus,** Mirallers,5. (Evenings until 02.00, closed Wednesday.) The difficulty in finding this little bar, tucked into the narrow streets of the old quarter, keeps it the preserve of discerning locals. Despite a golden eagle hovering over the bar, this is understated, and its good contemporary music makes for a great atmosphere.

**El Otro Bar,** València,166. (Sunday-Thursday until 02.30, Friday and Saturday until 03.00.) Loud music and a good atmosphere; expect a weekend crush.

**Pastís,** Santa Mònica,4. (Nightly until 02.30.) Inside this minute bar the French aperitif Pastis has been translated into the Spanish post-prandial *copa*. The French theme is all pervasive, from the music to the prints, photos and objets d'art which adorn the room. Low lights have glowed here for over 50 years, and during which time, you are proudly informed, it has never been dusted. Down one of the key red light streets, there is plenty of street life to be detected through the window.

**Les Puces del Barri Gòtic,** Montsió,7. (Nightly until 24.00 weekdays and 02.00 weekends). With rough hewn stone walls and floor, this unpretentious bar attracts a lively stream of drinkers.

**4 Gats,** Montsió,3. (All day, every day 09.00-03.00). Opened in 1897, this is something of an institution in the old town, although it relies more on past glories than present (it was a favoured watering hole for writers and artists at the turn of the century). Interesting for art lovers, this was Puig i Cadafalch's first building, and the front room has numerous drawings of famous locals like Picasso and Francesc Macía; the back room was site of Picasso's first exhibition, and is today hung with identical copies of his paintings. A busy atmospheric place for a drink, this serves snacks and full meals all day until 02.00.

**(Opposite)** Spreading out the spoils. The Galician Bar Celta overflows with the best selection of back street tapas.

**Targets,** Consell de Cent,411. (Evenings until 03.00, closed Sunday.) Part of the Group Pub chain, this civilized bar has a smooth, comfortable interior. Run by Jordi and Chus, an especially friendly and accommodating pair, it has a low-lit ambience.

**Tetería Jazmín,** Maspons,11. (Open 18.00-01.30, Friday/Saturday until 03.00, closed Monday.) Just off Plaça del Sol in Gràcia, this original Turkish bar specialises in teas, including ginseng, Arabic or herbal infusions. Light snacks of salads, couscous, falafels and tiny Arab cakes are also served. The feel is bohemian and intimate, the interior Islamic; wall hangings, scattered cushions and engraved brass tables complete the theme, while Turkish lanterns cast mottled shadows around the room.

**Los Tilos,** Passeig dels Til.lers (Daily 13.30-03.30, Saturday/Sunday 12.00-04.00.) Uptown and smart, this is frequented on summer evenings for its large, leafy garden which backs onto the Güell Pavilions and Gaudí's Dragon Gate.

**Universal,** Marià Cubi,182. (Nightly until 03.00, Friday/Saturday until 03.30.) A pioneer of the modern design movement, this music bar stands out in a street full of trendy venues (another just opposite, **Mas i Mas** is worth a visit). Downstairs is vast and dark with frantic music, strobe lighting and videos. Upstairs, with its elegant high ceilings, is cooler and calmer with small tables.

**Vall d'Ouro,** Paris,198 (corner with d'Enric Granados). This excellent café operates from 05.00 to 02.00 daily and crowds usually start gathering just before it opens. A cheery spot for pre-dawn breakfast which prides itself on its irresistible *chocolate con churros*.

**Zsa Zsa,** Rosselló,156. (Nightly until 03.00, closed festivals.) Recently opened, this has a bizarre look, where a metallic, spot-lit interior is softened by Iranian wall hangings. Its loud music, expensive image, fresh approach and lethal cocktails, make it a favourite with yuppies. And some of Barcelona's best designer loos can be found here.

## Nightclubs

**ARS Studio,** Atenas,27. Zona Alta. (Nightly until 04.30.) This is the hottest acid club in the city. Not a place for conversation, there are constant videos and the huge dance floor is all frenetic action. Best at weekends but expect to fight your way through to the central bar.

**Artículo 26,** Gran de Gràcia,25. (Nightly until 4.30, Friday and Saturday until 05.00, and weekend afternoons 18.00-22.00.) A hi-tech disco with plenty of neon and playing popular hits, this attracts a clean-cut crowd. Additional entertainment includes early evening concerts, a large video above the stage and various distractions like basketball, billiards and table football.

**Centro Ciudad,** Consell de Cent,294. This fashionable club has a vast interior with dancing downstairs (one of the best sound systems) and billiards upstairs. Overall, the tone is glossy with a bank of televisions surrounding the bar, and the odd comfortable sofa. Its size makes for an airy feel with the emphasis on black and chrome.

**Cibeles,** Córcega,363. (Open Thursday-Saturday nights until 04.00 and weekend afternoons 18.30-21.45, closed August.) Alternating live music with disco, an evening here could be hit or miss; the disco tends towards the straight and stodgy. A standard, airy interior with plenty of seating around the dance floor.

**La Cavo del Drac,** Tuset,30. (Open 23.00-02.00, no live jazz Monday, closed Sunday and July to September.) Beneath an average tapas bar, this place is well known for its excellent jazz. Tuesday is Blues night, Wednesday Dixieland, Thursday traditonal jazz; Friday and Saturday are the highlights, when visiting musicians appear, and then it's best to book.

**Distrito Distinto,** Avinguda Meridiana,104. Just by Clot metro and on the road out of town, this is hard to spot but well worth the journey. One of the hottest gay clubs which only starts sizzling around 03.00. It has a wild interior design and fantastic murals, whose topical theme changes regularly. And those flagging can be revived by its croissant bar.

**Fibra Optica,** Beethoven,9. (18.00-21.30 and 23.30-05.00.) There is a heavy emphasis on acid and rap in this big, three-tiered modern club. A good, frenetic and fun place.

**Harlem Jazz Club,** Comtessa de Sobradiel,8. A lively jazz venue in the heart of the Gothic quarter.

**Karma,** Plaça Reial,10. (Nightly until 04.30 or 05.00 at weekends). This sweaty disco absorbs most of the characters from the square once the bars are closed. Cheap, hectic and smoky, although you can escape to the outdoor terrace. Appealing mainly to funkies and junkies, weekends see this impossibly packed.

**KGB,** Alegre de Dalt,55. (Open 22.00-04.00 and 05.30-08.00 nightly, no second stint on a Sunday.) Stark and sparse, it's the last port on the club circuit. Early visitors will feel the space; it picks up in the second stint which pulls in a well-dressed crowd of nocturnal trendies. A cool, streetwise joint, where there's more talk than dance.

**La Paloma,** Tigre,27. (Evenings until 02.30-03.30, also Sunday 18.00-21.30, closed Monday-Wednesday.) Wonderfully sumptuous, with a gilt Rococo interior, this dance hall attracts a startling range of dancers. Oldies out for a whirl in their glad rags, and displaying some adept footwork, brush shoulders with Barcelona's young and swinging. The uplifting band plays strictly well-loved, old melodies. Hilarious as a bystander, yet the infectious atmosphere brings even the most self-conscious to the floor.

**Martin's Disco,** Passeig de Gràcia,130. (Nightly until 04.30, or 05.00 on Friday/Saturday.) A gay male preserve, women pay almost double and are banned from the mysterious upper rooms. A frenetic strobe accentuates the wild, flirtatious scene, and the pulsating music makes this a great place to dance. Shows are occasionally held, and videos are played upstairs.

**Otto Zutz,** Lincoln,15. (Nightly until 04.30, supposedly members only after 02.00, but you are usually let in for a fee.) This combines the sensation of space with an electric atmosphere. Dancing is serious business, and the music a relief from the insistent acid elsewhere. Fashionable but informal and unaffected, the upstairs balcony has seats where (rare in Barcelona) there's the chance to talk. When it is not being forcibly closed down, this is one of the best clubs around.

**Ozono,** Gran Vía de les Corts Catalanes,593. Lively until sunrise and beyond, this is another popular acid disco.

**Satanassa,** Aribau, 27. (Nightly until 04.00.) Only recently opened, this is one of the grooviest nightclubs in town. The fantastic interior features wild murals and freaky mannequins. Great music, and not only fashionable, this is a friendly and highly atmospheric place which fills up from 23.00.

**Studio 54,** Paral.lel,64. (Friday/Saturday nights until 04.30; under 25s on Saturday and Sunday afternoons from 18.30-21.30.) Everything you'd expect from a proper discotheque, this is a great dancing alternative to Paral.lel's cabaret shows. Hectic, sweaty and trendy — dress is sexy, fluorescent and minimal. And teenagers are promised a wild Sunday afternoon in this strobe-lit set up.

**Velvet,** Balmes,161. (Nightly until 05.00.) A promising entrance reveals a disappointing scene. Oppressively popular, its music is largely '60s, and the interior smacks of a mediocre disco. Don't miss a visit to the hi-tech loos — this club's most entertaining feature.

**Verdi,** Verdi,32. (Open Tuesday-Saturday until 04.30, Sunday 18.00-21.30.) Above the cinema is one of the city's most friendly, unaffected clubs. This has a good-sized dance floor, but is fairly short on seating. A handy place to end an evening in Gràcia, it also holds weekly live music: Tuesday salsa/samba; Wednesday samba; Thursday pop/rock.

**Yabba Dabba,** Avenir, 63. (Until 03.30, closed Sunday.) A tiny club with outsize design and Egyptian overtones, this has a monumental candelabra, zebra bar stools and mottled walls. It blasts funky music, and the minute dance floor dictates a private party feel. Promising more than it delivers, but still worth a visit, the bar staff look more raring for a night out than the customers.

When Sardana dancers descend on one of these Gothic squares, you'll have to do some fancy footwork to dodge the swiftly forming circles. The crowd may look receptive, but we've yet to see a visitor fitting in.

## Traditional Dancing

Catalan folk dancing may not be a spectacular event but it has charm, restraint and a certain dignity lacking in its southern Spanish rival. **Sardana,** diametrically opposite to the firey flamenco of Andalusia, has its emphasis on solidarity. Bridging the generation gap, anyone can join the wide circle where, with hands held high, tiny steps accompany lilting, mournful music.

Thought to originate from Cerdanya in the Pyrenees, this sedate dance has taken on a profound significance in the province, and to an extent embodies the struggle for independence. Under Franco it was upheld in a spirit of defiance, as a visible aspect of Catalan culture that even he couldn't stamp out.

And this spectacle gives dancing around your handbag a whole new meaning; inevitably guarded within each circle sit a stack of personal possessions. You can see it danced in the squares several times a week, when locals flock to make up a merry throng — Plaça de Sant Jaume at 11.00 and early evening Sundays and festivals, or (once the underground car park has been completed) in front of the Cathedral on Sunday mornings.

There are many places which exploit the mystique of true *flamenco* and dish up a comercialised version with dinner. Being of Andalusian extraction, it has no tradition in Barcelona, but there are a few places where one can see an authentic display:

**La Macarena,** Nou Sant Fransesc,5. Deep in the red light district, and open for 60 years, this lively place has a highly charged atmosphere.

**Los Tarantos,** Plaça Reial,17, (tel: 317 80 98). Another old favourite, here the two-hour shows start at 22.00 and 24.00.

**El Patio Andaluz,** Aribau,242, (tel: 209 35 24). Reputed to be one of the best, shows start at 22.00.

**El Tablao de Carmen** operates in Poble Espanyol.

## Music Halls and Cabaret

The music hall tradition in Barcelona is long, strong and continues unabated. Quick to follow the Parisian lead, risqué shows and chorus girls have had broad appeal since the turn of the century.

**El Molino,** modelled on the Moulin Rouge, and a Modernista creation of 1913, is the oldest and boldest. Possibly the only original *café-concert* still surviving, it was built in 1913.

Spectacles here combine an extravaganza of costumes (and staggering headgear) with comic sketches, and lewd song and dance routines. Talent varies, and while the lead players are surprisingly skilled, some of the chorus look bored and sulky. A gaudy red and gold interior and raucous audience complete the bawdy feel. And if participation is not a prospect you relish, keep away from the stage and centre aisle. Highly recommended for a frivolous night out, where understanding Spanish is not a prerequisite.

Evening curtain rises at 23.00, and although there's no entrance charge, don't stint on the obligatory first drink as it always costs 1,500 pesetas (2,000 on Saturday). Matinées, which kick off at 18.00, are at least half the price. El Molino is at Vilà i Vilà,99 (tel: 241 63 83); Metro Paral.lel, closed Mondays except festivals or eve of festivals. Similar shows can be found at the **Arnau** or **Barcelona de Noche** (both also on Paral.lel) or at the **Belle Epoque** in Muntaner,246 (tel: 209 73 85), shows are after 23.15, closed Sunday and you should book.

**Bodega Bohemia,** Lanacaster,2-4. (Evenings until 03.00, also Sunday and festival afternoons, closed Wednesday.) Dripping with nostalgia and living up to its name, this seedy cabaret bar has been going for nearly a century. Here saucily-clad old timers and an antique pianist perform amid fairy lights and personalised bric-a-brac. Wonderfully kitsch, this decaying place is highly entertaining and not to be missed.

**El Llantiol,** Riereta,7 (tel: 329 90 09). (Tuesday-Saturday shows begin at 12.00 or at 19.00 on Sunday with a children's show in the morning; closed Monday.) This cabaret venue mixes magic tricks, with song and dance, and risqué comedy. Foreigners should keep a low profile, as they invariably make a tempting target for jokes. Entertaining and relaxed, this is definitely worth a visit, but best to book a table at weekends.

This is the last stop on the cabaret circuit for raddled old performers. Whether the acts strike you as hilarious or pitiful, the intriguing Bodega Bohemia is a true eye-opener.

For a hard-core cabaret, visit **Bagdad** (Conde del Asalto,103, tel: 242 07 77) a plush, comfortable club with the expected mirrored ceiling and a glitsy, eastern decor. The two daily shows (23.00 and 01.15) attract a rowdy crowd, including plenty of couples, and this is a favoured spot for stag and hen nights. No longer so extreme since the departure of the donkey and the well-endowed dwarf, this theatrical show still features transvestites, nuns, whips, knife throwing and live sex. It's expensive, and usually crowded and there's no shortage of audience participation, so pick a ringside slot at your peril. There are many similar shows elsewhere; a seedier option is **Eurosex** near the bottom of the Rambles. The **Mercé** show (at the Central Market) operates in the early hours, and now designates certain nights on which men must be accompanied by women.

## Concerts and Opera

**Palau de la Música Catalana,** Amadeu Vives 1, (tel: 268 10 00) Staggering and larger than life, first sight of this building simply demands a reaction. Here Domènech i Montaner quite surpassed himself, designing the most Modernista building ever conceived. And, not only unique, it is quite unrepeatable — the level of craftsmanship no longer exists.

This incredible concert hall was created (1905-8) to solve a surprisingly practical problem: to provide a permanent site for the Orfeó Català. Firmly regional, this choral group has come for many people to symbolise the Catalan spirit and culture. It is significant that the Palau should not only be a public work for all to enjoy but, like the wider spirit of the movement, one that reaches beyond the visual to embrace the other arts. As relevant today as the day it was built, this is a living and progressive musical centre, not just a monument to a past golden era.

The main red brick façade contrasts a stunning double row of multi-coloured mosaic pillars, each one individual, with the solemn busts of famous composers. The mosaic frieze on the upper part of the main façade depicts the Orfeó Català, and shows the peaks of Montserrat (another potent Catalan symbol) in the background. Topped by a cupola, even the richness of the exterior doesn't prepare you for the interior.

Flowers are the key inspiration — handmade mosaics, undulating floral patterns, brilliant stained and etched glass and liquid stone carvings make up this decorative extravaganza. On columns, walls, panels, ceilings and roof, never a space is left fallow. Huge ceramic roses bedeck the roof and a riot of maiolica collages keep your eyes flitting. While from the luminous ceiling a coloured glass centrepiece hangs like a pendulous breast.

Flanking the right of the stage is Beethoven, while on the left presides Anselm Clavé, (founder of the society in the late nineteenth century).

Humour is never far away, the back of the stage has protruding stone busts, which tail off into cheeky mosaics of ladies in swirling

---

**Uniting Notes**

Often a focus for repression, the Catalan National Anthem has had a dramatic life. This song originated in 1640 during the violent revolt of the reapers *(segadors)* against domination by Castile. Since then Els Segadors has been adopted by the Catalans as a symbol of solidarity, and to honour all those suffering injustice.

The national feeling that this inspires was best personified by the Orfeó Català, the famous choral group for whom the Palau de la Musica Catalana was built. They were so popular and incited such strong feelings of nationhood that for nine years (1937-46) Franco banned the group not only from singing Els Segadors, but also from giving any public performances. Wholly fitting therefore — and illuminating the Catalan character — was the poignant moment in 1960 when the audience at the Palau spontaneously rose to sing Els Segadors. In dignified defiance of Franco's minister, they sang their unofficial anthem. The next day Jordi Pujol (the Catalan president) was imprisoned for three years, even though he had not been present.

---

dresses. Representing the 18 musical muses, each lady fingers a different instrument; the whole ensemble by mosaic artist Lluís Bru and sculptor Eusebi Arnau is highly original. The ground floor is named after Lluis Millet who founded the Orféo Català in 1891 and there is also a bust of the Catalan cellist Pau Casals, a great favourite of Palau audiences.

Purists claim the music isn't up to the standard of the Berlin, Paris or London orchestras, but nevertheless superb, the unbeatable acoustics and fantasy of the setting more than make up for this. The concert season runs from October to June. You can write in advance from September for the season's programme. Guided tours in English are organised on certain days of the week; call for the times.

**The Liceu,** Spain's leading opera house and Europe's largest, sits mid-way down the Ramblas. Attracting a trail of celebrated artists, opera tickets are a hot commodity, often reserved well in advance. It opened in 1847, built on the site of a seventeenth-century Trinitarian monastery, whose foundations support today's bar. This glamorous and sumptuous venue trails a tumultuous history which reflects some of Catalunya's political and social struggles. And it remains a thriving cultural attraction of which Barcelonans are justifiably proud.

The season (September-June) alternates opera, ballet and concerts. Renovations underway include the construction of a new stage, which will enable productions to be rotated. The house holds some 3,000 seats and tickets are obtainable direct from the box office, or by requesting a booking form (write to Gran Teatre del Liceu, Departament d'Abonaments i Localitats, Sant Pau,1, 08001, tel: 318 91 22). But last minute seats can be found, as 10% of tickets are held back until the day of the performance after 17.00, or four hours before the event, when queues form outside the box office. Alternatively, tickets can be reserved through some international agencies.

---

### Stage Fright

Equally notorious for its behind-the-scenes action, the Liceu has historically been centre stage for some significant drama. In 1861, only 14 years after opening, fire blew up in the costume workshop and wrecked most of the auditorium and stage. Although uninsured, a hasty decision was made to reconstruct the house around the original shell, and its doors reopened in 1862.

In 1893, more off-stage drama firmly closed the Liceu doors. At the beginning of the new season, during Act Two of Rossini's William Tell, an anarchist hurled two bombs into the stalls, killing 20 people and wounding many others.

Yet it was the rivalry between the Liceu and Teatro Principal (or Teatro de la Santa Cruz) which so boosted theatrical culture that 23 operas were performed here in under three years. Supporters of these factions became known as 'liceístas' and 'cruzados', and came to personify the escalating battle between the generations and classes. The 'cruzados' were a staid and aristocratic lot while their rivals were a younger, industrial crowd. This conflict, and such intense theatrical activity, only ended when the management of both theatres was merged.

---

## Touring Bands

A city of music, Barcelona is a key stop on most group's European tours, and as much a focus for experimental as internationally-famous bands. Tickets can usually be bought from record shops, or the grey ticket booths, *taquillas* dotted about town. Surprisingly big names are engaged by the town hall for the Grec summer and the biannual 'Bienal' music festivals, as well as the free-for-all fiesta entertainment. (The Bienal takes place in Autumn for one month and is specifically for young amateurs throughout the arts.) A venue to keep an eye on is Zeleste, a large warehouse with the latest live sounds most days. Open air concerts are a regular feature on

Montjuïc and in Plaça de Toros Monumental. Very big stars appear at both or at the Barça stadium and occasionally the Velodrom, the city's open air cycle circuit. For the latest gigs, scan the *Guía del Ocio*.

# Cinema

English language films, carrying Spanish subtitles, are shown at various venues around the city: **Verdi** cinema in Verdi,32, Gràcia (tel: 237 05 16) Metro Fontana; **Casablanca** in Passeig de Gràcia,115 (tel: 218 43 45) Metro Diagonal; and **Capsa,** Pau Claris/Aragó (tel: 215 73 93) Metro Aragó. And the hottest international flicks don't take long to reach Barcelona's screens. The International Film Festival takes place annually around the end of June or early July: for information call 215 24 24. The Festival of Fantasy Film is held in Sitges during the first half of October: for information call 317 35 85.

# Billiards

Although billiards and pool tables can be found all over the city, enthusiasts are catered for in a number of interesting bars:
**Antinoo,** Torrent de l'Olla,141, Gràcia. Open 18.00-03.00. As well as billiards, this has live music on Wednesday (23.30), and samba and jazz nights.
**Snooker,** Roger de Llúria,42. Open until 02.30, closed Sunday.
**Ticktacktoe,** Roger de Llúria,40. Open until 02.30. This post-Modernist bar has a smooth restaurant and a swanky, uptight feel.
**Veledromo,** Muntaner,211. An old-style central bar, not to be confused with the concert venue.

# Theatre

The city's main theatre is the **Poliorama** at Rambla,115 (tel: 317 75 99). One of the best venues for experimental drama is **Mercat de les Flors** at Lleida,59 (tel: 426 21 02). Originally the flower market, this incredible building is now used for fringe theatre productions and contemporary dance. **Teatre Lliure,** Montseny,47 (tel: 218 92 51) is another important experimental venue where Chamber music concerts and poetry recitals are also held. From the beginning of

September to the end of December, a theatre festival is held in the Mercat de les Flors and in **The Romea,** Hospital,51 (tel: 317 71 89).

## Casinos

Casinos are banned from within the city of Barcelona, but there are three fairly nearby, all of which have restaurants. For more information about casinos in Catalunya, call 204 80 14.

**Gran Casino Barcelona,** Sant Pere de Ribes. Around 42 kilometres from Barcelona, near Sitges, this is an attractive, late nineteenth-century building, open daily 18.00-04.00 or until 05.00, Friday, Saturday and eve of holidays.

**Casino Castillo de Perelada,** Perelada (Girona). This castle is situated 20 kilometres from the French border and dates from the fourteenth century. Open daily 19.00-04.00, though Saturday, Sunday and eve of holidays, it opens at 17.00.

**Lloret de Mar,** Lloret de Mar (Girona). Situated 70 kilometres from Barcelona, within the largest Costa Brava development, this is open Sunday to Thursday 17.00-04.00, or until 04.30 on Friday, Saturday and eve of holidays.

SEVEN

# Sightseeing

The days and opening hours of Barcelona's sights vary drastically, and seem to be a law unto themselves. Weekdays *(laborales)* means Monday to Saturday, and the usual closing day is Monday. Holidays signify the annual public holidays or *festivos* (as distinct from other additional saints days and fiestas) and these are January 1 and 6, Good Friday, Easter Monday, May 1, June 24, December 25 and 26. However, many museums stay open on all but the vital three — January 6, December 25 and 26.

## Gothic Quarter

Metro Liceu/Jaume 1 or bus 16,17,19,22,45.

It is worth allowing some time to wander around the Gothic quarter on both sides of Vía Laietana as this narrow enclave possesses some fascinating alleys and ancient façades, full of history and character. The cluster of streets around the Cathedral are packed with architectural interest (and tourists), but don't overlook the area around Santa Maria del Mar and Passeig del Born, as there are many, if less obvious, gems to be sought here.

### Barcelona Cathedral
Pla de la Seu, (07.30-13.30 and 16.00-19.30.)

Dominating the Gothic quarter, the Cathedral's ornate spire is widely visible and its presence loudly proclaimed every quarter of an hour. Founded in 1298, on the site of a Romanesque and an even earlier Roman church, the rather fussy main façade was not completed until the end of the last century. This is shown to best advantage when illuminated at weekends.

The more attractive interior is large but quite compact, its finest features being the graceful colonnade which sweeps behind the high altar, and its fan vaulting, with vast carved bosses. The main nave is blocked by a central wooden choir, which has elaborate, golden

In true Barcelona fashion, the cathedral comes into its own after dark, when
strategically placed spotlights pick out the finest features.

painted decoration and Gothic tracery. This is historically important as the site where Emperor Charles V met with the Chapter of the Golden Fleece in 1519. Henry VIII attended this famous gathering, and you can see his, and many other kings', coats of arms.

The crypt chapel below the altar (built by a Mallorcan architect) is of considerable local importance for housing the sarcophagus of Barcelona's patron saint, Santa Eulàlia. The alabaster tomb, depicting scenes of her martyrdom, was carved in 1327 by a pupil of the great Italian sculptor Nicola Pisano. Nearby, on the wall to the right of the altar, hang two painted wooden sarcophagi of the patrons of the earlier Romanesque Cathedral.

The verdant cloister was a slightly later addition which, edged by shallow chapels, contains a fountain, palms, magnolias and a gaggle of sacred geese. Numerous tales surround these noisy birds, whose ancestors were first installed here by the fourteenth-century canons. According to the legend their whiteness symbolises the purity of Santa Eulàlia; others claim they were put here to echo those of the Roman capitol, as a tribute to Barcelona's ancient heritage.

Treasures of the **Cathedral Museum,** which you enter from the cloister, include a Gothic tabernacle and the silvergilt throne of Marti I, the Humane, on which the Monstrance (a casket which displays the consecrated bread) is placed during the Corpus Christi procession.

A cool retreat from busy streets, but this pretty, leafy cloister is not always tranquil. Gaggles of tourists and the 'holy' shrieking geese are hardly conducive to contemplation.

**Casa Pia Almoina** (right as you leave by the Cathedral's main entrance) is a severe, fifteenth-century building with tiny high windows, and was originally founded as a community residence for the canons. Part of this was built for the Pia Almoina, an eleventh-century organisation established to feed a hundred paupers each day.

**Casa de l'Ardiaca** (once the archdeacon's house, now the archive library), beside the Cathedral in Santa Llúcia, is a fifteenth-century house with shallow vaulting and low arches. Note the early carving on the pilasters around the door and the much later letterbox of swallows, a tortoise and ivy leaves. The tiled courtyard with its tall palm and shaded bench makes a pleasant resting place. The upper gallery has fine pillars whose capitals show incredibly life-like carving of marmots and shepherds, eagles and griffins. (Visitors are not allowed inside.)

Keep an eye out for sculptural capitals, whose carving can be impressively life-like. Here marmots crawl around the pilasters of Casa de l'Ardiaca, close to the cathedral.

Close by in the Carrer del Bisbe Irurita and again, one that you can only see from the outside, is the thirteenth-century **Palau Episcopal.** This originally backed onto the Roman city wall, but the stark façade over the Plaça Nova was a late-eighteenth-century addition. Sitting where the bishops' vegetable garden once lay, this has a grand courtyard and some beautiful stained glass. (The patio is open 09.00-14.00 Monday to Friday.)

Plaça Sant Felip Neri, at the end of Carrer Montjuïc del Bisbe and often overlooked, is one of the old town's sweetest squares. There is a pretty church here, and outside usually becomes the playground for the resident primary school.

The Catalan flair for decoration is most apparent when the functional is transformed by elaborate details. This delightful letterbox adorns Casa de l'Ardiaca.

**Museu del Calçat,** Plaça Sant Felip Neri. (Tuesday-Sunday 11.30-14.00.)

Nestling modestly in this quiet square is one of the world's three footwear museums (others are in France and Switzerland). This quaint and fascinating collection is housed in two rooms of the Master Shoemakers' Guild, the origin of which was a brotherhood formed in 1202. Official activity stopped in the nineteenth century but traditionally loyal members continue to meet here weekly.

Shoes, boots and sandals from all over the world comprise the main display, and date from the first century AD to the twentieth century. Examples once sported by famous feet include the silver evening shoes of Catalan singer Nuria Feliu, the lace-ups of the master cellist Pau Casals and the boots which took Catalan climber Carles Valles up Everest. Surprisingly, the designs worn by Roman feet look remarkably like the fashionable sandals flaunted today.

This tiny museum also proudly holds a *Guinness Book of Records* entry for the world's largest shoe. Made in honour of Christopher Columbus, it was designed to exactly fit the enormous foot of his statue by the port, and weighs over 23 kilograms.

Back on Carrer del Bisbe Irurita is the narrow **Plaça de Garriga i Bachs,** dedicated to the five loyal Catalans who were killed resisting the Napoleonic forces (though it would seem to have been designed specifically for buskers). The central statue was created in their memory and their tale is immortalised in the series of hand-painted tiles. Further along this street, the neo-Gothic bridge created this century, links the Generalitat to the President's residence (on the left).

If you wander down Carrer Pietat, look above the east door of the Cathedral for The Pity, the beautiful Flemish-style wooden relief, which gives this street its name. Just a few yards down the narrow Carrer Paradís at the Centre Excursionista de Catalunya, a tiny plaque indicates that this — the highest point of the ancient city — was once the site of Augustus' Roman Temple **(Temple Romà d'Augusti)**. Just inside, large as life, stand three of the original fluted Corinthian columns, which have been incorporated into the inner courtyard.

These can be glimpsed at any time through the glass panels, or when the centre opens between 18.00 and 22.00. Earlier this century there were supposedly many more which may have been casually absorbed or demolished. Astonishingly disregarded — certainly many cities would proudly display Roman columns still standing erect and intact — it would seem that Barcelonans have become blasé.

Yet this is perhaps less surprising given that the whole area is an archaeologist's dream. Overflowing with history, beneath today's pavements a network of tunnels links many of the principal buildings. And further evidence of ancient settlements, along with Roman and Visigothic relics, is uncovered with amazing regularity.

At the end of Carrer Pietat, the **Arxiu de la Corona D'Aragó** (archives of the crown of Aragon) sits on Carrer dels Comtes. This sixteenth-century building is also known as the Palace of the Viceroys and, like the other royal buildings, forms part of Plaça del Rei. You can wander into the courtyard and up to the first gallery, but it is principally recommended for the modern bronze by Josep Subirachs. A relief after the glut of Gothic architecture and sculpture, this bronze door (to the left of the patio) shows the sculptor playing with concave and convex forms, and the historical allusions include a map of Europe.

**Museu Frederic Marès,** Plaça Sant Iu,5-6. (09.00-14.00 and 16.00-19.00, closed Monday and holidays.)

Previously the palace of the Counts of Barcelona, this is another extension of the royal buildings in Plaça del Rei. The present contents were donated to the city by the Catalan sculptor, Frederic Marès. This important collection includes Roman relics, and sculpture from the twelfth to the eighteenth century, as well as Romanesque and Gothic panel paintings and artefacts.

The sculptor was born in the border town of Portbou in 1893, and, at the time of writing, is still making designs. He lives above the museum (second floor), and on Wednesday between 12.00 and 14.00, allows his rampant collection of sentimental, personal objects acquired over many years of travel to be viewed. This is well worth a look and anyone interested in the Spanish fan will find almost an entire upper room devoted to this accessory.

Around the corner, **Plaça del Rei,** as the forecourt of the medieval palace of the Counts of Barcelona, is of significant historical and architectural interest; the main hall (Saló del Tinell) of the palace sits at the back, and is famed for being the site where Queen Isabella received Christopher Columbus on his return from discovering the New World (1492). To the left hovers the five-tier tower of King Marti the Humane (though this is a misnomer as it was built well after his reign in 1555); its lofty sweep has unfortunately been interrupted by later construction.

Evening floodlights pick out the finer features of this architectural hotch-potch, including the stained glass of the Gothic Chapel of Santa Àgata, running along the right side. This grand setting is frequently brought to life as an open air theatre for concerts and festivals.

**Museu d'Història de la Ciutat,** Plaça del Rei. (09.00-20.00, closed afternoons on Sunday, Monday and holidays.)

The history of the city museum is housed in the elegant Casa Clariana-Padellàs, a late fifteenth-century mansion on the corner of Plaça del Rei. This was originally built in the Carrer de Mercaders, and was subsequently moved to this spot, piece by piece.

Work on the building's foundations in 1931 revealed staggering Roman remains which now constitute the museum's underground rooms. These extensive cellars, undoubtedly the highlight, are cleverly constructed so visitors can tread the ancient residential streets and see mosaics, urns and carvings in situ. Upper rooms chart later urban development, and include a particularly comprehensive display of maps.

Also part of the museum, connected by a passage, are the

fourteenth-century Royal Palace buildings in Plaça del Rei: the great stone Tinnel Hall and the Chapel of Santa Àgata. Tall and slender, this chapel has an intricately painted wooden ceiling and two layers of pointed stained glass windows. Both these buildings are frequently used for temporary exhibitions. (This museum is in the throes of major renovation; there are no leaflets in English and all exhibits are labelled in Catalan/Spanish.)

## Ajuntament

At the nerve centre of the Gothic quarter, in Plaça de Sant Jaume, sit the Ajuntament (town hall) and Palau de la Generalitat (home of the Catalan Autonomous government). Often opposed in policy, they are significantly sited on opposite sides of this commanding square. The Ajuntament dates from the fourteenth century, and combines Gothic, neo-Classical and modern architecture. Although currently closed to the public, visits may become possible in the future.

The main façade, destroyed by Philip V in 1714, was rebuilt in neo-Classical style. It displays the statues of Jaume I (left) and Fiveller, a fourteenth-century citizen widely admired for his determination and good sense. The lateral façade, originally a main entrance (in Carrer de la Ciutat) is Catalan Gothic with its characteristic pointed arches and gargoyles, each one different. When it's not smothered in pigeons, you can also see Sant Jordi (Saint George), a familiar figure around the square and one of Catalunya's throng of patron saints. If you're visiting the information office (to the left inside the main entrance) take a look at the various modern sculptures in the inner courtyard, including pieces by Miró, Marès, Llimona and Rebull.

## Palau de la Generalitat

Construction of this palace began in the fifteenth century, but continued for two centuries and shows a mixture of styles. The main façade stems from the early seventeenth century and typifies Catalan Renaissance architecture. Presiding over the entrance above the distinctive red and yellow striped flag of Catalunya, is Saint George, once again in murderous mood.

Inside, the most attractive feature is the upper, arcaded gallery which, built in the late fifteenth century, shows a sober, elegant side of Catalan Gothic. Beyond this a pretty courtyard is possessed by gruesome gargoyles and yet another statue of Saint George; here the medieval custom of cultivating orange trees is still preserved.

The palace contains some grand reception rooms with huge

frescoes both early and modern with scenes of Catalan history; there are fine Flemish tapestries, and some beautiful early sixteenth-century coffered and painted ceilings. Joining the palace to the President's official residence is the Pont del Bisbe. Visits to the Palace must be arranged in advance by writing to Relacions Externes i Protocol, Palau de la Generalitat, Plaça de Sant Jaume, Barcelona, 08002.

## Santa Maria del Pí

Plaça del Pí and the adjacent Plaça de Sant Josep Oriol form a recommended retreat from the surrounding bustling streets. A favoured spot for buskers and comedians, it is an entertaining place to linger, but don't overlook the charming Gothic church. Simple and pretty, it does a roaring trade in wedding couples.

There is just one large nave and no side aisles, although side chapels (some elaborately adorned) run along both edges. The apse has elegant, ribbed vaulting and, like the altar, is refreshingly plain. Behind this, richly-coloured stained glass (especially some stunning deep blues) provides ample decoration. While a vast rose window illuminates the flat-fronted façade.

## Carrer de Montcada Metro Jaume I. Bus 16,17,22,45,100.

Although mainly frequented for the Picasso museum, the whole of this street is worth investigating. A fashionable centre in the sixteenth and seventeenth century, it was originally the preserve of the aristocracy, and then the rich bourgeoisie, and is lined with small Gothic palaces.

A few are open to the public (others can be glimpsed through open doors) and these, with their tiny inner patios and elegant first floor galleries, provide a good example of medieval Catalan architecture. At the far end, the last street on the left is the narrowest street in Barcelona, and is aptly named the 'street of flies' (Carrer de las Mosques). This area contains some interesting contemporary galleries, and is rapidly becoming a centre for art and antiques.

## Museu Picasso, Montcada,15-17. (10.00-20.00, closed Monday.)

Housed in two fine Gothic mansions, specifically converted in 1968, the museum is the result of donations by the artist and his great friend Jaume Sabartes. Although patchy, it is a significant collection which further illuminates the extraordinary genius of Pablo Picasso (1881-1973). And despite containing none of his best known pieces, and few in the Cubist style so often associated with him, it is Barcelona's most visited museum and highly recommended.

Works from the period Picasso spent in Barcelona, from age 14 to 23, make up the majority. You can see the remarkable skill he had developed by the age of ten — tiny portraits of his family, and figurative oils and sketches, including a revealing group of early self portraits. Here is proof, if any were needed, that Picasso's draughtsmanship was quite superb.

He was clearly affected by his introduction to the Parisian art scene during his trip in 1900; and certainly adept — his experiments show the influence of Toulouse-Lautrec, Cézanne, Degas, the Nabis, and the Impressionists. There are some pieces from his celebrated Blue Period (1901-4), then a gap until 1917 (the year he returned to Barcelona) represented by a few works, in particular *The Harlequin*.

The collection then leaps to 1957, with two rooms devoted to Picasso's vibrant adaptations of Velásquez's royal portrait *Las Meninas*. There are at least 50 variations — wild, colourful contortions of the Princess Margareta Maria, Isobel, her lady-in-waiting, the dwarf, the page and the dog. Graphic works are displayed on the top floor, including a few studies of his wife Jaqueline and the famous doves of peace. There is also a varied selection of ceramics donated by his wife.

The illustrated chronology of his life is helpful, but there is no information or catalogue in English. The museum café has a trendy interior with a small but tasty menu.

**Museu Textil i d'Indumentaria,** Montcada,12-14. (09.00-14.00 and 16.30-19.00, closed afternoons and holidays, and all day Monday.)

Almost opposite the Picasso, spread over another couple of Gothic palaces, is the peaceful textile and costume museum. The ground floor is devoted to textiles dating from the fourth century, and early scarves with religious or historical scenes. Upstairs is an impressive collection of clothing and accessories from the sixteenth century to the present.

There are elaborate silks and satins with incredibly intricate designs, even some seventeenth-century embroidered socks. On the second floor the exhibition ends on a more frivolous note, with an outrageous dress from 1987, constructed from chicken wire adorned with lurid pink bunches of thread and plastic hair rollers.

Just slightly off the typical tourist track, the Santa Maria del Mar is the finest church in Barcelona.

The basilica's faintly neglected facade belies a gloriously airy interior. The highlight is its enormous and elegant sweep of fan vaulting, as seen here.

**Santa Maria del Mar,** Plaça Santa Maria. (10.00-12.30 and 17.00-1930.)

This enormous basilica — built in the early fourteenth century from funds raised by local merchants — at one time stood close to the sea. (This was before the development of the harbour in the eighteenth century, dregs from which then formed the triangular area of Barceloneta.) A shining example of Catalan Gothic, the main façade has been sorely neglected and is in dire need of weeding.

The heavy, fortress-like exterior hides a wonderfully elegant, spacious interior. The keynote here is verticality; graceful octagonal columns making a circular sweep behind the altar, end in lofty fan vaulting. One of the highlights is the superb stained glass, particularly the enormous rose window over the main door.

A fire in 1936 during the civil war destroyed the vast organ and the Baroque altar, but the result enhances the beautiful bones of the building. And the present altar sitting on a plain dais is charmingly simple. If you visit any church in Barcelona it should surely be this.

## Along The Rambles

Metro Catalunya/Liceu/Drassanes; Bus 14,18,38,59,100.
Set back from Santa Anna, tucked into the small courtyard of Placeta de Ramon Amadeu, with a flower stall at its gate, the church of **Santa Anna** (09.00-12.30 and 18.00-20.30) is all too easy to overlook. This sweet church was founded in 1881 and has a rather odd layout. It has a central octagonal dome, and very deep side chapels, one of which is dedicated to sport (see Sporting Spirit, page 146).

**Palau de la Virreina,** Rambla,99. Metro Liceu.
Set slightly back from the Rambles, this eighteenth-century palace was designed for the Viceroy of Peru and lived in by his widow, the Virreina. Showing the influence of Louis XIV-style architecture, it has a grand first floor, pilasters spanning two storeys, and a rooftop sprinkled with classical urns. This now houses the cultural wing of the town hall, the ground floor having an information centre and ticket office for all Ajuntament run entertainments. Some of the upper rooms have been set aside for temporary art exhibitions.

**Museu de les Arts de l'Espectacle,** Nou de la Rambla,3. (11.00-14.00 and 17.00-20.00, closed Sunday and holidays.) Metro Liceu.

The forbidding Palau Güell sits in a seedy street just off the Rambles. Built between 1886-8 this was an early Gaudí project, and his first for patron, Eusebi Güell. To compensate for its cramped location without views, Gaudi created tremendous interior interest. Inside, the palace is endowed with a feeling of space, and seems to miraculously expand as you wander between rooms — it actually covers some 2,000 square metres.

Columns in the basement (once the stables) support the building, and there are numerous others throughout the house. The main salon was originally a chapel and concert hall, and almost all the rooms are elaborately decorated, with distinctive ironwork and panelled ceilings. But the most extraordinary sight (and quite out of context in the old quarter) is the roof terrace which has 18 sculpted chimneys and ventilation pipes decorated with odd pieces of coloured ceramic. This has been declared by UNESCO as part of the worldwide architectural heritage. Today this is the centre of the Theatre Institute, containing their library and archives, and occasionally holding temporary exhibitions. The portraits which hang inside the place depict mainly Catalan actors and actresses.

**Museu de Cera,** Rambla,4-6. (Monday-Friday) 10.00-13.30 and 16.30-19.30, Saturday, Sunday and festivals 11.00-20.00.) Metro Dressanes.

Just up from the port at the foot of the Rambles, the wax museum is an escapist's place to spend an hour or two. This has some highly convincing models, and some more or less successful trickery. All the usual world-famous figures feature (along with some fictional ones), and great atmospheres are created in the dungeons and in the rides underwater or into space.

**Museu Marítim,** Porta de la Pau,1. (Tuesday-Saturday 09.30-14.00 and 16.00-19.00, Sunday and holidays 10.00-14.00.) Metro Drassanes; bus 14,18,59,64,19,100.

Perhaps more interesting than the exhibits it houses is this well-preserved medieval dockyard building, where the galleys and boats were once built. Today's exhibits include maps, navigation equipment, original local fishing boats and some splendid reconstructions, notably Don John of Austria's Royal Galley.

Moored close by, and worth visiting, is a 1950s replica of the Santa Maria, the ship in which Columbus discovered the New World. Its authentic interior seems shockingly small given the scale of his discovery, and underlines the courage and resilience of the early explorers.

# Parc de la Ciutadella

Metro Arc de Triomf/Barceloneta/Ciutadella; bus 14,16,17,36,39,
40,45,51,57,59,64,100.
The whole park makes a pleasant visit. For a description see Parks,
Chapter 8.

**Museu d'Art Modern** (09.00-19.30, Monday 15.00-19.30, Sunday
and festivals 09.00-14.00.)
Situated in the same building as the Catalan Parliament, this
collection mainly features Spanish, and particularly Catalan artists.
It opens in the latter part of the nineteenth century, in which works
by Maria Fortuny Marsal feature, notably his famous *Battla de
Tetuan*. And various city scenes of that period are intriguing — see
Pla de la Boqueria or Born market transformed.

A few whimsical turn-of-the-century, pre-Raphaelite style works
are followed by a collection of Art Nouveau furniture: dressers and
ensembles with marquetry (inlaid pictorial patterns on wooden
veneers) and decorative panels. There are colourful Modernista
mosaics and pieces by Josep Puig i Cadafalch (architect of Casa
Amatller) which were designed for that house. Not to be missed are
Pau Gargallo's sculptures which show the influence of Matisse, and
increasingly of Cubism on his work; look out for his telling stone
caricature of Picasso.

As a whole the museum is more interesting to those familiar with
Catalan art, although it does show how all the major styles and
movements permeated Europe. It is disappointing in having so few
contemporary works; there are almost none from the last 50 years.
The small cluster of modern canvasses hanging just inside the
entrance includes two by the Catalan favourite Antoni Tàpies.

The highlight is a fascinating installation in an inner courtyard by
Josep Guinovart i Bertran made from 1976-9. A jungle of vertically
inspired wooden rods — like totem poles, spears, javelins,
rattlesnakes tails — and a cascade of white paper shapes; here
phallic symbolism is rife and, reminiscent of a Red Indian burial
ground, there is an eerie feel.

**Zoo** (Summer 09.30-19.30, Winter 10.00-17.00)
Spread over Ciutadella park are Barcelona's fine zoological
gardens; these, which are of medium size, opened in 1892. Here
more than 45 species of tree cast valuable shade over the paths and
elegant sculptures, including the *Lady with the Umbrella* and *Saint
Francis of Assisi,* the zoo's patron saint. (Not surprisingly, but out

of character, Saint George keeps a low profile in this sculpture garden).

The five star attraction is Snowflake, the world's only albino gorilla, but other highlights include Ulysees the Icelandic killer whale (one of only three in Europe), and a terrarium with snakes from all over the world. One important strand of this zoo's philosophy is to promote the reproduction and reintegration of endangered species.

---

### The White Gorilla

One of Barcelona's most treasured residents is Floquet de Neu (Snowflake), the only albino gorilla in the world. This pampered adult male has had three wives (Ndengue, Bimbili and Yuma) but still prefers Ndengue, mother of his first son. Entrancing to watch, with his blue eyes, white fur and pale pink skin, he inspires an international fan club, and the zoo receives numerous letters each year requesting his details.

Snowflake was discovered in 1966 (aged two) in Western Africa's dense Ntem jungle, near the Cameroon border, and was donated to Barcelona's African investigation centre. Since arriving in the city he has been showered with attention to ensure good mental and physical growth, and has consequently developed a domineering and impetuous character.

Although Snowflake has sired 20 babies, only six have survived and these, like their mothers, do not share his lack of pigmentation. Now the zoo is hoping to save the white gorilla from extinction. A promising genetic recipe for white offspring may be to mate son and daughter, or better still father and daughter.

---

**Museu de Zoologia,** Passeig de Picasso. (Tuesday-Sunday 09.00-14.00, closed Monday and holidays.)

Built as the Café-Restaurant for the 1888 Universal Exhibition, this is a curious-looking, red brick building by Modernismo supremo Domènech i Montaner. Its castellated roof line is decorated with huge blue and white ceramic shields depicting animals, insects and plants.

Sitting at the edge of the park, it forms a logical extension to the nearby zoo. A taxidermist's delight, exhibits include numerous species of rare stuffed animals, birds and insects.

# Eixample

## Modernismo and Gaudí

The architectural monuments for which Barcelona became especially famous begin around the end of the last century with the *Modernismo* movement. This embodies many of the characteristics of Art Nouveau, but moves further and wider than the purely aesthetic. The revolt against the drab practicality of industrialisation, which was echoed all over Europe, is especially evident here in the rich indulgence of decoration and a taste for the exotic.

Concentration of this style in Barcelona was the result of a unique combination of factors: resurgence of national pride and prosperity, freedom from the limiting city walls (pulled down in 1860) and all the possibilities that the development of Eixample afforded the bourgeoisie. Citizens rich from trade in the Americas were ready to show off their new wealth, and at the same time aristocrats flocked back from the provinces to live in Barcelona.

As much as anything it was the amazing Catalan ability to look confidently to the future, not back to traditional styles. From around 1880 until the First World War, *Modernismo* affected almost all aspects of life. It was the result of an awakening in everything from music and literature to fashion, intellect, and even politics; and this period of potent creativity reached its high point in Barcelona's buildings.

Today many places have hardly changed, and the insatiably curious can find feasts all over town: beautiful carved doorways, original Art Nouveau-style plasterwork, frosted windows with stylised floral decoration, or sinuous patterns cut into curved stone. The greatest concentration of these buildings are found in Eixample, which was still under construction when this movement burst its banks. And a walk along any of the grander boulevards, such as Rambla de Catalunya, Balmes and Diagonal, will yield many surprises.

But to throw yourself in at the deep end, head straight for Passeig de Gràcia (metro Passeig de Gràcia), especially to one block (numbers 35 to 43) known as the *'manzana de la discordia'* or block of discord. (This is an architectural joke because *manzana* means apple as well as block, and this prestigious block — like the infamous apple over which Cain and Abel fought — supposedly had *Modernismo* architects vying to build here.) It contains representative buildings by each of the three protagonists in the Modernismo movement: Antoni Gaudí (1852-1926), Lluís

Domènech i Montaner (1850-1923), Josep Puig i Cadafalch (1869-1956) — as well as one by another prolific architect, Enric Sagnier — all constructed at the beginning of the century.

---

### Sung in Stone

A charming addition to the splendid *Modernista* interior of Casa Lleó-Morera is the Catalan children's song, and history of the Morera family, illustrated by Eusebi Arnau's voluptuous overdoor carvings. On the first floor, to the right above the main entrance, the legend begins with a fiesta, in which a king receives fruit from a page. Moving anti-clockwise, the king and courtiers set off hunting with a falcon, its keeper and a hound. Alone at the palace, the prince is shown with his nurse and a spinning wheel.

Returning to the hunt, a wild boar is pursued by dogs and archers. Back in the palace (round to the left), the nurse has lit a fire, fallen asleep, and the baby prince is burning in his cradle. A contrite nurse is next shown praying to the Virgin and Christ child, begging for the baby's return and pledging the king's crown in exchange. Along the passage, the court page offers the nurse some money, which she rejects saying gold can never revive the babe.

Meanwhile the hunt draws to a close and a kid has been caught. Turning around we see a miracle has been pulled off, the baby prince has sprung back to life. The king and queen are reunited with their son, unaware of the drama, while the nurse looks on joyfully. Finally above the entrance, the nurse (on the left) pleads with artisans, who make a gold crown for the Virgin and a little silver one for young Jesus.

---

**Casa Lleó Morera** is a mature work (finished in 1906) by Domènech i Montaner, leader of the *Modernismo* movement. Here, commissioned by the wealthy Morera family, the architect was able to indulge his decorative fancies using top quality materials to alter the existing house. The façade is decorated with wrought iron and diverse mythological animals, and the whole is crowned by a colourful cupola.

The second floor circular balconies are interesting: those in the centre, with male and female heads facing each other, symbolise two marriages, one young, one mature; the side balconies depict four women each holding a symbol of progress — a lightbulb, a record player, a camera, the fourth is hidden in the woman's hand. Above, the skyline is punctuated with elaborate spikes rather like asparagus tips.

The spectacular interior has a lift like a confession box, and you can visit the principal floor (afternoons only) as this now houses the

Tourist Board. Known as the *floralista* style, undulating, flowery ornamentation abounds, and designs are combined in plaster, sculpture, marquetry, mosaic and ceramics.

The porcelain reliefs and mural mosaics are a masterpiece, wholly typical of the *Modernista* richness, and anticipate the peak Montaner reached with the Palau de la Música. Perhaps most stunning is the brilliant, pictorial stained glass. And the voluptuous stone carvings of Eusebi Arnau above the doors depict (beside the most vivid Saint George yet) a traditional Catalan song (see box above).

**Casa Amatller** at number 41, was created in 1900 by Josep Puig i Cadafalch, and forms a jarring contrast in its harsh angularity. Beside Casa Batlló, its flat front appears restrained; and this flatness is relieved only by a protruding window, and a first floor balcony whose brackets are a bunch of iron flowers. Of medieval inspiration, it has a dramatic castellated roofline like a Dutch gable, pointed features and flowing carving.

The yellow and white façade has graphic patterns made from ground marble overlaid on stone, and the top is decorated with ceramic shapes. On weekdays you can enter the courtyard to view the jagged brass lanterns supported by dragons, superb stone carving around the stairs of animals and insects, and the splendid luminous coloured glass ceiling which lights the stairwell.

Upstairs houses a library of books and photographs, and a small museum of Hispanic Art. This is a mixed collection with a few paintings, tapestries, furniture, and a fairly large collection of antique glass. These were all gathered by the original patron Amatller, who had made his money manufacturing chocolate. His bust which (along with those of his father and daughter) sits in the tiny museum, was carved by Eusebi Arnau, the leading *Modernista* sculptor responsible for the whole mansion.

Although relatively unknown, this is freely open to the public (10.00-14.00); and it is well worth venturing inside if only to glimpse Puig i Cadafalch's luxurious interior. Note the mosaic passages, beams painted with snaking flowery motifs, and in the library, the yellow and green floral glass woven into Gothic arches and tracery.

Next door, with **Casa Batlló**, Gaudí moved beyond anything hitherto explored (1905-7). Unlike the others here, this building was designed as a piece of sculpture in itself. Startlingly organic, the luminous façade of broken glass and plates is wonderfully fluid and full of movement. The plasticity of the windows and pillars vividly resemble animals' skin and bones. And this creepiness is extended by the metal balconies which appear like eye masks.

Its life-like qualities culminate in a scaly roof which symbolises an arched dragon's back, the crowning ripple of blue ceramic bobbles, its spine. Stuck in the dragon's tail, and forming the dramatic mosaic chimney, is the five-pronged cross so favoured by Gaudí. Some see this as simply religious, others as the cross of (none other than) Saint George. (Gaudí's fixation with dragons sparked his creative fire in numerous works, but seems distinct from the cult of this tiresome patron saint.)

It demands a long look to fully appreciate the humour and visual trickery so typical of Gaudí. Although this sinuous, shimmering front is entirely original, his task here was to alter an existing house rather than design from scratch. Its deliberate asymmetry was not only challenging old styles, but also the result of Gaudí considerably demolishing one room (top left) in order not to ruin the skyline for Casa Amatller. (Visits to the interior require a permit and are reserved for specialists.)

Another example of Gaudí's compulsive visual teasing in silhouette. Seen from within, this cobweb gate forms the entrance to La Pedrera, his most organic and provocative creation.

**La Pedrera,** Passeig de Gràcia,92. (Closed Sundays)

Even that extraordinary block won't quite prepare you for **Casa Milà.** More popularly known as **La Pedrera,** the stone quarry, this was designed at the height of Gaudí's powers and maturity; it broke away from the existing style and forms of *Modernismo,* and stunned Barcelona. Architecturally unique, in 1984 it was declared by UNESCO a World Heritage building.

A close look at the façade is tantalisingly confusing — your eye is led a merry dance and drawn up numerous blind alleys. Just where you expect to find one pillar supporting another (in the time-honoured way) the weight appears offset, the whole highly asymmetrical. The movement and plasticity are both inspiring and disturbing, and everywhere constructional norms are defied. He has achieved a brilliant architectural unity — and far from limiting his creativity, here functional considerations complement his imaginative ebullience.

Gaudí also needed to overcome the emphasis given to the street's chamfered corner (part of Cerdà's recently designed grid system). The resulting undulating façade, which rounds the corner but at no point forms one, is a masterstroke. This stone curtain, which is asymmetrical in three dimensions, hangs from a steel structure. And so wholly organic, here the ironwork literally grows over the balconies like seaweed.

Gaudí's sense of fantasy veritably raised the roof. He transformed the chimneys and skyline of La Pedrera into a surreal sculpture garden.

Quite belying their appearance, Gaudí's buildings were the result of painstaking, mathematical ingenuity. And infinitely more important than the decoration, are the architectural breakthroughs he achieved. His experiments with falling drapery enabled him to produce a fluidity that could also bear weight. Most important to twentieth-century construction was his use of the parabolic arch. This design produced a hitherto unsolved distribution of weight, improving the continuity between the roof and walls, with the base taking the greatest load.

The rooftop reaches the realms of fantasy; here necessity provoked the imaginative disguises of contorted pinnacles. The larger towers hide the ventilation towers and staircase, while the smaller twisted pillars are chimneys; and in the onion-shaped domes it's easy to see Gaudi's love of Moorish design. The whole is really a sculpture terrace, where Gaudí was experimenting with collage effects, using broken bottles and tiles. As with so many of his grand projects, the architect had envisaged a dramatic addition to this roof which was never carried out.

The whole was built for the Milàs as a residential block of flats; the attic, designed as the ventilation area, was only converted in 1954 into 14 new apartments. This had the disastrous effect of blocking the vents, and thereby ruining the cooling system. The straight columns with helmeted tops are chimneys for the new apartments added in 1954 and soon to be demolished.

This twisted turret, coated in broken tiles, actually hides a staircase and ventilation tower on top of La Pedrera.

La Caixa de Catalunya purchased the building in 1986 with the purpose of restoring it to its original splendour. Apart from the recent cleaning, restoration plans include the demolition of the flats, stripping back the attic plaster to reveal the brickwork of Gaudí's famous parabolic arches, and installing a permanent display of Gaudí furniture (from the museum in Parc Güell). La Caixa publishes information in many languages and operates six free guided tours from Tuesday - Saturday except holidays daily to visit the inner courtyards and roof at 10.00, 11.00, 12.00, 13.00.

---

**A Provocative Madonna**

Throughout his life, Gaudí became increasingly preoccupied with religion, and for the roof of the Pedrera, he had designed an enormous statue of the Virgin to dominate the skyline. His patron (Milà) rejected this idea, however, frightened of provoking a revolutionary attack. It was during this period in 1909, that anarchists were planting bombs around the city, aimed particularly at the state, the rich, and the church.

In July of that year the escalation of violence culminated in what is remembered as the *"Setmana Trágica"* (Tragic Week), when anarchists set fire to a great number of churches in the city. Yet Gaudí was so incensed by Milà for thwarting his plans that he is supposed to have abandoned work on the building, and left the remainder to be completed by an assistant.

---

Within the grid of Eixample lie many other *Modernista* buildings. If you continue up Passeig de Gràcia to number 132, **Casa Fuster** rounds the corner into the narrower Gran de Gràcia. Here Domènech i Montaner makes use of stunted columns with overblown capitals and protruding semi-circular windows.

His earliest work for the publishing house Montaner i Simon (1880) is found on Aragó (between Passeig de Gràcia and Rambla de Catalunya). This is in the process of incorporating the Fundació Tàpies, named after the famous Catalan painter Antoni Tàpies, which will include all his private collections, as well as pieces of oriental art, and will become an artistic centre due to open in 1991.

Another building completed by Domènech i Montaner is the **Palau Montaner** (Mallorca,278), a grand mansion which is now the headquarters of the Government Delegation in Catalunya. However, his most sensational creation, and widely considered the greatest representation of *Modernista,* is the **Palau de la Música Catalana.** Tucked into a rather cramped area of the old town, near the top of Vía Laietana, this is all too easily overlooked, but it should be seen *at all costs* (see Concerts and Opera section, chapter 6).

Another famous landmark, and again remarkable for its curious style, is Puig i Cadafalch's **Casa Terrades**. This block, which fills an awkward triangular space left by Diagonal, is more popularly known as the *Casa de les Punxes* or House of Spikes. Here Puig i Cadafalch was experimenting with verticality, and his sharp turrets appear like a German schloss. Planned in 1903, this is the architect's largest work, and with its gabled roofline and rich ornamentation, it certainly creates a startling effect.

**Museu del Perfum,** Passeig de Gràcia,39. (Monday-Friday 10.00-13.30 and 16.00-19.30, closed holidays.) Metro Passeig de Gràcia; bus 20,21,22,24,28,39,43,100.

The entrance to this unlikely museum is through an upmarket cosmetics shop. Hoarding the world's most comprehensive collection of vanities (other similar displays are in France, Germany and the USA), its exhibits number about 5,000 receptacles for perfume, cream and cosmetics. Gathered from around the world and made from all manner of material, these take every conceivable shape, hue and size including a heart, a boot and a horn.

Displayed chronologically, the earliest treasures are Egyptian (dating from around 3000 BC), the latest being the seductive packages manufactured by today's houses. Also here are Roman bottles made from pale opaque glass with rainbow threads, big nineteenth-century European eggs enclosing little bottles, and Art Nouveau luxuries. This tiny museum also guards the source of some famous fragrances: bottles belonging to Queen Victoria and Grace Kelly, as well as those of Marie Antoinette, disguised inside a pocket book. And there's even a bottle designed by Dalí.

**Museu de la Música,** Diagonal,373. (Tuesday-Sunday 09.00-14.00.) Metro Diagonal; bus 6,15,22,24,28,34,39,100.

Housed in a *Modernista* creation of Puig i Cadafalch, this collection of musical instruments includes a particularly comprehensive range of guitars.

**Sagrada Família** (09.00-20.00 daily, until 21.00 July and August, or 19.00 in winter) Metro Sagrada Família; bus 19,34,43,50,51,54, 100,544.

Only partly built, Gaudí's Temple of the Holy Family still justifies its fame as the sight which epitomizes Barcelona. Jutting into the sky, it was intended as the city's tallest building, but is now dwarfed by the Besós Thermal towers. The first stone was laid in 1882 and, offering a rare glimpse of a church in mid-construction, some say the last won't be down until well into the twenty-second century.

It has always been funded by public donation and entirely hand carved, which in part explains the delay. Much of the crypt, apse and Nativity façade were built by Gaudí himself, who at one stage actually lived on the site. The source of much controversy, some argue its interest will be diminished when work is completed; but love it or hate it, this is a must for any visitor.

This startling monument, like a monstrous vertical maze, can't be fully appreciated without braving the towers. From here the architecture unfolds every possible shape, sometimes quite liquid, packed with plump curves, and elsewhere angular. The spiral climb, up passages resembling fossiled shells, is a dizzy experience. Although the frequent alcoves are some respite, vertigo replaces claustrophobia as gaps crop up at foot or shoulder level when least expected. Still more disorientating are the views which switch as you walk between towers; from here a clear landmark is the lake in Gaudí park (which allows a more distant perspective of the Sagrada).

Once planned in Gothic style by the architect Francisco del Villar, the design was given to Gaudí when del Villar resigned in 1883. Although Gaudí's original designs were neo-Gothic, the Sagrada really defies architectural labels. It has three major symbolic façades, the south (and main one) celebrates Heavenly Glory, the east depicts the Nativity, and the west Christ's Passion and Crucifixion.

Its 18 towers represent the 12 apostles, four Evangelists, the Virgin Mary, and Christ (the highest one). The ground plan comprises a nave, four aisles and a transept making up a Roman cross, and encircling the church is an outer cloister. Rich symbolism surrounds the Nativity doorway where the stone has a muscular, voluptuous texture depicting organic images, some reminiscent of teeth and leaves. Continuing this theme are the towers topped with perky floral mosaics.

The assembly of sculptures on the Passion façade are by the contemporary sculptor, Josep Subirachs. These, which will take many years to complete, are to depict the final days of Christ's life from the Last Supper to his burial. Those visible to date are the flagellation and the Crucifixion. The former, which in Subirachs' words "represents the loneliness of man", will be flanked by "the Betrayal of Judas" and "the Denial of Peter".

The pillar to which Christ is bound is made of four sections which represent parts of the cross, and "the old world that Christ has come to change". But this is dislocated to signify Christ's impact on the world. The steps symbolise the three days preceding the Resurrection. Above hovers Christ on the cross. Powerful, angular and provocative, these are out of key with the rest of the architecture and have caused a stir.

In the Sagrada museum are models and photography of its various stages of construction. But revealing an overall flavour of Gaudí's work is the short free film which shows how astonishingly prolific he was.

---

### A Deadly Attraction

Barcelona's 44 museums, which leave little ground unturned, bolster her reputation as Spain's broad-minded capital. Whether your special subject be holography, footwear, football, robots, cosmetics, bullfighting or the postal service, there's a museum dedicated to your field.

Most peculiar of these is one of the world's rare funeral museums. Here a holiday could be spent boning-up on the history of the hearse; exhibits range from the horse-drawn carriages, once used for Barcelona's funeral processions (such as the gilded French-style Imperial model) to '50s motor cars like the Hispano-Suiza. Extending to funereal fashion, there is also a collection of mourning wear; and this unlikely attraction even produces its own postcards.

By night, you could continue in the same spooky vein at the 666 discotheque (Llull,145) where low tables are made out of coffins. (The Museu de Carosses Fúnebres is at Sancho d'Avila,2, open weekdays 09.00-13.00 and 16.00-19.00, mornings only on Saturdays.)

---

# Gràcia

**Casa Vicens,** Carrer de les Carolines,24. Metro Fontana.

Gaudí's first private commission (as opposed to his early civic works) of 1878-85, is a complete departure from previous tendencies, and heralds the start of the *Modernista* movement. Significantly commissioned by a tile merchant, rough brick with bands of colourful ceramic make up the lower part. Then using turrets, balconies and a two-tier front, decoration becomes increasingly feverish, until the upper part is almost entirely faced with a rash of yellow, green and white tiles.

Red castellated brickwork, and exotic pointed windows and

minarets add to the Moorish feel. The emphasis on ceramics, wild, wrought iron and bright colour foreshadows many of his later works and other *Modernista* buildings. But this first experiment is altogether more angular and less plastic than Gaudí later dared.

The whole house has a fortified air, accentuated by the fence and gateway made from roundels of sharp leaves topped with gruesome spikes. Tortured ironwork features all over the house, although it is less organic at this stage. This is the first sign of Gaudí's early familiarity with metals (his father was a coppersmith and kettle-maker) and savage ornamental railings and metalwork were quickly to become a Gaudí trademark.

**Parc Güell,** Carrer Olot. Open weekdays: 10.00-18.00; weekends: 09.00-20.00. Metro Lesseps; bus 24,25,31,32,74,100.

Laid out on a hillside rising behind Barcelona, this was envisaged by Count Güell as a fashionable garden suburb, to house a community in a peaceful location. Perhaps it was just too far from the city centre (the bourgeoisie turned their noses up at it) or perhaps, in true Gaudí style, it was simply too ambitious. Nevertheless Güell's generous patronage gave Gaudí free rein to indulge his extravagant imagination without the limitations of city streets. That the grand scheme was never realised is an extra bonus to Barcelona's citizens, who now have a fantastic public park to enjoy.

The gatehouses, showing a curious mix of whimsical and Moorish design, are often referred to as gingerbread houses. Their fairytale quality is wholly appropriate and sets the tone for what is to come. The ceramic surfacing on these roofs, and on the stairway with its giant lizard, is the first example of broken mosaic which Gaudí was to elaborate in Casa Batlló (1905), and a few years later (1908) in this park's wavy bench.

Humorous and delightful, this park has wonderful plants and shady seats along a network of paths. These zig zag upwards through numerous tiers and past terraces bedecked with stone-sculpted palm trees. There are avenues of stone columns which slant alarmingly, like the roots of a great tree, and which, not only typify Gaudí's provocativeness, but were planned as covered walkways for the residents. All of these features appear to imitate nature, as filtered through an extraordinary, surreal mind.

The great parapet to which all paths lead, was intended as the meeting place for the new community. Its highlight, the undulating, multi-coloured mosaic bench, has an abstraction which is well ahead of its time. (The snaking contours were supposedly taken from the outline of a naked workman seated on layers of plaster.)

This is supported by a dramatic hall of 86 columns, a forest of fluted pillars ending in precariously-poised ceramic bosses. Arab overtones are evident again, as a jungle of columns was often a feature in mosques, and here Gaudí planned the community's marketplace. It incorporates an ingenious drainage system, in which water empties down the hollow columns into an enormous underground cistern.

Apart from the gatehouses, only two of the intended houses were created, and one of these was bought by Gaudí. Currently run as a tiny museum, this is a bit of a hotch-potch, containing *Modernista* furniture, some by Gaudí and some by contemporaries, which is soon to be installed in La Pedrera; there is also some more classical, French-inspired furniture from Palau Güell and another Güell/Gaudí creation, Casa Calvet. The ceiling upstairs is prettily painted in Art Nouveau floral patterns in pastel colours. And Gaudí's bedroom is preserved, including his wardrobe and an old iron bed.

## Montjuïc

To reach this hill by public transport, there are three options. Either take the AERI cable car from the harbour to the Miramar, or take a funicular train from Paral.lel metro station to half way up (near the Miró gallery), from where you can take a cable car on to the top. Alternatively the 61 and 100 buses run up the hill. There is also a free bus from Plaça d'Espanya to Poble Espanyol. (See Bus section, Chapter 3.)

**Fonts de Montjuïc.** Metro Espanya; bus 61,100.

An old favourite for postcards, but nonetheless worth seeing, are the fountains in front of the National Palace. Although a blatant tourist attraction, the sound and light show held here is really pretty impressive. To musical tones, these fighting fountains dance the night away amid clever spot-lighting in almost every imaginable colour. They are illuminated on Thursday, Saturday and Sunday nights from 21.00 to 24.00, and their musical accompaniment plays between 22.00 and 23.00. (In winter, Saturday and Sunday only from 20.00-23.00, music from 12.00-22.00.)

**Museu d'Art de Catalunya,** Palau Nacional. (Open Tuesday-Sunday 09.00-14.00, closed Monday and holidays.) Metro Espanya (and climb past the fountains up the front steps); Bus 61 or 100.

Set dramatically on the hillside, and framed by the two spikes of the park gateway, the Palau Nacional, which contains this museum, was built for the 1929 Universal Exhibition. The Catalan art museum is one of the most important in the province. It is the one locals are most proud of, and is best known for its significant collection of medieval art.

It opens with eleventh to thirteenth century Catalan religious works, the highlight being frescoes rescued from Romanesque churches in the Pyrenees. Once brightening the rounded apses of enchanting and remote little village churches, they have been painstakingly reconstructed here beside a photograph and plan of the church from which they were prised. Also interesting are some superbly carved Romanesque capitals, and two murals of local maps from the same period, depicting the churches and monasteries of medieval Catalunya.

The Gothic section is equally rich, with some dark and brooding panel paintings, often framed with Gothic tracery, human masks, griffins and cherubs. There are many typical altarpieces with stylised figures and the ubiquitous gold tooling, especially for the haloes. Incredibly gory scenes are depicted, of saints and sinners being flayed, raked, or boiled to death — poor Saint Vicenç crops up again and again in agonising scenes.

Few cities escape without a sound and light show. These enormous fountains flash through rainbow lasers, and weekend gatherings become vibrant affairs.

The final phase is a magnificent selection of paintings, drawings and sculpture from the Renaissance and Baroque periods. Represented here are international figures like Tintoretto and Dürer, and Spanish geniuses like Velásquez and Zurbarán, also numerous Dutch genre pictures hung among Catalan works clearly show influence on local art. A whole room is dedicated to the greatly acclaimed Catalan Antoni Viladomat and the other local favourite Pere Pau Montaña.

Upstairs a neat summary of ceramic art from all over Spain is provided by the **Museu de Ceràmica.** Ranging from primitive pots from the Balearic islands and late twelfth-century Arabic wares to contemporary works. There are wonderful early tin-glazed earthenwares on show and plentiful lustreware, made popular by the Spanish Muslims, from the fifteenth to the eighteenth century. The diverse collection includes history friezes, tiles with domestic, religious and artisan scenes, some vibrantly-coloured dishes from Lléda and bright blue, green and yellow pictorial maiolica.

**The Barcelona Pavilion,** Plaça Font Màgica. (Open daily 10.00-19.30.) Metro Espanya.

Reconstructed close to the fountains at the foot of Montjuïc is the highly acclaimed German exhibit which startled the world at the 1929 Universal Exhibition. Designed by Mies Van der Rohe according to the Bauhaus architectural concepts, this remains a historical milestone, and heralded the start of the Modern movement.

Emphasising the simple and linear, this use of new building materials — chromed steel and glass in conjunction with reinforced concrete — gave architecture a hitherto unknown weightlessness. It shows a highly sensitive use of space; open sides and opaque glass screens break down the distinctions between exterior and interior. And the semi-translucency of these are reminiscent of the paper screens in Japanese buildings. (Adjacent to the pavilion, the COOB Olympic building, with its heavier industrial look, provides an interesting contrast.)

Equally important, and still in place, is the Barcelona Chair, which perfectly echoes the new approach to design and materials expressed in the architecture. This X-frame chair has an elegance and simplicity which belies its technical and design brilliance — a clear move away from heavy wooden furniture. The patio contains a bronze copy of a Georges Kolbe sculpture. (Recommended mainly for those interested in the development of architecture.)

**Poble Espanyol,** Avinguda del Marquès de Comillas. (Open all day until the early hours.) Metro Espanya (and walk up the hill); bus 9,13,27,50,100. A free bus service is operated from Plaça d'Espanya.

Possibly the least appealing and potentially expensive sight on Montjuïc is the Spanish village which was built for the 1929 exhibition. Interesting in concept but tacky in reality, the entire range of Spanish architecture is condensed here in 18 reconstructed streets, several squares and a Romanesque church. You can also see various regional crafts carried out, such as hand blowing glass *porróns.* Local delicacies can be sampled at international prices, and you'll find everything from *chocolate con churros* to tapas and paella.

Shops vary from the good to the abysmal, but the whole place rings of last minute gifts. Facilities run to a bank, information centre and a 20-minute audio-visual show entitled 'Barcelona Experience'. At night, Poble Espanyol throbs with club-crawling tourists mixing cocktails with *flamenco,* disco or jazz. All guaranteed action and, to an extent, education.

**Fundació Joan Miró,** Plaça Neptú. (Tuesday-Saturday 11.00-19.00 (until 21.30 on Thursday), Sunday and holidays 10.30-14.30; closed Monday.) Bus 61 from Plaça d'Espanya; cable car from the beach or the port, or funicular train from Paral.lel metro (daily in summer; Sundays and holidays only during rest of year).

Opened in 1975, this gallery contains a versatile collection of sculptures, collages, paintings and drawings from the childhood sketches to the final works of Joan Miró (1893-1983). Also a contemporary art centre, it reserves an exhibition area for young artists and holds regular films, videos, recitals and lectures. Particularly helpful is the explanatory section of illustrated boards, which puts Miró's life and achievements in perspective; and beside these are cards in various languages which you can borrow.

Aptly housed in the sleek, spacious design of his friend Josep Lluís Sert, this gallery has great views, and is one of few that is suitable for wheelchairs. Using skylights to provide natural light, and built around a central patio, there are exhibits both inside and out, while the concrete shell is white in typical Mediterranean fashion. Yet the architectural simplicity does not detract from the haunting quality of Miró's art.

Ranking with Dalí as Spain's foremost Surrealist, his distinctive work relies on primary colours and persistent themes of women, insects, birds and umbrellas. Some of the most fascinating pieces are his sculptures, many in bronze and often incorporating everyday materials like stone and root or household utensils. Once again, the favoured theme is female, and she can be spiky and wiry or receptive and generous. His highly individual style never becomes tired; perhaps most appealing, and impossible to bypass, is the artist's infectious humour.

An illuminating addition is the collection of dedication pieces by friends and contemporaries of the artist, featuring paintings by Leger, Calder, Robert Motherwell, a little drawing by Matisse, a typical Henry Moore reclining figure and a brilliant metallic sculpture by Anthony Caro. Works reminiscent of most of this century's key movements, include a tiny Cubist bronze, a large canvas by the other Catalan genius Antoni Tàpies, and of course, drawings by Josep Lluís Sert. This gallery's restaurant has an imaginative menu and is certainly the best place to eat on Montjuïc.

**Museu Arqueològic,** Plaça Santa Madrona. (Tuesday-Saturday 09.30 - 13.00 and 16.00-19.00, Sunday and holidays 10.00-14.00, closed Monday.) Metro Espanya; bus 55.

This contains the relics of Catalan inhabitants from Paleolithic to Visigothic civilisations. It also houses Greek and Roman ceramics, mosaics and sculptures.

**Museu Militar,** Montjüic Castle. (10.00-14.00 and 16.00-19.00, Sundays and holidays 10.00-19.00, closed Monday.)

Funicular railway or cable car to the summit; bus 61,100. Exhibits include weapons, tin soldiers and military uniforms, though more widely appealing are the views from the castle.

# Pedralbes

**Museu/Monestir de Pedralbes,** Baixada Monestir,9. (Tuesday-Sunday 09.30-14.00, closed Monday and holidays.) Bus 22,64,75,BC,BI,SJ,100.

This is one of Barcelona's prize Gothic sights for both architecture and sculpture, and is certainly worth the journey. Founded in 1326 by Queen Elisenda de Montcada and King James II, its main feature is a grand three-storey cloister. Visitors can wander through the chapter house, infirmary and refectory. And in the chapel you'll find murals by the medieval Catalan artist Ferrer Bassa.

It is convenient to combine with a visit to the Palau Reial de

Pedralbes (nearby at Diagonal,686), though you will need to make a prior arrangement (tel: 203 75 01). This palace was built in the 1920s for Alfonso XIII, and contains interesting furniture, paintings and sculpture, notably a gallery of Royal portraits. In late Autumn, the gardens hold an annual display of roses grown by locals.

**Museu del F.C. Barcelona,** Arístides Maillol. (October-March) Metro Collblanc/Maria Cristina; bus 7,15,54,56,57,100.

Here you can view the football stadium from the presidential box, and see trophies, photographs and prizes as well as an audio visual show about the history of the club.

# Tibidabo

A trip up this legendary mountain, which looms over Barcelona from the north-west, is recommended as much for its fresher air as for its spectacular panorama. On a clear day (rare in this polluted city) you can see across to Montserrat, up to the Pyrenees and over the water as far as Mallorca. Take the Sarrià line train or bus 17 (both from Plaça de Catalunya) to Avinguda Tibidabo. From here take the blue tram — great for the nostalgic — which connects with the funicular railway to the top. (These run frequently between 07.15 and 01.00.)

Aside from a few cafés and souvenir shops, the amusement park with its dramatic funfair rides is popular with local teenagers. There is a mechanical dolls museum with an enchanting collection of nineteenth-century puppets and toys, a display of crazy mirrors, and Tibistory which depicts the history of the mountain.

In summer all these are open from 16.30-00.30 weekdays and from noon at weekends; entrance is cheaper after 20.00. In winter they only open on weekends and holidays, from 11.00 until 20.00 or 21.00. (Forthcoming opening times are not fixed, and it is advisable to check with the tourist office first.) At the summit the modern, rather over-the-top church, with a monumental statue of Christ against the skyline, is interesting merely for its views.

**Museu de la Ciència,** Teodor Roviralta,55. (Tuesday-Sunday 10.00-20.00.) Avinguda Tibidabo train station; bus 17,22,58,73,100 and tram.

Part way up Tibidabo in a peaceful residential spot is Spain's only science museum. Founded by the Caixa de Pensions, this hi-tech, cool and well-designed museum is geared up in a way that many others are not. As well as basic leaflets, there are also computerised information points which clearly explain certain exhibits in English. Each room has its individual theme, which include optics, waves, perception, mechanics and computers.

Solid family entertainment, it's pitched at the right level for adults or children, and succeeds in making science accessible and fun. Every display, inviting hands-on participation, leaves hoards of absorbed children — a rare sight in any museum — and this interactive element helps overcome language difficulties. Discover the secrets of a solar eclipse, see Catalunya by satellite, analyse your diet on computer, or observe tropical fish magnified on video. Also here is one of Barcelona's two planetariums, but the commentary for its half-hour show is only in Catalan or Spanish. (The other planetarium is at Escoles Pies,103.)

The night of the long knives — the cathedral bells disturb close residents every quarter of an hour.

No suffering in silence, Catalans sieze every opportunity to make themselves heard. This outsize tower, which dwarfs Gràcia's Plaça de Rius i Taulet, holds the legendary bell that rang incessantly in angry protest against the Troop Levies of 1870.

EIGHT

# Sports and Activities

## City Beaches

Beyond the network of narrow streets in Barceloneta at the bottom of Passeig Nacional lies the city's primary beach. Constantly popular, weekends see this bristling with activity — families and lovers, lads with their beers and boogie boxes, hawkers and gawpers. And although litter is collected daily by beachcombing machines, predictably, this stretch of sand is horribly dirty.

As with city beaches worldwide, tales abound of washed up syringes and contagious disease; and while this may have an element of truth, it is possible to avoid the scum, especially where the current is swifter. Barceloneta is an entertaining, convenient place to sunbathe or escape the hot city streets, and showers are posted at regular intervals along the sand. The beach is just a five minute walk from Barceloneta metro or a more adventurous (and expensive) route is the cable car which drops you on the sand. You can pick this up at Montjuïc Miramar or from Barcelona pier near the Columbus column. Alternatively there are two public pools nearby (see Swimming Pools below).

Probably the finest, and certainly the greatest concentration of fish restaurants are found at Barceloneta. Restaurants with tables on the sand are a favoured spot with families for Sunday lunch, especially for vast seafood paellas. These are equally popular at night when, imbued with candlelight and soft breezes, they take on a romantic atmosphere.

One of the largest projects currently underway is the demolition and reconstruction operation for the Olympic village at Poblenou. The transformation of this old industrial quarter in the north-east into Parc de Mar, will provide Barcelona with around seven kilometres of new beaches by early 1992. This valuable stretch of seafront was previously cut off to the public by rail tracks which, now obsolete, are being removed to expand the city seawards.

Another beach can be found at Badalona, a large suburb to the north. This is less crowded, cleaner than Barceloneta, and more peaceful the further you walk from the station. Trains from Plaça de Catalunya take around 20 minutes. Or, further afield, many of Catalunya's beaches lie only a short drive or train journey from Barcelona (see Part IV: Around Catalunya).

# A — Z of Sport

Geographical diversity has played a significant role in securing Barcelona's nomination as the next Olympic site. With easy access from the city to mountains, inland lakes and sea, Catalunya is endowed with excellent sporting opportunities. Facilities throughout the province are being sharpened daily in anticipation of 1992, and the Olympic legacy is bound to be additional public amenities. With a city centre as tightly confined as Barcelona's, predictably, many sports locations are found on the outskirts, and aren't always easy to reach.

### Bowling
Bowling is possible well into the night, and the city has three alleys:
— Pedralbes Bowling, Avinguda del Doctor Marañón,11 (tel: 333 03 52). Open from 10.00 until 01.30, this also runs classes.
— AMFF Bowling Centre, Sabino de Arana,6 (tel: 330 50 48). Open from 11.00 until 01.30, this offers a free initiation course.
— Boliche, Diagonal,508 (tel: 237 90 98). Open from 18.00 to 02.00, this alley is located at the back of a fashionable bar.

### Bullfights
Barcelona's two mighty bullrings face each other staunchly from either end of the long Gran Vía, which slices through the city centre. Unmistakable, they are clad in rusty-red brick with the distinctive minarets and Moorish overtones found on so many *Plaça de Toros*. Although bullfighting has never been as popular among Catalans as it is in southern Spain, it still has a following in some of the local villages.

Within the city, however, there is only limited interest in this controversial sport, and the flagging industry is buoyed up largely by tourism. Fights take place every Sunday at 17.30 during the season (March to September), or 18.00 in July and August. The Monumental bullring at Gran Vía de les Corts Catalanes,743, has its box office at Muntaner,24 (tel: 253 38 21) and occasionally draws a full house for pop concerts. (The one just beside Plaça d'Espanya is no longer used for bullfights and is soon to become a trade fair centre.)

## Cycling

There is a noticeable absence of cyclists pedalling the city; cobbles, dangerous driving, thefts and traffic fumes combine to keep bicycles off the road. A free cycle track can be found in Horta at Passeig Vall d'Hebron (tel: 427 91 42). Open 08.00-22.00 daily.

## Football

Camp Nou, home of Barcelona F.C., makes British football grounds look like provincial railway stations (at lunchtime). With a capacity of 120,000, it is Europe's biggest stadium, and Saturday league matches regularly attract more fans than the F.A. Cup at Wembley.

The club claims to be the richest in the world. It is possibly the money rather than the allure of the Camp Nou that has attracted so many big names... Maradona, Cruyff, Koeman, Venables, Lineker and Laudrup all hang in the 'Barca' hall of fame.

A handful of spectators stand behind the goals, but the real equivalent of the British terraces is the *Entrada General* section on the upper tier of the stadium. These are the cheapest, unnumbered concrete seats. The view is excellent, but if you want somewhere slightly more comfortable and a bit less crowded, seats on the *Lateral* (east) stand are the best value. *Tribuna* seats are covered and more expensive.

You'll see a few incongruous woolly hats, but Spanish football is basically a different experience to the British game. Violence is almost unknown, and a match can be a night out for the girls too. Essential accessories are long plastic horns (with which people seem to communicate across the stadium in some strange elephantine code) and huge cheese sandwiches wrapped in tinfoil to eat at half time.

One thing that's never different: you find exactly the same grumblers, wisecrackers and touchline-coaches as on British terraces. It won't take you long to learn the Spanish for "Where's your glasses, referee?". That apart, the things to shout are 'Bravo', 'Vale', 'Shoota' and (of course) 'Goooooaaaalll.'

Matches are advertised widely in the local press, and for most games it is possible to buy a ticket at the gate. But matches against Bilbao or either Madrid team (Real Madrid and Atletico Madrid) inspire a huge turnout, and for these it's worth buying tickets about three days in advance. This can be done either at the ground, or from Taquillas de Venta. These grey ticket booths dotted around the city centre (there is one on Plaça de la Universitat and the corner of Aribau) sell tickets for many entertainments.

Traditionally the two Barcelona teams, Barça and Espanyol, are arch enemies, but Barça is always streets ahead. Infinitely more potent is the rivalry between Barça and Real Madrid. Permeating every aspect of life, this tension between Spain's two foremost cities makes sparks fly and goals strongly fought.

The season runs from September to May, and weekend matches kick off around 17.00. The football stadium is at Camp Nou, Avinguda Arístides Maillol (Metro Collblanc/Maria Cristina); to reserve tickets, call 330 94 11. (There is a recommended football museum, see chapter 7.)

---

### Sporting Spirit

Traditionally a heavily religious nation, it would appear that today's uniting force is football; and indeed Catalans are verging on the obsessional about every kind of sport. Yet curiously they manage to mingle the two quite happily. It is customary, for example, for any cup (be it the League or the King's) won by Barça football team to be ceremoniously offered to their patron saint, the Black Virgin of Montserrat.

The mixing of sport with the divine is neatly summed up by a modern little chapel inside the church of Santa Anna. This was offered by the Catalan Sports Federation to the Black Virgin. Here her likeness sits on an altar emblazoned with the five-ring Olympic symbol, and surrounded by candles reminiscent of Olympic torches. Even stranger are the murals on either side of contemporary sports figures. Athletes of every denomination — football, cycling, hockey, skiing, riding, hiking, swimming, tennis — compete for wall space with the Lord and two angels behind the altar.

---

## Golf

Catalunya has a good sprinkling of golf courses and for a full list of the region's facilities, see *Golf in Catalonia* (published in English and available from the tourist office at Gran Vía de les Corts Catalanes,568). Some of the closer venues are:

— The Prat Royal Golf Club, Apartado de Correos,10 (08820) in El Prat de Llobregat (tel: 379 02 78). This international competition venue has three 18-hole courses, and is 15 kilometres from Barcelona. Facilities include a restaurant, pool, nursery and electric cars.

— Sant Cugat Golf Club, Sant Cugat del Vallès (tel: 674 39 58).

Fifteen kilometres from Barcelona (accessible from the A7), this has one 18-hole course, a restaurant, children's facilities and a pool.
— Vallromanes Golf Club, Apartado de Correos,43 (08170). Montornès del Vallès (tel: 568 03 62). Twenty three kilometres from Barcelona, it has one 18-hole course, a restaurant, sauna, pool and tennis courts.

## Gyms and Health Clubs
— Gym Gràcia, Mare de Déu dels Desemparats,2-4 (tel: 213 50 63). Open Monday-Friday 07.00-22.00, Saturday 09.00-14.00. This is a fully-equipped gym where non members can use the solarium and sauna, or take massage and body treatments.
— El Timbal, Portaferrisa,13 (tel: 302 73 47). Open 10.00-14.00 and 17.00-21.00. This specialises in gym and fitness, and holds classes in dance and theatre.
— California Look, Plaça de Ramón Berenguer el Gran,2 (tel: 319 87 25). Open 07.00-22.00 Monday-Friday, until 14.30 weekends and festivals. This fitness centre has a weights circuit, aerobics, body building and jazz classes, a sauna, solarium, masseuse and beautician. It is open to anyone on a daily basis and also operates short-term memberships (from two weeks).

## Hiking
Being a mountainous region with diverse geography and some notable historic sights, hikers are promised endless challenges. A big advantage is the climate which, on the whole, remains mild, and hiking affords a radically different perspective of the province. Up in the hills, there's no shortage of lonely villages and unspoilt country, surprisingly close to the sardine-packed coast.

The province has around 3,000 kilometres of well-maintained footpaths. If you are considering hiking, you should buy a specialist guide book, or see the Generalitat's booklet *'Long Distance Footpaths'* (available from the tourist office in Gran Vía de les Corts Catalanes,568) which outlines good routes. And don't embark without a water bottle, hat and compass.

## Hunting
Traditionally popular in the mountainous north is the shooting of partridge, duck, hare and wild boar. Here game appears as regularly on the menu as it does on the wall, and many a Pyrenean restaurant feels inadequate without a token boar's head trophy. Those interested should contact a travel agent.

## Microlighting, Flying and Parachuting

There is a good flight school between Pals and Torroella de Montgrí, sign posted off the GE650 road near the Costa Brava (at Rio de Oro,24). This offers microlighting rides, but it's best to call Carlos Manich and book, as sessions are in demand (tel: 204 84 13 or 908 13 74 24).

Parachuting is possible at three places in Catalunya. A large school, and host to the 1989 World Championship is the Centro de Paracaidismo Costa Brava, at Empuria-brava, (open 08.00-20.00 daily). This has excellent facilities and offers various courses including a freefall tandem jump for first timers. Tuition can be booked by writing to: Apartado de Correos 194, Empuria-brava, Girona province (tel: 972 45 01 11).

A bit further afield, the most important centre for flying and parachuting is Aeródromo de la Cerdanya in Alp village. Another parachuting centre in Aeródromo Sabadell, is just a short way from Barcelona. For all information on flying in Catalunya call the Civil Aviation office on 379 24 54 or 317 01 78 or 379 27 62.

## Riding

You can hire horses at the Riding Hyperclub, found two kilometres short of Castelldefels, just off the C245 from Gava, where there are good woodland rides. Or the Barcelona Riding School in Sant Gervasi at Ciutat de Balaguer,68 (tel: 417 30 39) offers lessons and courses. There are also various organised treks around the province lasting from one to ten days, for information call Equitur: 339 41 00.

## Skating

Skaters have two choices: Roger de Flor,168 (tel: 245 28 00) or the Camp Nou Football Club at Avinguda Arístides Maillol (tel: 330 94 11).

## Skiing

The Catalan Pyrenees has peaks reaching 3,000 metres, where 12 ski resorts have now been developed; and you can expect these to be white between December and April. Travel agents within the city will arrange a trip for you, and full details about the resorts are listed in the Generalitat's brochure *Esquí Alpí a Catalunya* (available in English from the tourist office in Gran Vía de les Corts Catalanes,568).

*Tren de la Neu* (snow train) is a special train for skiers wanting to do a day trip. This runs on Sunday during the ski season, leaving

Sants station from 06.00 for Ribes de Fresser (from where you are connected to Núria resort) and to La Molina resort.

## Squash

It is usual to call and reserve a court:

— Squash Barcelona, Avinguda Doctor Marañón, 17 (tel: 334 02 58). Open 08.00-24.00 daily.

— Tibidabo Squash Club, Lluïs Muntadas,8 (tel: 212 46 83). Open Monday-Friday 09.00-23.00/Saturday 10.00-22.00/Sunday 10.00-17.00

— Vall Park Club, Carretera de Sant Cugat,79 (tel: 212 67 89). Open 08.00-24.00.

## Swimming Pools

There are a few central public swimming pools, some of which close for an afternoon siesta:

— Barceloneta Swimming Club at the sea end of the Passeig Marítim (tel: 309 34 12). Metro Barceloneta. This has an indoor pool, open daily 07.00-21.00.

— Baños San Miguel, Platja Sant Miguel. Metro Barceloneta. Located much further along the seafront out of town, this has an outdoor pool open daily 09.00-18.00.

— Parc de la Crueta de Coll at Castellterçol in Zona Alta (tel: 213 25 14). Metro Vallcarca and Bus 100. This has an outdoor pool which is only open in summer (June to mid-September); weekdays 10.00-16.00, Sundays and holidays 10.00-19.00. In winter the lake has pleasure boats.

— Can Caralleu Sports Complex, Esports, in the north part of Sarrià (tel: 204 69 05). Reina Elisenda train station. This has an indoor and outdoor pool, and is open daily between 08.00-09.00 and 14.00-15.00.

---

### Kept at Arm's Length

Assumptions that the human physique is still evolving have recently been lent further weight. Today's brawny atheletes — or at any rate swimmers — have breached previous Olympic measurements, and standards acceptable as recently as the 1970s are now obsolete.

To their cost, the Barcelona Olympic Committee have discovered how the swimmer of the '90s is a decidedly taller and more broad-shouldered being. To accommodate these, adjustments must be made to each of the eight swimming lanes in Picornells Olympic pool on Montjuïc. And these three extra metres (bringing the pool to 25 metres wide) provide official evidence of increased arm span.

— Ronda Swimming Pool, Ronda de Sant Pau,46 (tel: 329 98 06). Metro Paral.lel. This has an indoor pool, is open weekdays 07.00-21.00, and is probably the most centrally located.
— Sant Andreu, Riera d'Horta (tel: 346 56 03). Metro Horta. This is an outdoor pool which is only open in summer. Its surrounding garden is generally crowded with local teenagers, and it stays open until 20.00.
— Bernat Picornell on Avinguda del Estadi,34, by the Olympic rings (tel: 325 92 81). Bus 61 and 100. This has an outdoor pool open daily in summer, 10.00-15.30.
— Montjuïc Swimming Club, Reina Amàlia,31 (tel: 241 01 22). Metro Paral.lel. Although called Montjuïc, this is not on the hill. It is an indoor pool, open Monday to Friday 11.00-13.30.

## Tennis

Public tennis clubs are:
— Can Caralleu Sports Complex, Esports (tel: 203 78 74). Train station Reina Elisenda. Open 08.00-23.00.
— Vall Parc Club, Carretera de Sant Cugat,79 (tel: 212 67 89). Open 08.00-24.00. Best reached by car or taxi, as buses only run to Passeig de Vall d'Hebron, from where it is a one kilometre walk.

## Water Sports

With around 580 kilometres of coastline, Catalunya is well equipped for water sports although you are best to travel outside Barcelona to find windsurfing, water skiing and boat hire. Barceloneta beach does have a surfing hire centre which operates in summer but this is not an ideal site as it is enclosed and lacks wind.

Boat hire and water sports are possible at the province's recreational ports. Most of the large Costa resorts offer the usual possibilities of water skiing, jet skiing, wind surfing and pedalo hire, such as at Roses, Estartit, Aiguablava, Blanes, Arenys de Mar; and to the south at Castelldefels, Sitges and Tarragona. (For a complete list of boating facilities see The Sports Harbours of Catalonia the Generalitat's brochure, available from the tourist office at Gran Vía de les Corts Catalanes,658.) In season white-water rafting is possible on various rivers in the Pyrenees and most travel agents can advise on this.

The marina beside the commercial docks on the Moll d'Espanya is managed by two private yacht clubs. Reial Club Nàutic (tel: 315 11 61) occasionally has moorings available to non members. Facilities at Reial Club Marítim (tel: 315 00 07) include a bar, swimming pool, and restaurant. The latter is an upmarket venue with unbeatable views of the port, which is the only part open to the public (closed Sunday night and Monday). There is a public zone in the harbour available to anyone who turns up, call 318 87 50.

# Parks

One park not to be missed is Gaudi's Parc Güell (see Sightseeing, Chapter 7.)

### Parc de la Ciutadella

At the edge of the Gothic quarter and bordering Barceloneta lies the city's major park. Designed by Josep Fontserè, it is appealing for its peace and well-cultivated greenery as well as important cultural attractions. The focal point is the lake, a scenic circuit which attracts joggers and where boating is possible. Patrolled by vigilant park keepers, this has well labelled trees and some diverse wildlife: the lake is haunted by pampered ducks and swans, while the odd exotic bird — parrots and parakeets — can be spotted in the tree tops.

Most famed of the statues are *Desconsol* by Llimona in front of the Catalan parliament and the *Lady with Umbrella* by Roig Solé (in the zoo). But the main lure for photographers is the fountain, an early Gaudi project, with sculptures by Nobas and Vallmitjana.

The park's name originates from the citadel built here by Philip V, most of which was destroyed in 1869. But standing firm is the governor's palace, chapel and Baroque arsenal which now houses the Catalan Parliament and Modern Art museum. Also here are some buildings put up for the Universal Exhibition of 1988, including one by Domènech i Montaner, which now houses the zoological museum. (For a description of the zoo and museums in this park, see Sightseeing, Chapter 7.)

### Botanical Gardens

These beautiful gardens are one of the foremost of their type in Spain and are open to visitors. They exist for scientific research, to educate people about western Mediterranean flora and vegetation, and to protect endangered species. Containing a diverse collection of plants, with some exotic examples from throughout the world, these form part of the Botanic Institute. Also here is a notable collection of eighteenth-century herbs.

Another day of retirement glides by in Joan Miró park. The Spanish take their leisure time seriously.

**Parc del Laberint**
Tucked away in the outskirts of the city is perhaps the most pleasant and peaceful leafy park. Laid out in 1792, this public garden was originally an aristocrat's plaything, and incorporates his Islamic-looking house. The spectacular formal gardens are neo-Classical in design with stairs and statues, fountains and follies. Based on a similar park in Paris, the highlight is a maze of cypresses after which it was named.

**Parc de Joan Miró**
Alternatively called Parc de l'Escorxador, this lies where the slaughter house once operated. The focal point is a pond out of which protrudes Miró's dramatic Woman and Bird sculpture. Skirted by high-rise blocks and one of the bullrings, the park adds welcome space and greenery to an otherwise cramped area.

Within its palm, pine and eucalyptus dotted confines are children's playgrounds; these are also a special haunt of the elderly who meet here for regular petanque sessions, and you can usually see a game early evenings and on Saturdays. This French sport, popular throughout Spain, is particularly so in Barcelona.

**Parc de l'Espanya Industrial**
Located in Sants, this park was designed by the Basque architect Ganchegui, whose aim was to create twentieth century Roman baths. The park has a central boating lake, on the edges of which are towers serving as lights and *miradors*. It also boasts novel sculptures, such as the dragon by Andrés Nagel, and works by Anthony Caro and Pablo Palazuelo.

**Parc de la Creuta del Coll**
Situated on a hill in the north of Horta, this park is a thoroughly advanced piece of contemporary urban planning, conceived by architects Martorell and Mackay. Tremendously spacious, covering 16 hectares, this contains a lake where you can go boating in winter, and which becomes a swimming pool in summer.

Above this a dramatic hanging sulpture by Eduardo Chillida is suspended, and a small artificial beach lies along the lake's edge. Other interesting modern sculptures include works by Ellsworth, Kelly and Roy Lichtenstein. This is also one of the stops on the bus 100 route.

# Funfairs

Barcelona's two mountains (Montjuïc and Tibidabo) are both topped by extensive funfairs. Tibidabo offers numerous rides, some of which are strategically perched so punters can simulate throwing themselves off the top. Broadly, this is open in July and August from 16.30-00.30, and from 12.00 at weekends; daily in Spring and Autumn from 11.00 until 20.30 weekdays, or 21.30 weekends and festivals; in winter it opens only on weekends and festivals from 11.00-20.00.

A more popular version, again with wild views, crowns Montjuïc Here the attractions are extreme and violent, marginally cheaper, and closer to the city centre. It is accessible either by cable car from the port, and another connecting cable, or by funicular from Paral.lel metro. Open 18.00-24.00, from 12.00 on Sunday, during summer (June 14 to September 11), and closed Monday; and in winter on weekends and festivals only from 12.00-20.00. Here there is also an open air theatre where summer concerts are held.

# Spas

Catalunya has plentiful spas or *balnearios,* some only a short distance from Barcelona. Each spa is recommended for different disorders, so it is worth calling to check first. The closest are in Caldes de Montbui, around 28 kilometres from the city (take the A2), and all those listed below are located there.
— Balneario Broquetes, tel: 865 01 00
— Balneario Termas Victoria, tel: 865 01 50
— Balneario Termas Solà, tel: 865 00 95
— Balneario Termas La Salud, tel: 865 00 98

# Tours

Tours can be an expensive ticket to skim the surface; but for those wanting a quick overview, there are a few short excursions which are helpful and worth the money.

In summer, an instant antidote to claustrophobia and a guaranteed breath of fresh air is the half-hour boat trip on *golondrinas* (or swallows) around the harbour. This is interesting as an offshore perspective of the city, as well as for a close up view of the port and the marina's luxury yachts. The only drawbacks of this round trip are the insistent accordianist and the disappointing destination.

The **100 Bus** is a good way to orientate yourself, as this takes in all the major sights, and you're free to spend the day hopping on or off at any of the stops. This air-conditioned service (which runs from 24 June to 17 September, leaving Pla de Palau from 09.00-19.00) stops at 15 key sights on a wide circuit, and buses run at 40 minute intervals.

The stops include the port, the Gothic area, Plaça de Catalunya, Passeig de Gràcia, Sagrada Família, Tibidabo, Montjuïc (Poble Espanyol and Olympic area), Parc Güell, Crueta del Coll and the Monastery of Pedralbes. A 'Barcelona Singular' ticket costs 300 pesetas and allows unrestricted travel all day on bus 100, the Tramvía Blau and funicular up Tibidabo, the Montjuïc cable cars and funicular railways. With this bus you have automatic discounts at Poble Espanyol and Tibidabo. Ask for its special map at any tourist office.

Travel agents and the larger hotels can often arrange guides. Or for good, English-speaking guides contact the Asociacion Profesional de Informadores Touristicos, Plaça de Ramon Berenguer el Gran,1 (tel: 345 42 21).

## Selected Courses

— Too Much, Mejía Lequerica,10-12 (tel: 339 71 30). Courses in rock, *sevillanas* and break dancing.

— Theatre Estudio Nancy Tuñon, Sant Magi,17 (tel: 238 10 17). Drama courses.

— Albahaca, Escuela de Cocina, Berga,23 (tel: 217 19 44). This runs various cooking courses including low-calorie, microwave, pastry making and market cooking.

— Kraken, Subacuaticas Club Actividades, Juan de Sada,34 (tel: 411 01 38). Courses in sub aqua diving.

— Shiatsu Association, Mare de Déu del Coll,25 (tel: 217 70 97). Courses available with flexible hours.

— Leonardo da Vincy, Cucurulla, 9 (tel: 317 26 27). This organises a plethora of activities — such as courses in drawing, painting, sculpture, ceramics and photography.

— Yoga, Diagonal,558 (tel: 200 39 85). This offers long-term, short summer, and weekend courses.

— Integral, Plaça Urquinaona,2 (tel: 318 30 50). Various natural health courses including massage and aromatherapy.

### A Chancy Business

Rivalling even football in widespread popularity, you will find lottery sellers and stalls littered all over the city. Gambling, something of a national pastime, is now big business in which staggering amounts of money change hands. The fever for lottery started during the financial crisis of the 1930s. The most popular is Lotería Primitiva, with ONCE coming a close second.

ONCE was set up to employ blind people and, with coupons clipped to their chest, hawkers' cries are a familiar sound along the street. One number costs just 100 pesetas and two and a half million pesetas are paid out every day. Foreigners may run into this hobby fairly early as ONCE booths are sometimes confused with telephone boxes.

Live entertainment lies in store at the Boquería market. Here the leading roles are played by knife-wielding, shrieking fishwives.

NINE

# Shopping

Most of the city retailers prize their siesta and open between 09.00-14.00 and 16.30-20.00, but department stores now forgo this traditional luxury. And as with other aspects of Spanish life, you'll need to adapt to a slower shopping pace, for no sale is complete without a chat. Sales are usual from the second week of January until the end of February and again during July and August (expect the Catalan word *'rebaixes'* splashed across shop windows). Shops invariably close on fiestas.

There are relatively few tourist shops, but an alarming number of windows displaying every conceivable type of knife — you may find it easier to buy a sword than a fan or flamenco doll on a trip down the Rambles. Many antique and artefact shops are tucked into the narrow streets around the Cathedral, and trade a mixture of genuine, reproduction and modern artisan pieces. This area is also peppered with ceramic, stamp and candle specialists. But beware the usual smattering of tourist trash.

A main theme on the street are the enticing *pastelerías,* selling tarts, cakes and *cava* (local champagne — see Food, Drink and Restaurants, chapter 5), and whose smells linger on every corner. One delicacy not to be missed is the *ensaimada* — a moist whirl dusted with icing sugar which originated in Mallorca. There's also a prevalence of shops which deal solely in daintily-packaged confectionery. The Catalan fondness for sweets is sometimes attributed to the Moorish influence; certainly the sticky almond fudge *turrón* is an old Arab recipe — and superbly sickly.

## Clothes

In the capital of Spanish fashion, you will find some dazzling bazaars and boutiques. Indeed the enterprising and commercial Catalans appear quick to adopt the latest in contemporary ideas. Exclusive fashions and mass market trends rub shoulders with sedate styles along the street. The early evening ritual of window gazing is a wholly Spanish pastime and here shopping is seen as a real treat.

High street fashions are generally of higher quality than their British equivalents. Boldly designed leather shoes and bags are plentiful and remarkably good value. A wide selection of these can be found along Gran de Gràcia. Another favourite with Spanish shoppers are the accessory emporiums, whose business exists on shoe laces, hair clips and costume jewellery.

---

### A Miraculous Feat

Shoes are among the best buys in Barcelona, and shoemakers are well represented with their very own patron saint and a personal chapel in the Cathedral. Curiously honoured as the patron saint of shoes, Saint Mark's story is depicted on the wall of Barcelona's footwear museum (a copy of the original painting from Manresa Cathedral).

Legend tells how Mark, arriving in Alexandria with sore feet and worn shoes, sought to repair the damage at a local shoemaker. While working, the craftsman injured his hand but was miraculously cured by his client. So astounded were the shoemaker and his two assistants that all were converted to Christianity. And later the well-shod saint appointed his shoemaker the first Bishop of Alexandria.

---

Eixample has a number of sophisticated shopping arcades (a good one is Bulevard Rosa, Diagonal,609 and Passeig de Gràcia,55); so for chic designer stores head towards these streets. The latest in vogue is probably to be found between Carrers Aragó and València; try Zara (one branch on València) or Union Bay which is on Passeig de Gràcia.

Many modern styles, at less extortionate prices, are available along the lower end of Rambla de Catalunya and off Portal de l'Àngel. The Gothic area (between Ferran and Plaça de Catalunya) is packed with smaller, cheaper boutiques and glittering accessory stalls, many catering for the younger market. Gralla Hall, an arcade in Portaferrissa, has much the most imaginative styles.

One of the first proper fashion shops with new designers (like Roser Marc) was Jean Pierre Bua on Diagonal, near Francesc Macià. Fashionable male designs by Toni Miró are sold at Groc on Rambla de Catalunya (corner of València), and Adolfo Dominguez has a shop of his own designs on Passeig de Gràcia (corner of Provença). Gonzalo Comella on Passeig de Gràcia, is another worth trying. For quality men's clothes, Massimo Dutti is the Spanish equivalent of Savile Row tailoring, with especially good value shirts, and has branches at Diagonal,602 and Vía Augusta,33.

# Food and Drink

Trading regulations in Britain ban the imports of any uncooked foods, but while you're here the ubiquitous smoked hams and sausages are always a good buy. You can hardly avoid *jamón serrano* (the unsmoked English-style ham is known as *jamón York);* but try its more succulent (and expensive) counterpart, *jamón jabugo* — commonly eaten on bread rubbed with olive oil and tomato. As well as the standard *chorizo* (cured sausage) or *lomo* (smoked pork loin), a Catalan speciality is *fuet,* a slender stick of salami, the best of which comes from Vic.

Slices of dried, smoked tuna or cod's roe are also popular salty snacks. As one of Spain's leading exports, olive oil is usually of good quality and value, as of course, is the baffling variety of olives. Fresh and salted anchovies make a popular tapa throughout the province, especially those from L'Escala — and don't dismiss the tinned variety.

Cheese-wise, the soft, unsalted, white *mató* is peculiar to the province, and is often eaten with dried fruit and nuts (known as *música*) or honey *(mel i mató).* Another delicacy which is either eaten separately or accompanying cheese is *membrillo,* a gelatinous slab of quince flesh.

Catalans especially favour goat and sheep cheeses, and mountain varieties are often spiced up with parsley, garlic or pepper corns. Pyrenean cheeses have a high reputation as do those from Valladolid. Another Spanish favourite is *Cabrales* cheese, strong and rich, which comes steeped in a tin of oil. *Manchego* (from La Mancha) is also tasty, and regularly appears diced as a tapa.

For high quality food and wines visit one of the many specialist delicatessens in Eixample: Gran Colmado at Consell de Cent,318, is open until midnight and is highly recommended for edible presents. It has fine wines (local and international), spirits, preserves and freshly-prepared delicacies — but expect to pay for such quality.

One of the most sophisticated food stores in Barcelona is Semon on Ganduxer,31 which stocks a superb selection of liquor, meat, cheese and sweetmeats. Mauri at Rambla de Catalunya,102, is another luxurious delicatessen, specialising in cured meats, pastries and preserves. And you can taste these delights on the premises, as all three double up as cafés or restaurants.

# Markets

Meandering through the covered food markets can be as revealing as anything about the Spanish way of life. Not least of the surprises will be the displays of every single part of the animal. Whether it be brains or bull's testicles, the Spaniards won't waste an iota. Marvel at the multidude of unfamiliar sea creatures or the sheer size of the creamy, quivering, spongy tripe.

Inside a fine wrought-iron railway style hall, **Mercat Sant Josep** sits half way up the Rambles. More popularly known as the Boqueria, this offers the greatest variety, steepest prices, and is the most flamboyant public food market. Not only is it a carnivore's delight, all the other fresh produce is colourful and succulent: local, exotic and dried fruits, gargantuan vegetables, cheeses of every shape and hue, and fresh herbs. Snacks at the basic stands can be uncommonly tasty and **La Garduña** restaurant at the back is also good value.

There are a number of other paler versions dotted around the city: Mercat Sant Antoni on the Ronda de Sant Pau, has cheap clothes around the outer edge and food in the centre, the enormous Mercat Santa Caterina in the Barri Ribera is good value, and in Gràcia is Mercat Abaceria Central in Carrer de Puigmartí. All these sell fresh produce Monday to Saturday, from 08.00-15.00 and 17.00-20.00 (the Boqueria doesn't shut for lunch), and variety is always greater in the mornings.

**Mercat Central,** located some way outside the city behind Montjuïc, is the site of all the major wholesale markets — fish, flower or fresh groceries. A hive of activity throughout the night (and selling alcohol through the small hours), this is a fascinating place to gaup at the enormous sharks; but operating solely for traders, goods are only sold in bulk.

Every day is market day in the **Rambles,** but probably more for looking than buying. The flower stalls are reasonably priced, although in the summer heat cut flowers make a short-lived luxury. Beyond these are the bizarre pet stalls teeming with screeching

**(Opposite) Top:** This kaleidoscope of mosaic columns is just one exuberant feature of the extraordinary Palau de la Mùsica, the crowning achievement of the Modernista leader Lluís Domènech i Montaner.
**Bottom:** Love it or hate it, you can't ignore Gaudí's Sagrada Família. Orwell condemned it as the most hideous building in the world, while Dalí hailed it as 'supremely creative bad taste'.

parrots, chaffinches, hens, fish and dejected rabbits. At the port end of the Rambles a market operates on weekend afternoons; here stalls selling jewellery, trinkets and hippie clothes compete for pavement space with palmists and tarot readers.

**Els Encants** flea market, Plaça de les Glòries. Open Monday, Wednesday, Friday, Saturday from 08.00-20.00 (until 19.00 in winter). Take the metro to Glòries, and walk over the bridge. This is the largest second-hand market full of trash and treasure, where, given time, you can find some wonderful bargains. A colourful array of stalls selling everything (cheap and well worn goods) including the kitchen sink. Costumes, hats, wigs, jewellery, antiques, records, domestic wares, tools, even car and bicycle parts. Bartering is vital, and it's best to arrive early, as it runs out of steam by late afternoon.

**Gothic Quarter Antiques Market,** Plaça del Pi. Open every Thursday (except August) 09.00-20.00. Sift through the domestic junk and you may strike lucky. Try to catch the **Honey Market,** held here on the first Friday and Saturday of every month, which sells myriad honey products: honey wines and spirits, pollen tinctures, honey shampoo and beeswax candles, as well as locally made cheeses, cheesecakes and handmade chocolate. (This also sets up in Tarragona's Rambla Nova on the second Saturday of each month.)

For a glimpse of local ritual wander past the **Coin and Stamp Market** held every Sunday morning in Plaça Reial. Operating from 09.30 until 14.30, this is a serious affair where keen collectors feather their nest. An **Antique Coin and Book Market** opens beside Sant Antoni market on Sunday between 10.00 and 14.00, great for the lovers of rare or early editions of books and magazines.

Cheap paintings are displayed every weekend in Plaça de Sant Josep Oriol, and there is an art market in Plaça del Roser on the last Sunday of the month 10.00-15.00 (except July and August). The Sagrada Família district painters exhibition in Plaça Sagrada Família is open weekends and holidays 10.00-15.00. For ceramics, glass, iron work, enamels, textiles and lace edging, try the craft fair

**(Opposite)** These enchanting Gaudi gatehouses surpass Walt Disney, and set the scene for the fantastical spread of Parc Güell beyond.

held in the gardens of Turó Parc, Avinguda Pau Casals, on the first Sunday of each month (except August and September).

Plaça del Pí is an endless hive of activity. When not otherwise engaged by fiestas, impromptu concerts, weddings or art fairs, this square supports local crafts, such as the travelling honey market above.

## Jumble Sales and Second-Hand Items

Perhaps surprising to the British (whose nose for a bargain seems more highly tuned than their dress sense) the Spanish are less keen on wearing second-hand clothes. In general they are proud dressers, preferring new and smart outfits; thus second-hand shopping is in its infancy, and considered vaguely distasteful. One of the main outlets is **La Kalle** at Verdi,12, which sell groovy imported bargains for both sexes.

Jumble sales organised by the church are held in Plaça Bona Nova several times a year. If you want to throw anything away, call Engrunes (tel: 372 46 54) a co-operative for the unemployed. For second-hand items, try the free magazines available at most kiosks: *Util, Mercapress,* and *Segona Ma.*

## Department Stores

These are generally open conintuously from 10.00-21.00 Monday to Friday and 10.00-21.00 on Saturday. Spain's leading chain store is El Corte Ingles, which has branches at Plaça de Catalunya and Diagonal, 617-619. Particularly recommended is its scrupulously clean supermarket and delicatessen. It also has a travel agency and an overseas mailing service for any purchases made there.

Galerias Preciados is its main rival which offers competitive prices and similar services to the above. Branches can be found at Portal de L'Angel,19-21 and Diagonal 471-473.

## Books and Magazines

English language newspapers can be bought at the majority of street stalls, and well into the early hours from the brimming kiosks on the Rambles. Here you can buy anything from Tolstoy to *Tintin,* alongside blatantly displayed pornography — no shifty brown paper bags here. English books are stocked at a number of places: Francesa, Passeig de Gràcia,91; English Bookshop, Calaf,52; Herder, Balmes,26. A good travel bookshop with some English titles is Altair, Balmes,69. Cheap second-hand English books can be found at Simon & Ko, Granja,13.

## Galleries

Barcelona has a collection of almost 50 contemporary art galleries, concentrated between Balmes and Rambla de Catalunya around Consell de Cent. Early evening sees this area thronging with artists, dealers and enthusiasts for regular exhibitions and private views.

Some of the most important traditional galleries are located in the Barri Ribera. Within the triangle formed by Montcada, Princesa and L'Argentería, many contemporary galleries and antique shops are opening up, and this is rapidly becoming a key artistic area.

## Late Night Shopping

It's possible to shop all night at the **Drugstore,** Passeig de Gràcia,71. (24 hours a day). This includes a supermarket, tobacconist, book store, photography and gift shops, billiards room and restaurant.

Justifiably popular as a rare place to shop around the clock, it's tacky, brightly lit and expensive but pleasant for late night coffee at the tables outside.

**7-11** is the only all-night supermarket, and is located beside the Sagrada Família on Mallorca,410.

**Drugstore David,** Tuset,19-21. This has 53 shops open daily from 09.00-05.00.

**VIP'S,** Rambla Catalunya,7. This comprises 22 shops open Monday to Thursday 09.00-02.00, Friday 08.00-03.00, Saturday 09.00-03.00, Sunday 09.00-01.30.

---

### Juggling the Sexes

Grabbing every visitor's attention, as much for its dramatic pouring effect as its extraordinary appearance, is the long-spouted, glass *porrón*. Originating in Catalunya, these are only traditionally found here or in parts of neighbouring València. This curious jug has always been a serious drinking tool, from which locals perfect their aim and vye to catch its thin jet of liquid from further and further away.

*Porróns* come in two shapes, either with a straight funnel or one curving backwards. At one time it was usual for women to drink from the upright variety, with the arched necks kept as the masculine preserve; and it was also popular for the appropriate shape to be given as a christening present.

The sexual symbolism remains unexplained, but in the past, households of spinsters and bachelors were always careful to use the right shape. The curved versions are now most widely found, mainly because they are less prone to spilling when the bottle is fully tilted back. Today the original process of hand-blowing glass *porróns* can be seen in Poble Espanyol.

---

## Souvenirs

The trinket centre is Poble Espanyol on Montjuïc. This theme park was created for the 1929 International Exhibition, and has since become a shopper's paradise catering exclusively to the tourist trade. It offers local crafts from each area of Spain, but reeks of artificiality at tourist prices.

For gifts with local flavour consider a drinking *porrón,* often competitively demonstrated by the local talent in bars; experts pass this long-spouted glass jar around and, without touching their lips, send alcohol streaming down their throats from a great height. *Botas* are the archetypal souvenir, although with some justification, as these porous leather pouches are highly effective for keeping liquids cool.

Ceramics can make some of the better buys: those sold around the Cathedral are generally custom made, and just a little exploration will uncover bargains. Best value and more interesting selections can be found in various villages outside the city, such as La Bisbal, outside Girona, or in Breda at the foot of Montseny. Silver can be cheap in Spain, and an interesting place to buy jewellery is Gem Art, on the corner of Marqués de l'Argentería and Comerç. This houses the world's biggest collection of rubies and opals, and here you can buy reasonably priced silver and gems, and even design your own jewellery.

*Sardana* music is a popular memento, although it is something of an acquired taste and can sound better in Catalunya. Knives have a tradition here and both the domestic and the pocket varieties are worth purchasing. Tobacco remains cheap and there is no shortage of specialist shops.

## Good Finds

— Makoki Comix, Plaça de Sant Josep Oriol. Vast array of comics.
— El Rey de la Magia, Princesa,11. Founded in 1881, it claims to be the second oldest magic shop in Europe.
— Fantasy Shop, inside Gralla Hall, Portaferrisa,25. Original, one-off, colourful clothes, hats and shoes.
— Gemma Povo, Banys Nous,5, and Pau Claris,183. Original artefacts, especially wrought iron, hand-blown glass and furniture.
— Vinçon, Passeig de Gràcia,96. Invariably popular and becoming something of an institution, this household store is upmarket and stylish with unusual gifts.
— Marron Glacé, Passeig de Gràcia. Contemporary fashions by top designers, with a few second-hand clothes.
— 2 Bis, Bisbe,2 Bis. Good for presents of modern crafts, china and glass.
— Herminia, Nou de la Rambla,13. Theatrical clothes.
— Aloe, Junta del Comerç,2. Indian clothes and accessories.
— El Mercadillo, Portaferrissa,17. Two floors of cheap boutiques, and upstairs there's a hairdresser and a patio for drinks.
— Vins i Caves la Catedral, Plaça de Ramón Berenguer el Gran. A broad selection of alcohol with an interesting *cava* cellar.
— The Body Shop, Provença,245. The only one in Barcelona.
— Viadiu, Comtal,20, Honey specialists.

— Torruela, Gran de Gràcia. Excellent cheese shop.

— La Portorriquea, Xuclá,25. Fresh ground coffee and fine biscuits.

— Escribà, Rambla,83. Inside this *Modernista* house is one of the most tempting *pastelerías* around, selling dainty sweets, pastries and savoury snacks.

— Look de Luxe, Portaferrisa,17. Groovy shoes.

— La Botiga del Sol, Xiquets de Valls,9, Gràcia. Health shop with books, music, supplements, food and ecologically sound products.

— Musical Emporium, Rambla,129. Specialises in classical guitars and sells international instruments and sheet music.

— Tanv 13, Jaume I,13. Cheap Indian and hippy styles with the odd bargain.

There are several alternative New Wave shops selling music, tee-shirts and fashion accessories; these often publicise offbeat gigs and events. Try New.ton, Riera Alta,8; TLF, Joaquim Costa,51; or Flag, Joaquim Costa,2.

— Edison's, Riera Baixa,4-10. Two record shops in the same street, one selling British and US imports, the other stocks second-hand records with good sections for Spanish sounds such as *salsa, sardana* and *flamenco.*

—Cafés El Magnifico, L'Argentería,64 and Grunyi,10. Specialists in coffee and tea from all the finest plantations in the world since 1919.

— Rosario Puig Casado, Canuda,3. Flamenco clothes, accessories and hats for adults and children.

— Sorribas, Asturias,48. Health food products.

Don Carlo, Casanova,228. Italian pasta freshly made on the premises, with dishes and sauces to take away.

— El Port, Ample,23. Popular ceramics, with some original and hand painted items, slightly cheaper than most pottery shops.

— Artero, Call,17. Wide selection· of knives, especially good for well-made kitchen varieties.

— Compañia de Baile, Plaça del Pí,5, and Bulevard Rosa at Diagonal,615. Good for beachwear, robes, towels and tee-shirts.

— Travel Photo, Plaça Rius i Taulet,3. Photographic shop with a good selection of different films, and a number of camera accessories.

# Hair and Beauty

— La Pelu, at L'Argentería,70-72, and Verdi,29, Gràcia. Open until 23.00, this offers hairdressing and beauty treatments.
— Maurice Mességué, Muntaner,292-294. Tel: 209 49 36. Beauty and body treatments (using wild herbs and natural cosmetics) including massage, make-up, waxing and electrolysis.
— Iranzo, Tuset,1. Tel: 200 15 20; or Passeig de Gràcia,100. Tel: 215 73 13. Expensive and one of the best hairdressers, for men and women.
— Llongueres, Rambla de Catalunya,16. Tel: 302 73 25; or Passeig de Gràcia,78. Tel: 215 41 75. A good, reasonable value unisex salon.
— Arycasa, Ausias Marc,17. Tel: 317 02 41. Hair and beauty.

State-of-the-art climbing frame. Barcelona's artworks are especially accessible to the public; here children in Gràcia show hands-on appreciation of modern sculpture.

The last word in police protection. Whether sporting shades, shorts or raincoats, the multi-layered Spanish force is adept at seasonal adjustments.

TEN

# A — Z of Information

### Addresses

In Spanish addresses, the house number comes after the street name, followed by the floor number, and finally the apartment number. You sometimes find a longer walk than expected to the relevant floor — a legacy from those days when nobody lived on the ground floor which was generally occupied by shops or warehouses. Thus, above the ground floor is the *principal,* and above that (effectively two floors up) lies the *primero,* or first floor.

### Banks

Banks are open six days a week, Monday to Friday 08.30-14.00, and Saturday 08.15-12.30 but generally closed on Saturdays in summer (June to September). Out of hours, go to Banc de Santander which has an automatic money exchange on the corner of Carrer Ferràn and Plaça de Sant Jaume. This can be used with bills of the following denominations: English — five and ten pounds; French — 100 and 200 francs; Belgian — 100 and 1000 francs; German — ten, 20 and 50 marks. Additionally, several of the central exchange booths stay open until 19.00. Some of those available late and on fiestas include:

Airport: 07.00-23.00 daily.
Sants station: 08.00-22.00 daily, and until 23.00 in summer, (closed on summer Sundays from 14.00-16.00).
Banc de Bilbao, Rambla 52, open daily 08.15-20.35 from June to September, closed Sunday in winter.

In summer La Caixa has two branches open at extra times for exchange: both of these are currently open Tuesday-Friday (15.00-19.00) and on weekends as follows:
Plaça de Catalunya (next to Banc de Bilbao): 10.30-16.30;
Montcada,31-33: 10.30-18.00 Saturday, or until 18.30 on Sunday (closed for one hour at lunchtime). Likewise at the Sagrada Família and Plaça d'Espanya. (Opening times not yet fixed.)

## Credit Cards — Information/Emergency numbers
Visa: 315 25 12 (24 Hours) Diners Club: (91) 302 14 28 American Express: 217 00 70 MasterCard: 315 25 12 or (91) 435 49 05

## Foreign Banks
Barclays Banks are at Passeig de Gràcia,45 (tel: 487 06 07); Ronda Universitat,27; Diagonal,601.
Lloyds Banks can be found at Rambla de Catalunya,123 (tel: 237 42 40); Diagonal,601; Calvet,16-22.

## Beach Etiquette
Topless bathing is usual on the city beaches and in the larger resorts, but nudism is confined to certain places along the coast. Some of the smaller and less accessible villages may be more conservative. Sleeping on the city beach is not allowed and you are liable to be moved on by the police.

## Churches
Most of the city churches are Catholic and mass is held between 07.00-14.00 on Sunday and saints days, and in the evening between 19.00-21.00 on Saturday, Sunday and saints days. Barcelona's only Anglican church is Saint Georges, Sant Joan de la Salle,41, in Pedralbes; this celebrates a holy eucharist on Sunday at 11.00 and on Wednesday at 11.30. Catholic mass in English can be heard at Paroisse Française, Anglí,15, at 10.30 on the first and third Sunday of the month.

Other religious representations include: The Al-Widadiyah Mosque at Balmes,13; Evangelical churches at Paral.lel,167 and Aragó,51; and the Synagogue of the Jewish community at Avenir,24.

## Complaints
Spanish law obliges all hotels, restaurants, campsites and petrol stations to keep complaint forms. These are also obtainable from tourist offices, or from the Direcció General de Turismo (Passeig de Gràcia,105, 08008). Complaints should be made within one month of the incident.

## Customs and Duty Free Allowances
There are no limits to the amount of currency you can bring into Spain, but if you intend to take out more than 100,000 pesetas in Spanish bank notes or foreign currency worth 500,000 pesetas, the excess must be declared when entering the country.

Duty free allowances are lower than duty paid (items bought in a normal shop) and these are shown in brackets. Quotas for items brought into the UK are: one litre (1½ litres) spirits or liqueurs in excess of 22 per cent alcoholic strength; two litres (three litres) fortified or sparkling wines and some liqueurs; two litres (five litres) still table wine; 200 (300) cigarettes; 100 (150) cigarillos; 50 (75) cigars; 250 grams (400 grams) tobacco; 60 cc/ml (90 cc/ml) perfume; 250 cc/ml (375 cc/ml) eau de toilette and purchases worth £32 (£265). Allowances are subject to change — so do check if in doubt.

## Drugs

The whole of Spain suffers from drug abuse, and Barcelona, as a port and swinging city, predictably has a severe problem. The current crisis is heroin, which is blatantly available, especially in the red light district, and great quantites of cannabis *(chocolate)* which enter the south of Spain from Africa every year.

Hashish is illegal, but is nonetheless visibly consumed; dealing, however, is a serious offence and the larger amounts incur severe penalties. Pushers are at work all night in the Rambles, around the port area and in Plaça Reial where this thriving trade continues in defiance of increased police presence. And many an unhappy tourist walks off with licorice not *chocolate*.

## Electricity

220-volt alternating current, using round two-pin plugs, is gradually becoming standard in Spain; travel adaptors for British square three-pin plugs are available at most electrical shops. Electrical wiring running off 125 volts lingers in many of the older buildings, but this can easily be converted using a transformer.

## Embassies and Consulates

Foreign embassies are located in capitals, whereas consulates are based in the provinces. Broadly, the Embassy performs a political function and conducts its native country's public relations.

Consulates exist to help their citizens abroad (although there are limits to what they can do), and deal mainly with passport and visa affairs. They will issue emergency passports, contact relatives or friends, and advise on transferring money. In a crisis, the British consulate can also advance money against a sterling cheque (with banker's card), provide a list of local lawyers, doctors or interpreters, and contact next-of-kin in case of an accident or death. They will also contact arrested or imprisoned British nationals, and occasionally make a loan for repatriation to the UK. The Consul cannot pay hotel, medical or other bills, or arrange preferential treatment in hospitals and prisons. Nor do they give legal advice, interfere in local judicial proceedings or obtain work permits.

The **British Consulate** in Barcelona is at Diagonal,477 (tel: 322 21 51); the **United States** Consulate is at Vía Laietana,33 (tel: 319 95 50); the **Australian** Consulate is at Gran Vía Carles III, 98 (tel: 330 94 96); the **Canadian** consulate is at Vía Augusta,125 (tel: 209 0634).

## Emergencies and Medical Care

Professional and efficient, the Spanish medical service is thoroughly impressive; and like all members of the European Community, Spain has a reciprocal arrangement with Britain which provides free health cover for visitors. (Leaflets SA40 and SA41 from the DSS will tell you more.) For reclaiming money spent on medical bills abroad, you'll need form E111, also from the DSS (see Planning Your Trip, chapter 2).

It is, however, wise to take out health cover as part of your travel insurance. ASTES, the widely recognised Spanish tourist insurance, covers private medical expenses and hospitalisation and is available from many travel agencies.

**Pharmacies** keep normal shop hours, but there are a number open late and at weekends, as well as a duty pharmacist open all night. The address of this is listed on a placard and displayed in the window of every other pharmacy; they can also be found in the daily paper under *'farmacias de guardia'*.

**Optical care** in Barcelona is of a high standard. The city has the famous Barraquer eye clinic at Muntaner,314 (tel: 209 53 11) which is excellent, but since it is private, consultations are expensive. High street opticians are efficient, reasonable value and provide free eye tests. Optica 2000 (on the corner of Santa Anna and Canuda), using computerised equipment, can produce glasses in just one hour.

## Hospital Emergency Services:

Hospital Clínic, Casanova,143 (tel: 323 14 14). This is the main city hospital (with a metro station of the same name right outside), and visits usually incur a small charge.

La Cruz Roja (Red Cross) Hospital, Dos de Maig,301 (tel: 433 15 51).

Hospital de Sant Pau, Avinguda Sant Antoni Maria Claret,167 (tel: 347 31 33).

Hospital General de Catalunya, Sant Cugat del Vallès (tel: 675 12 12).

**Emergency Telephone Numbers:**
National Police: 091 Traffic accidents: 092 Doctors: 212 85 85
Nurses: 417 19 94 Ambulances: 329 77 66/300 20 20 Fire Brigade:
080 Alcoholics Anonymous: 317 77 77

## Expatriates

Barcelona's expatriate community has been very large for the last
ten or more years, and there are a number of organisations which
exist for foreigners in Barcelona. The British Council Institute at
Amigó,83 (tel: 209 63 88) has a library and organises cultural events.
The British Society of Catalunya arranges social gatherings for
British citizens and their families. Membership forms may be
obtained from the British Consulate.

The theatre club is open to all English speakers (contact Patricia
Gill: 323 23 32). The American Women's Club, for English
speaking women from all over the world, arranges regular activities,
further information from the Club House, Loreto,10 (tel:230 00 06).

*Look Now* is a glossy upmarket magazine for expatriates which
has interesting features and lists financial advice (on importation,
housing, shopping, tax etc).

## Flat Share

Finding longer-term accommodation in the city is difficult; try the
classifieds in the *Vanguardia* or use a flat sharing agency. A cheaper
and often easier alternative (since advertisements are in English), is
to check the various noticeboards where rooms are regularly
advertised. Worth trying are: International House, Trafalgar 14; the
British Institute, Amigó,83; and the American Institute, Vía
Augusta,123.

## Free Education

Lectures and conferences are held at the Central University in Plaça
de Universitat around 16.00-16.30 during the summer. These are
cultural talks designed for foreigners studying Spanish but are open
to everyone.

The cultural office of the Caixa (Centro Cultural de la Caixa) in
Vía Laietana (corner of Sant Pere Més Alt) offers free use of its
facilities; you can play with their computers, videos, or make use of
drawing equipment, etc. Various seminars and short courses are also
run from here. These are cheap, perhaps lasting a week, on subjects
such as how to make a video.

At the Centre Permanent d'Artesania in Passeig de Gràcia,55 (tel:
215 71 78) you can see examples of handicrafts and artisan work

from all over Catalunya. Located next to Bulevard Rosa, between Aragó and València, exhibitions are also held here.

### Hitch-hiking
Hitching is legal in Spain, but as in all countries, you should take sensible precautions. Avoid hitching in isolated spots at night, particularly if alone and female. You are much less likely to be picked up in the city centre than out of town or on the coast. More reliable alternatives are the agencies which connect you with drivers who have extra space in their cars: Auto Stop (tel: 412 14 14); Eco Stop (tel: 389 08 16); Barnastop, (tel: 318 27 31). These are cheap, and rates are generally governed by international agreements.

### Hygiene
It's hard to ignore the oppressive dirt in Barcelona and coastline pollution, the legacy of intense industrial activity, makes many swimmers head for clearer waters. But in other ways, hygiene is not neglected, and a surprising side of Barcelona's nightlife are the high-powered hoses which come out in the early hours with the rubbish collectors to spray down the streets and dustbins.

Food hygiene is a debatable subject; obviously it's wisest to wash fruit and avoid tapas which have been left uncovered too long. Typhoid has not quite been eradicated in Spain but, although occasional incidents attract headlines, the chances of contamination are incredibly slim.

AIDS is fast becoming an acute problem; condoms and syringes are available cheaply from every pharmacy. Part of the Hospital de Nuestra Senora del Mar (by Barceloneta beach) has been designated specifically for AIDS victims, and here patients can seek free help. There is also an AIDS department in Hospital Clínic which has a minimal charge. For a confidential helpline telephone: 339 87 56.

### Information and Support
There is a 24-hour telephone general information service run by the Ajhntament — dial 010. Operated by over 30 people during the day, it is usually possible to speak to someone in English, French, German or other languages; if the appropriate person or answer is not available daytime calls may be put through to the tourist board.

Also useful for visitors is the Connection Agency run by Montse Sunyer (tel: 318 05 17). This is a support service for foreigners, which, for a small charge, can assist in a whole range of problems from finding accommodation with local families, to tracing lost property, or cutting keys on a Sunday.

From mid-June to mid-September, you may occasionally see "Red Jackets" — officers specifically employed to provide on-the-spot information for tourists. These people patrol sections of the city in pairs from 09.00-21.00 daily, and can be found along the Ramblas, in the Gothic quarter and Passeig de Gràcia.

## Language

Although Spanish (Castilian) is understood everywhere, the main language throughout Catalunya is Catalan. This is an ancient Romance language, which is broadly a mixture of French and Spanish; speaking even a few words will win warm smiles. Officially banned under the Franco regime, this language has since resurfaced with gusto (see Language, chapter 1).

Part of this enthusiasm can be detected in the renaming of roads in Catalan. The changes are mostly slight and present no problem, but older maps may show the central artery as Avenida Generalissimo Franco instead of the renamed Avinguda Diagonal (the original pre-Franco name). Businesses and shops use either language according to their political affiliations, hence addresses can be confusing.

Cities have been re-christened in Catalan, Gerona has become Girona, Lérida is now Lleida. Likewise with houses and streets: *Plaza = Plaça* (square), *Calle = Carrer* (street), *Paseo = Passeig* (boulevard), *Avenida = Avinguda* (avenue), *Palacio = Palau* (palace), *Iglésia = Església* (church). Other key words to note are *Tancat* (closed), *Obert* (open), *Gràcies* (thank you), *Si us plau* (please), *Adeu* (good bye), *Ho'sentu* (sorry), *Quant costa?* (How much does it cost?). (For a list of Spanish/English words, see Appendices.)

## Language courses

Foreigners visiting the city are presented with a myriad of possibilites for learning Spanish or even Catalan, and schools can usually fix lodgings with a local family.

**Barcelona University,** Gran Vía de les Corts Catalanes,585 (tel: 318 42 66/318 99 26). This offers Spanish language and culture from October-May, intensive Spanish language courses during the summer or Catalan language courses (termly, or monthly in July and August).

**Official Language School,** Avinguda de les Drassanes, 08001 (tel: 329 34 12). Spanish or Catalan courses as well as many other languages.

**International House,** Trafalgar,14, 08010 (tel: 318 84 29). This well organised school offers intensive courses at all levels for two weeks or longer. Conversation and individual classes are also possible.
**Inlingua,** Rambla de Catalunya,33, 08007 (tel: 318 23 38)
**Barna House,** Rambla de Catalunya,112, 08008 (tel: 218 78 46)
**Linguarama Ibérica,** Gran Vía Carles III,98, 08028 (tel: 330 16 87)
**C.L.I. Consultas Lingüísticas** Preben Yamashita, Llibreteria 18-20, 08002 (tel: 321 21 64).

It is also possible to take Spanish courses at the British, French, German and North American Institutes.

## Laundry
Numerous places around the city will do your laundry - look out for the sign *tintorería* — and these usually do a same-day service wash. Often dry cleaning *(bugadería/limpiar—seco)* is done at the same place. *Lavanderías automaticas,* the cheaper, self-service variety are much rarer.

## Lost Property
Recovering lost property is never the easiest task, but those feeling optimistic should try the *Objectos Perdidos* at the Ajuntament (Town Hall), Plaça de Sant Jaume (tel: 301 39 23). This is a store for property left in the bus, metro, taxi or street.

## Luggage
Left luggage offices and lockers *(guarda equipajes)* can be found at Sants station, Passeig de Gràcia-Aragó RENFE station, and at the Maritime stations.

## Media
Unlike the British, Spaniards do not avidly consume newspapers, and there is no equivalent to the tabloid press. *El País* is the main national newspaper which, although published in Madrid, has a special edition for Catalunya. This is thoroughly supportive of the socialist government, but nevertheless has good journalism with strong foreign news coverage. Its rival in Madrid is *Diario 16,* but in Catalunya is *La Vanguardia.* This and *El Periódico* are the two most popular provincial papers, both written in Spanish.

*La Vanguardia,* slightly right of centre but fairly independent, is expanding around Spain. *El Periódico,* despite its larger headlines and photographs, is a serious paper with left wing views, supporting central government. *Avui* is written entirely in Catalan, published in Barcelona and wholly supports the Catalan government.

Television, on the other hand, is regarded as a top priority accessory, and despite the dubious quality and limited choice, the Spanish are obsessional viewers. There are currently three TV channels, although the present media explosion is expected to bring several more. TV3, the highly regarded Catalan station, broadcasts the British news at 18.45 daily. TV1 and TV2 are the national channels.

International newspapers are widely available especially from the kiosks along the Ramblas or in Passeig de Gràcia. A useful publication is the *Guía del Ocio,* a weekly entertainment listing which details restaurants, bars, clubs, musical events and shows and the *Guía del Pais. Vivir en Barcelona* is a more glossy and less comprehensive monthly version.

## Mosquitoes

Although keen on the sunburnt flesh along the Costas, mosquitoes seem to bypass Barcelona.

## Motoring

An international driving licence is needed in Spain (the European pink variety is acceptable) and it's advisable to carry this and your green card with you at all times. On the spot traffic fines are growing, and are occasionally levelled at visitors who have no local contact address. You must be 14 to drive a motorcycle under 75cc, and 18 to ride or drive a vehicle over 75cc. Seat belts and crash helmets are compulsory (although horse-riding hats are occasionally sported — sometimes even backwards — by the less self-conscious).

Speed limits are 120kph (75mph) on motorways, 100kph (62mph) on main roads and 60kph (36mph) in built-up areas. Cars with trailers or caravans have a limit of 80kph (50mph) on open roads. Parking in Barcelona is beset with problems and the safest option is an underground parking lot. Generally rates are 130-175 pesetas per hour and 900-1,400 pesetas per day.

Barcelona is surprisingly short of petrol stations; most are found on the outskirts of the city. Central ones are at the intersections of Paral.lel/Parlament, Passeig de Gràcia/Casp, and Roger de Flor/Arc de Triomf. *Super* is the Spanish equivalent to four star and *normal* to two star.

Unleaded petrol *(sin plomo)* is being taken up slowly in Spain. It is now slightly cheaper than super and available at Provença,1 (in front of Sants station), and at a few motorway services around the province. The nearest is on Castelldefels motorway (Km16) by Gavà, or heading north on the N11 (Km652) by Mataró. It is illegal to wash your car on the street, but there is a car wash on Gran Vía de les Corts Catalanes, near Urgell metro.

Garages open 24 hours include Detroit, Biscaia,326 (tel: 351 12 03) which has a workshop and round the clock towing service. Grúas García, Nou Pins,24 (tel: 350 75 35) also does 24-hour towing. There are orange emergency boxes on the motorways, from which you can call for an ambulance or mechanic. Simply press one of the two buttons which are marked with either a red cross or a spanner.

---

### Forcefully Dressed

At first sight, the multi-layered Spanish police force may seem baffling, but the clue to their duties can be unravelled by the colour of their clothes. Dressed in blue, are the Guardia Urbana, municipal officers responsible for civil affairs and who, despite their guns, more than live up to their approachable reputation.

Clad in beige, and next up the line, are the Policía Nacional, whose concern is crime throughout the country. Top of the rank, most feared and least to be meddled with, are the Guardia Civil. In olive green, this national force focuses on the higher profile crime and terrorism. On an altogether more blissful beat are the beach branch (a *costa* sideline of the Guardia Urbana). Sporting sunglasses and police shorts, their uniforms are the most revealing of all.

---

## Police

Theft is rife and the more conspicuous foreigner makes a prime target. Professional thieves operate the main tourist areas nightly, often in pairs and using sophisticated techniques. Bags vanish magically — beware of street pedlars whose role may be to distract you.

Never resist a violent attack, and report any theft immediately. Not only is this vital for insurance purposes, but there's also a high chance of recovery. Main police stations are at Ample,23 (tel: 301 66 66, ext. 360) at the port end of the Ramblas (access by Josep Anselm Clavé), and Vía Laietana,49 (tel: 302 63 25), both of which should have an interpreting service. The police are more attentive to robberies worth over 31,000 pesetas; it's not worth prosecuting for less, and petty criminals are soon back on the street for round two.

There is a police support service for tourists who have suffered an accident or crime 'Tourist Attention', Rambla,43, (tel: 301 90 60). This is open from 07.00-02.00 June to mid-October, and during Christmas and Easter. It gives legal and medical advice, and officers speak English, French and German. If you are destitute, and your

Consulate is closed, they will call a friend or relative and arrange for money to be sent to you care of the police station. They will also telephone to cancel lost credit cards.

Potential problems can be minimised by wearing a money belt or carrying bags cross-wise. It is best to carry photocopies of your passport or ID; these are generally accepted by banks for exchange purposes, but not always considered sufficient by the police. The worst areas of town to walk alone at night are the narrow streets of the old quarter, particularly the Barri Xines. Never leave your car unlocked, even for a moment; anything visible inside — stereos are a magnet — is liable to disappear swiftly. And a sensible precaution is to insure credit cards before you arrive.

### Post Offices

These generally operate between 09.00 and 14.00, Monday-Friday, though some open in the afternoon. Barcelona's main post office sits at the port end of Vía Laietana, at Plaça Antoni López (tel: 318 38 31) and opens 09.00-21.00 Monday-Friday and 09.00-14.00 on Saturday. Post from England tends to be considerably quicker than vice versa, and should you want a speedier service, try *Urgente.*

A Poste Restante or Lista de Correos service is available here for collection during the same hours, and for which you need identificaton. Stamps are also sold at tobacconists *(tabacs)* and at some hotels. Telegrams at the main one; there is also a 24-hour telephone telegram service: 322 20 00.

### Property

Speculators can obtain a list of agents dealing in Spanish property from: the National Association of Estate Agents, Avon House, 21 Jury Street, Warwick, CV34 4EH; Royal Institute of Chartered Surveyors, 12 Great George Street, Parliament Square, London SW1; or local tourist offices. The British consulate can supply a list of local lawyers and a guide in English for foreigners purchasing property in Catalunya.

### Public Holidays

There are 15 official public holidays *(festivos),* on which banks, shops and many restaurants close. (Eleven apply throughout Spain, two are for Catalunya and two more apply solely to Barcelona.)

January 1 and 6 (12th night) Good Friday, Easter Monday, May 1 (Worker's Day), June 24 (Feast of Sant Joan), August 15 (Assumption), September 11 (Catalunya's National Day), and 24 (Feast of the Mercé), October 12 (Spanish-speaking world's national holiday), November 1 (All Saint's), December 6 (Constitution Day), and 8 (Immaculate Conception), Christmas Day and Boxing (St Stephen's) Day.

Municipal facilities such as swimming pools may operate weekend hours or charge higher rates on these days. However, it is usual to find almost all museums and quite a few restaurants open on all but the major three holidays: December 25, 26 and January 6.

Although these are often a cause for celebration in themselves, they are largely distinct from the purely local fiesta, which is deeply ingrained in Spanish popular culture (see Catalunya and the Catalans, chapter 1). These are community celebrations, saints or feast days, which preserve local folklore and traditions, and are generally marked by processions and street parties held in a specific part of town.

### Students

Student concessions in Catalunya are rare, unless you are attending a Spanish University or college (except at the Dalí museum — a law unto itself). TIVE at Gravina,1 (corner with Tallers, tel: 302 06 82) is an agency which arranges travel for students, those under 26, and employed teachers of all ages.

### Tax

The Spanish equivalent to VAT is IVA. Foreigners who are not from a European Community country can reclaim IVA on single purchases of over 50,000 pesetas. To do this, keep your receipt, make sure it is stamped when you re-cross the border and claim the money in your own country. However, you should expect this process to take between six months and one year.

### Telephones

Public telephone boxes are blue, numerous and contain instructions in English; pay phones are also widely available in bars. International calls can be made from cabins marked Teléfono Internacional and calls to Europe cost a minimum of 100 pesetas. Dial 005 for the international operator (excluding Europe) or 008 for Europe. For international calls dial 07 and listen for the tone. Dial 44 for the UK, the STD code (omitting 0) and finally the number. (The USA's code is 1 and Australia 61). Some call boxes accept credit cards — just slide your card through the slot. There are two price bands, the cheaper rate is after 20.00 (until 08.00 the next morning) on weekdays, and between 14.00 on Saturday until 08.00 on Monday.

You cannot make reverse charged calls *(cobro revertido)* from a public telephone. Make these from a hotel, private phone or Telefónica (an office where you pay later with cash or a credit card). A surprising number of hotels don't allow reverse charged calls, and you should beware of crippling surcharges. Some hotels also charge calls at the peak rate regardless of the time. Reverse charged calls are billed at the rates of the receiving country.

The Telefónica is at Fontanella, 4, near Plaça de Catalunya (Monday-Saturday 08.30-21.00). Spain's prefix is 34 and Barcelona's code, 93 (omit 9 if calling from abroad). (Dial 010 343, from Great Britain, 011 343 from USA, 0011 343 from Australia.) A long intermittent tone signals a ringing phone; the engaged tone is shorter and more rapid. Dial 003 for Directory Enquiries.

## Time
Spanish time is one hour ahead of Greenwich Mean Time (and six hours ahead of Eastern Standard Time in the USA), and as in Britain, Spanish clocks are put forward one hour during the summer.

## Tipping
Hotel and restaurant bills usually include IVA which is not a service charge, but is the Spanish equivalent of VAT. Tipping is optional, but if you are pleased with the service in a restaurant or bar, it is usual to leave a small tip to make up a round number. In expensive restaurants, it is customarary to leave a tip of between five and ten per cent. Tip taxis a maximum of ten pesetas, station and airport porters often have a set rate, and cinema attendants expect around ten pesetas.

## Tourist Offices
Barcelona is well served by tourist offices: for information about the city you will find them at Sants station (tel: 490 91 71) open daily 08.00-20.00; FIRA de Barcelona, Plaça de l'Univers (tel: 325 52 35), open during some trade fairs and Av. Maria Cristina s/n (tel: 423 30 01 Ext 8356).

For information about the whole of Catalunya and Spain, offices are at the airport and Gran Via de les Corts Catalanes,658 (tel: 301 74 43, open Monday-Friday 09.00-19.00/Saturday 09.00-14.00). The town hall's information office is at Plaça de Sant Jaume (on the left just inside the Ajuntament) and for cultural information go to the Palau de la Virreina, Rambla,99. Poble Espanyol on Montjuïc has its own information centre.

## Travel Agents

A sample of Barcelona's many travel agents are: American Express, Passeig de Gràcia,101 (tel: 217 00 70); Happy Travel, Muntaner, 182 (tel: 322 54 00), TIVE, Gravina,1, (tel: 302 06 82). The latter is only for students, those under 26 and teachers.

## Water

Tap water within the city is heavily chlorinated and tastes unpleasant, but is not unhealthy; five-litre bottles of mineral water are cheap. Tea made with local water tastes foul — ask for it made with *agua mineral* or choose coffee which is strong enough to obscure the taste.

## Women Travellers

Women can expect the usual Mediterranean hassle which is, on the whole, harmless and friendly. It is customary for strangers of either sex to call women *guapa* (pretty), more often a term of endearment than a pass. Certain areas (such as the red light district and all around the old town) are best avoided if alone, on foot and late at night. For feminist books, go to Llibrería de les Dones at Lledó, 10.

## Work

Officially, Britons wishing to work in Spain must have a work permit, and the Spanish authorities are not keen to hand these out (no doubt due partly to 17 per cent unemployment in Spain). These can be obtained by contacting the Spanish Embassy in your home country. You also need a visa if you're staying longer than three months. Fruit picking and translation work are possibilities, but the most obvious option is teaching English. This is especially easy if you possess a TEFL (Teaching English as a Foreign Language) qualification. There are, however, a number of *idiomas* (language schools) which are known to take on teachers with neither experience nor qualifications.

For the well qualified, a good starting point is International House at Trafalgar,14 (tel: 318 84 29). Cic, Vía Augusta,205 (tel: 201 13 42) is a traditional language school which pays well and (a great rarity) even pays holidays.

Another option for casual work is to au pair; try Agencia Aupair, Passeig de Gràcia,118 (tel: 242 32 06); SAS International, Consell de Cent,226, (tel: 253 31 71); Intercambio Internacional Cultural, Passeig de Gràcia,86 (tel: 215 48 95). Modelling is also a possibility, contact La Agencia, Reina Victoria,1; New Group, Muntaner,475; or Natasha's, Diagonal,469.

# Introduction to the Region

The province of Catalunya is surprisingly diverse and covers an area just larger than Belgium. A journey into the surrounding countryside should not be missed, whether your preference is for the beach, the mountains or for any type of sport. And there are many places easily accessible for a weekend, overnight or even a day trip.

To the north, Catalunya is bordered by the Pyrenees which are appealing for their dramatic scenery and ski resorts; most beautiful and remote is the Vall d'Áran. In the west lies the industrial city of Lleida which, set among flat fruit plantations, is thought to be the least interesting part of the region. To the south the landscape changes again, and worthwhile trips include the vineyards of Penedès, the Cistercian monasteries of Poblet and Santes Creus, or down to Tortosa and the wide mud flats of the Ebre Delta.

The entire coastline to either side of Barcelona is dominated by industrial works or tourist developments. Here every yard of sand is exploited, but it is just possible to find some lesser-known, unspoilt beaches. To the south of Barcelona lies the **Costa Daurada**; this contains the infamous development of Salou, as well as the popular Catalan resort of Sitges.

Stretching as far as Blanes to the north lies the **Costa Maresme.** After this comes the **Costa Brava** which contains many of the largest developments; the most notorious site is Lloret de Mar, followed swiftly by Tossa de Mar. Both seethe with tourists in summer, and Lloret is supposed to have more hotels than Madrid. (Details of campsites near Barcelona can be found at the end of Accommodation, chapter 4.)

### Paradors

Paradors are nationally owned hotels which form a network across Spain, and although not the cheapest, invariably promise a comfortable night. The vast majority are housed in old buildings such as castles, monasteries and mansions, and as a result, often occupy spectacular locations. Listed below are a selection of paradors found in Catalunya.

Aiguablava (four star), Aiguablava, Girona province, (tel: (972) 62 21 62)

Parador de Vich (four star), Vic, Barcelona province, (tel: (93) 888 72 11)

Parador Valle de Áran (three star), Viella, Lleida province, (tel: (973) 64 01 00)

Castillo de la Zuda (four star), Apartado,157, Tortosa, Tarragona province (tel: (977) 44 44 50)

*Note:* All telephone numbers listed in Part IV are applicable from Barcelona, complete with area code. It is advisable to check times and stations for all public transport with the tourist office, as these are subject to frequent changes. Suggested hotels are included for all trips, but for the fullest listing, consult the *Guía de Hoteles de Catalunya,* obtainable from bookshops or from the Generalitat bookshop, Rambla, 118.

If travelling by train, arrive early to buy your ticket as queues can be horrific (see Arrival, Departure and Getting Around, chapter 3). In summer it's best to buy bus tickets a day early. For information about all transport, call 336 00 00.

ELEVEN

# North from Barcelona

Leaving Barcelona for the Costas Maresme or Brava, Montseny or France, the normal exit for the A7, N150 and N152 is via Avinguda Meridiana. This long and depressing thoroughfare, lined with grimy tenement blocks and the odd factory, is one of the worst faces of the city.

Alternatively for the N11 coastal road (and the short A19 which runs as far as Mataró), take the Gran Vía de les Corts Catalanes as far north-east as it runs. Traffic leaving Barcelona and Girona for the coast at weekends is atrocious, and in summer expect delays even on the most minor roads well away from the cities.

## Montseny

Remarkably overlooked by tourists, this part of the Prelitoral mountain range provides a welcome contrast to the sticky city streets. The foothills are just 40 minutes from Barcelona to Sant Celoni exit off the A7, and from here the landscape rapidly changes into green and craggy highlands. A slower, more scenic route is the N152. And revealing an unexpected side of Catalunya, a trip here is highly recommended, if only for its fresh air.

This small mountain range is covered almost entirely with forest — poplars, fruit trees and cork oaks. Rising to an altitude of over 4,000 feet, the area provides most of the province's mineral water. The narrow climbing road skirts sheer drops, and passes some dramatic scenery. Easy to combine with a day on the beach, a night in Montseny offers a peaceful escape from the grotty possibilities of the Costa Brava.

From Sant Celoni there are two main routes up the mountain. Either you continue to La Batllória and fork off for Breda, Riells and up to Arbúcies. Alternatively for Santa Fe and Les Agudes at the summit, you head uphill from Sant Celoni. Trains run as far as Breda (just off the C251 at the foot of the mountain). These leave from Sants or Passeig de Gràcia-Aragó stations and take around 50 minutes to Sant Celoni or just over an hour to Riells or Breda. From here buses connect to all the towns and villages.

**Breda,** a friendly little town with a pretty Romanesque church, is most often visited for its wide selection of ceramic stores. Seven kilometres uphill, at the end of the track, is the tiny hamlet of **Riells** — with just a couple of houses, one shop and a good value hostel. This is easy to reach by local bus or a cheap taxi ride from Breda station.

Particularly recommended for a peaceful day or two is Hostal Marlet, about half a kilometre before Riells (tel: (972) 87 09 43). Set in the lap of the hills, this is a well kept, family-run pension which serves simple but tasty local fare. Full board costs 2,900 pesetas per person. Around the swimming pool, the pretty garden has rose bushes, weeping willows and hydrangeas as big as your head. Popular in summer, it is open all week (June to September) but only on weekends during the winter.

### Sant Hilari de Sacalm

At the top of a steep road, the alpine feel is accentuated here by herds of Swiss cattle complete with bells. Pleasant and prosperous, it seems to be a magnet for elderly, retired folk. The water tastes so pure that it will come as no surprise to see the enormous bottling plant of Font Vella, just beyond the town. (From Breda carry on past Arbcies on the GE552 and then the GE550 — a windy road with stunning views.) La Hispano Hilariense runs two buses a day from Girona taking one hour ten minutes (tel: (972) 86 80 34). The same company also runs two buses a day from Barcelona leaving from Consulat,45, near the port (tel: 319 10 89) or from Plaça Palau (beside La Bolsa bar).

A civilised and comfortable night can be found in the three star Hotel Suizo, Plaça Verdaguer,8 (tel: (972) 86 80 00) close to the church, where a double with bath costs 5,000 pesetas. This pretty, old fashioned hotel with its log fire and homely feel, is only open from June to September. Hostal Torras (tel: (972) 86 80 96) in the main square is decent, reasonable value (a double with bath costs 2,970 pesetas) and also serves great food (although closed in winter).

The more basic Hostal Verdolet (tel: (972) 86 81 06) is the only one open all year; though not an inspiring place, it has a good view and double rooms for 2,640 pesetas. The tourist office here is at Carretera d'Arbúcies (tel: (972) 86 81 01).

### Viladrau

The miniature spa town of Viladrau has a refreshing atmosphere and is highly recommended for a quiet night or weekend. From Breda continue to Arbúcies on the GE552, fork into the GE543 and then the GE520 past some dramatic chasms. By public transport, the best way is to take a train from Sants or Catalunya to Balanyà which leaves more or less every hour. From here local buses (Autocars Prat) connect you the short distance; but these only run on Tuesday and Saturday at 12.00 and 17.00.

Set high on the mountainside and surrounded by woodland, this too has an Alpine feel; and, being well away from the usual trail, attracts discerning regulars. Primarily a spot to get away from it all, any exploration of the surrounding countryside will reveal endless lovely walks. One of those flawlessly pretty places, its tight cluster of streets house a well-heeled community. Pristine and peaceful, home cooking and early nights (don't try and eat too late) are Viladrau's attractions.

There are five hostels and surprisingly, given the low-key feel, these are often full. Try the wholesome and cheap Hostal La Barita (tel: 884 91 62); or Ca La Rita is great value for a decent and clean family-run hostel. Fonda La Moderna (tel: 884 90 61) is another civilised option for 1,390 pesetas a night.

# Garrotxa Region

An invigorating trip, and one that unfolds the staggering diversity of the Catalan countryside, is to drive up around the River Ter, through Ripoll and into the Garrotxa region (approximately 154 kilometres from Barcelona and 54 kilometres from Girona). From Barcelona, take the N152 to Ripoll, followed by the C150.

Trains from Sants and Catalunya stations run regularly throughout the day to Ripoll (a journey of around two and a half hours), and all pass through Vic. Ripoll is an attractive place where the façades of its houses lining the river make a pretty sight. The tourist office is in Plaça Abad Oliba (tel: (972) 70 23 51).

This mountainous country, bordering France in north east Catalunya, has lush vegetation, oak and beech forests, and some beautiful, remote spots which make good ground for hikers. Surprisingly, it is also a volcanic zone, and harbours over 40 extinct volcanoes. Due to the altitude and weaving road, almost every corner reveals a wide, hilly tapestry of soft blacks and greens, much of which is terraced. The drive is consistently scenic until Olot, today's regional capital, whose outskirts crop up as a sprawling, industrial disappointment.

**Castellfollit de la Roca** (on the C150) is an extraordinary town, and one that attracts its fair share of photographers. Here, the houses cling to a vast rock whose sheer, hacked face drops straight into the basin of the River Fluvià. Easiest, and seen to best advantage by car, it is also accessible by bus. From Girona, TEISA (tel: (972) 57 00 53) runs buses to Besalú, Castellfollit de la Roca, Olot and some to Ripoll. It also runs buses from Barcelona (Pau Claris, 118) daily at 09.30 and 19.00; on weekdays another bus leaves at 14.00. (These do not go to Ripoll.)

## Besalú

Further along the C150, the medieval village of Besalú suddenly materialises as something of a surprise. Most eye-catching is its twelfth-century fortified bridge which is constructed in two sections and turns at right angles into town. Thought to have been inhabited as early as the sixth century BC, it was also occupied by the Romans and Visigoths. Later, between the ninth and twelfth centuries it became capital of the area, and today has a population of 2,000.

Unspoilt, and with a strong personality, Besalú is a charming place to stop and simply stroll the old streets. A characteristic event, and one which guarantees a big turn out, is *sardana* dancing every Saturday in summer at 22.00 in Plaça de la Llibertat. The arcades of this square once sheltered a medieval market and you can find the tourist office here. Among the main sights are the twelfth-century Sant Pere monastery, which, made up of three naves, shows a curious brand of Catalan Romanesque, as well as the small Jewish baths. TEISA buses run here daily, see above.

Since there are only two hotels here, it's best to book. Both are good value at between 2,000-3,000 pesetas for a double with bath. These are Fonda Siques, Avinguda Lluís Companys,10 (tel: (972) 59 01 10) or Curia Reial, Plaça de la Llibertat,5 (tel: (972) 59 02 63). The cheapest restaurant in town is Can Quey in Sant Vicenç.

# Girona

The provincial capital of Girona, Catalunya's second city, is an attractive place which has been surprisingly overlooked by visitors to Spain. Built along the river Onyar (where it meets the Ter and the Galligants), it combines a manageable selection of sights (all within easy walking distance) with an air of respectability and tranquility. And, in contrast to the grime of Catalunya's capital, Girona is less oppressive with clear skies.

Surrounded by pleasant rolling countryside, it is highly accessible, being around an hour's drive from Barcelona, and just a short haul from numerous beaches. It was founded by the Romans over 2,000 years ago; and within its ancient city walls still possesses medieval houses and cobbled streets. The River Onyar has traditionally caused problems by sporadic flooding; to prevent further damage, a part which runs through the town centre has been shored up and its concrete banks painted by local children.

Flights from Britain to Girona (the airport is 12 kilometres from the city centre) are frequent and often very cheap, as the airport serves the bulk of the Costa Brava package industry. There are no buses or trains into the city centre, but expect taxis to cost around 1,000 pesetas. (See Arrival, Departure and Getting Around, chapter 3.) Buses leave Barcelona for Girona five times daily and these take either one hour 20 minutes or two hours 10 minutes.

By car from Barcelona, you should take the A17 which leads into the A7 direct to Girona (for the city centre, use the south exit), or the slower, coastal N11. Fast trains leave frequently from Sants station, from 05.55 to 21.50 and take around an hour and a quarter. The slower ones also stop at Passeig de Gràcia and Clot-Aragó.

On arrival, the best way to get your bearings is to walk along the top of the recently restored old city wall. From these ramparts you can clearly locate some of the major sights and have a good overview of the city settled in its surrounding countryside.

### The Cathedral

Built on top of the hill in Carrer de la Força, the Cathedral is Girona's prize sight. Dating from the fourteenth century, this Gothic building was erected on the site of an earlier Romanesque cathedral, and is best known for having the largest nave in Christendom. The approach, a 90-step climb, leads to the later addition of the dramatic Baroque façade.

Finished in 1733, this was constructed from nummolite fossilised stone (the same as that found on the Pyramids), which proves Girona lay under water thousands of years ago. Below the central rose window, statues of Saint Peter and Saint Paul flank the door, and the Virgin sits above. A statue of Saint Narcis (Girona's patron saint) stands on the second level.

The impact of the interior relies on its vast nave, with its splendid stained glass windows. Although building begun in the early fourteenth century, it was later delayed until 1416 due to an architectural debate which continued for over 50 years. To solve the dilemma of whether to have a single nave or a nave and two aisles, a meeting of European architects was held. Although the majority favoured the latter, the bishop and chapter cast the deciding vote — and hence the famous nave.

A lesser controversy now surrounds the walnut organ; this, which sits in the centre of the nave, was installed around one hundred years ago. And although blocking the altar view, its supporters claim it must stay for acoustical reasons.

Formerly part of Girona's original Cathedral, and dating from the twelfth and thirteenth centuries, is the elegant Romanesque cloister. Here the capital carvings depict Biblical scenes, the story of man, and some particularly vivid wildlife. From the cloister, you can see Charlemagne's tower, which built in the twelfth century, formed the Romanesque bell tower. Protruding from this, and an eye-catching detail, is the solitary witch gargoyle. Reputed to have cried against God during a holy procession, she was duly struck by lightning and transformed to stone as a grim lesson to others.

The southern Gothic façade is in the Plaça dels Apòstols, which was originally a cemetery, and whose floor is partly paved with tombstones. This doorway was constructed during the fourteenth century with restoration work this century. Here the stone is slowly disintegrating as a result of a mysterious cancerous disease.

The Chapter Museum houses a small collection of Romanesque and Gothic religious pieces. Its most important exhibit, and outstanding among the reliquaries, chalices and panel paintings, is the eleventh-century woollen tapestry. This tells the embroidered story of creation; Christ is depicted in the centre, surrounded by the events of creation and bordered by the months of the year.

Further along in Carrer de la Força, is the **Museu d'Història de la Ciutat** (open 10.00-14.00 and 17.00-19.00 daily). Aside from temporary art exhibitions, this contains exhibits from prehistoric times to modern day. The collection includes domestic and agricultural instruments showing some of the landmarks of social progress; here you can see the fifteenth-century cathedral clock mechanism and the machine which first lit Girona's streets. (It was in fact the first city on the peninsula to be illuminated by electricity.)

Girona's leading museum, and housing one of Catalunya's foremost collections of medieval and modern art is the **Museu d'Art de Girona.** Just by the Cathedral in Plaça dels Apòstols, this was once the Episcopal Palace (built between the ninth and sixteenth centuries) whose interior has original Romanesque and Gothic features (although the façade's doors, windows and the entry courtyard were Renaissance additions).

Exhibits are arranged chronologically and include altar pieces and religious artworks from around the province. Among the most treasured are the Virgin of Besalú, a fifteenth-century alabaster Gothic virgin and a fourteenth-century glazier's table. The latter was used to make the Cathedral's windows and provides an illuminating insight into the preparation of Gothic stained glass.

Offering an intimate glimpse into Girona's past are the **Banys Arabs** (Arab baths) which date from the twelfth to thirteenth centuries and were restored in 1929. Among the best preserved examples of Spanish public baths, these are similar to Roman baths and inspired later Arab versions. One storey high and built in Romanesque style, this, is one of Girona's prettiest sights and should not be missed.

---

### Eternal Brethren

In the bowels of Girona's history of the city museum — originally an eighteenth-century Capuchin monastery — nestles the gruesome legacy of a peculiar monastic practice. The cellar was used as a small mortuary, where vertical niches around three sides of a square once formed open enclosures for dead monks. Here, seated over air vents leading to drains, their bodies slowly dried until, several years later, their mummified corpses once again took to the cloth.

Dressed up, they joined the community for prayer, and even meals, to familiarise their living brothers with the concept of death. Although eventually forbidden by the Trent Council in the early seventeenth century, these monks clung to their sinister habits for some time longer. With other examples at Rome and Palermo, there are just three such cemeteries in the world.

---

Inside lingers an air of indulgence and luxury; here you can see a caldarium for hot baths and tepidarium or warm steam room. But most exquisite is the frigidarium, reserved for cold dips. Here, a central octagonal pool is encircled by elegant columns, while the whole room is lit naturally from a skylight above the pool. (Open 10.00-13.00 and 16.30-19.00, closed Monday, and Sunday and festival afternoons.)

One of the most fascinating aspects of Girona is its well-preserved **Call Jueu** (Jewish quarter). Here Carrer de la Força (originally the Roman city's artery) formed the main street between 890-1492. This community thrived in a convoluted warren of streets, at times separated from the rest of the city by doors that could only be opened by its inhabitants. On occasions housing up to three hundred people, it was the most extensive Jewish community in

Catalunya after Barcelona, and is one of today's best examples.

Meandering the sloping streets and winding alleys, you uncover frequent nooks, lovely courtyards and interesting doorways. One of the most atmospheric streets, Carrer de Sant Llorenç was re-opened 15 years ago and now holds an information office. Just off this is a pleasant bar with seats in a plant-filled courtyard; this is in the vicinity of the city's last synagogue which was built in the Middle Ages, but the precise location is unknown. Beside some of the doorways, you can still see a small scar; the Jewish custom was to keep a scroll here which was ceremoniously touched before entering the house.

La Plaça del Vi, so called in memory of the original wine market, is today's home of the Ajuntament (city council). This is one of many squares and streets which were named after the old city guilds and markets, such as Plaça del Col (cabbage square), Plaça de les Olles (cooking pot square), and Plaça dels Raims (grape square).

A colourful street is **Rambla de la Llibertat;** on Saturdays, this is ablaze with activity during the antique, flower and animal market. With many bars, it is a pleasant place to stop and has a distinctly gentler feel than Barcelona's sharp-edged Rambles. It runs beside the River Onyar, and between the houses, you will see an arch which leads to the Pont de les Peixateries (Fishmongers bridge). From this wiry structure, built in 1877 by Eiffel of Parisian fame, you can see the quaint façades of houses lining the water. Just at the end of the Rambla (at number 1) is Girona's central tourist office (tel: (972) 20 26 79); another is located in the station (tel: (972) 21 62 96).

**Sant Feliu** church, built between the fourteenth and seventeenth centuries, is one of the sights of which Girona is most proud. The Gothic nave is supported by heavy Romanesque columns and semi-circular arches, while the main façade was completed in Baroque style. Competing with the Cathedral for the skyline, the distinctive Gothic bell tower has a blunt top, whose peak was lopped off by lightning; this is circled by the points of eight shorter towers. Inside, there are eight Christian and pagan sarcophagi, the earliest of which date from the second century AD.

Nearby, just across the River Galligants is the Benedictine

**(Opposite) Top:** Catalans use any excuse to bring out the bunting and glad rags. Their national folk dance, the *sardana,* draws together young and old in a circle of solidarity. **Bottom:** Captured in a rare sedate moment, Plaça Reial is the focus of the old town and embraces all and sundry: this is the place to soak up the sun, scene and sangria.

monastery of **Sant Pere de Galligants.** This twelfth-century Romanesque building is outstandingly beautiful, well proportioned and atmospheric. The interior has a serene and spacious feel and is well worth a visit (open 10.00-13.00 and 16.30-19.00).

Suggested hotels include the three star Hotel Ultonia, Avinguda Jaume 1,22 (tel: (972) 20 25 24). Or a good value hostel is Bellmirall, at Bellmirall,3 (tel: (972) 20 40 09) between the University and Cathedral. This is small and spotless, but not a place for those bothered by quarterly Cathedral chimes. Alternatively, the one star Hotel Peninsular at Nou,3 (tel: (972) 20 38 00) has good service.

One of Girona's best restaurants is Pol Nord, at Pedret,120 (tel: (972) 20 09 27). Serving nouvelle cuisine, dishes are beautifully presented and unforgettable. Another sophisticated, but less expensive restaurant is La Penyora near the Ajuntament. This serves Catalan dishes, with cod as the speciality. Cheaper restaurants can be found along the Rambla and in the attractive Plaça Independencìa.

# Figueres

Undoubtedly the principal attraction here is the Salvador Dalí museum. After the Prado in Madrid, this is Spain's most visited museum, and a must for any visitor to Catalunya. The centre of Figueres is the wide Rambla with its twin rows of plane trees. The various cafés hugging the sides are as touristy as one would expect, with tables outside and most offering menus in four languages.

Travelling by car from Barcelona, you should follow signs for Girona. It is quickest to use the autopistas (A17, followed by the A7), but cheaper on the N11. Numerous trains run between Barcelona and Figueres, all of which pass through Girona, although usually there is no need to change here. The fastest takes about one hour and 40 minutes, but most are slower and can take up to an hour longer. The earliest currently leaves Barcelona at 05.55, and the last return leaves Figueres at 21.32.

There are connecting buses between Barcelona and Figueres, leaving five times daily. These take one hour and 20 minutes to reach Girona and connect with another taking 40 to 45 minutes to Figueres. There are some additional buses leaving at the same time

**Opposite:** Monks once used these impenetrable crags to shelter their high ideals. Today their retreat, the monastery of Montserrat, is a magnet for pilgrims and visitors alike.

which, by avoiding the toll roads, are cheaper but considerably slower (it is worth checking which is which at the ticket office). Since Figueres forms a junction of roads in this part of the province, it is often a stopping point for buses, from where connections run to resorts in the north and east.

## The Teatre-Museu Dalí

This was installed by the artist on the site of the old municipal theatre, and is as much a theatre as a museum. Inside and out, it defies description, being Dalí's last word in Surrealist adventure. It was opened in 1974 and is a superb treat, being, at once, fantastic, outrageous, absurd and hilarious. Here the artist uses every imaginable device to provoke a reaction and stun your sensations. Indeed, here, beneath the stage, the old charlatan's remains are buried.

Exhibits are arranged around a central courtyard which contains the most dramatic displays. Spiralling around, this museum covers several floors, and having no lifts, is not an easy place for disabled people. Full of visual trickery, it appeals to all ages and has many interactive displays. You should leave two or three hours to have a good view. (Open daily from 09.00-20.15.)

The genius of Salvador Dalí (1904-89) is difficult to quantify, and has been hotly debated since he first appeared on the art scene. Certainly it's original and provoking. He explored new art from Impressionism onwards, but showed that technically he was as precise and accomplished as the Old Masters. His cult reached its apogee in America — where the artist had lived for 15 years (1940-55), and where his inimitable Surrealism, with its Freudian and horrific images, was most appreciated.

Anything connected to him has been staggeringly exploited, whether it's his amoebic watches (an image which now adorns tee-shirts, plates, wall hangings), his man-sized ants, his jewellery or even perfume. And in true paradoxical form, the artist himself perpetrated this crazy business by flooding the market with 3,000 blank, signed lithographs for adulteration.

Close to the museum, and coming as a complete shock in this otherwise tame provincial town, is the old Gorgot tower converted by Dalí into his home, the **Torre Galatea.** It is not possible to look inside but, with its salmon pink walls decorated with bread loaves, and topped with gigantic egg sculptures and naked ladies, it has an even more startling exterior than the museum.

Although most visitors only spend the day in Figueres, it is a pleasant enough place to stay, with a handful of other activities.

There is a bullring, with fights every Sunday in summer (tickets from the tourist office), a toy museum on the Rambla, and a public swimming pool north of the city park just up the hill from the hospital.

The tourist office, at Plaça del Sol (on the Ronda Mossen Cinto), is open Monday to Saturday from 08.00 to 20.15 (tel: (972) 50 31 55). The post and Telefónica offices and local police are all well located in this same square. Maps are available from the train station (just beside the bus station) as well as the tourist office.

In the three star hotel bracket, there is Ampurdan, Carretera Nacional II (tel: (972) 50 05 62), with double rooms for 7,630 pesetas and an excellent restaurant; or Duran, Lasauca,5 (tel: (972) 50 12 50) at 8,000 pesetas for a double, whose restaurant also has a high reputation. The two star Trave, Carretera de Olot (tel: (972) 50 05 91), is a slightly cheaper option (at 5,000 pesetas for a comfortable double) and is the only one with a swimming pool. Pensions and guest houses are plentiful (the tourist office has a full list), the greatest number are located around the Dalí museum and in Carrer de la Jonquera.

As well as the better hotels, restaurants are easily found around the town centre and Can Yeroni in Carrer Castelló is popular with the locals. Figueres is not really a late place, but Café Emporium, below the Hotel Paris (on the right as you look up the Rambla), stays open for late night drinks. An entertaining place for a daytime snack is the small square alongside the Dalí museum which overflows with extraordinary sculptures.

### Surreal Gossip

Outrageous and attention-seeking, the personality of Salvador Dalí can never be wholly abstracted from his art, and Catalans are full of tales about his antics. One such runs that having sped to Paris to join the Surrealist movement, he then took a leisurely taxi ride around every brothel in the city, masturbating on his way. When he finally reached his destination — Picasso's home — and explained his delay, the elder artist praised him, and said he'd done well.

Subsequently, no love was lost between these two significant and contrasting figures on the Catalan art scene. Of Picasso's strong political persuasions the apolitical Dalí liked to provokingly remark, "Picasso is a communist, neither am I".

And one of his most absurd remarks was that he had been present on the Queen of England's wedding night. This wild claim was made on the grounds that the portrait he had painted of Lady Mountbatten was hanging in the bedroom where Queen Elizabeth and Prince Philip spent the first night of their honeymoon.

# Beaches: Costas Maresme and Brava

Heading north on the N11 you immediately hit the industrial towns of Badalona and then Mataró — and all the smells that go with them. Beyond these, however, a number of decent beaches can be found scattered between the enormous developments. Unfortunately the whole of this coastline is blighted by the railway track which clings leech-like to the shore, preventing access or expansion in various places.

The nearest good choice is Sant Pol de Mar, stretched across rocky coves, about 45 kilometres from Barcelona on the N11. It is also accessible by train from Sants, Catalunya, Clot-Aragó or Arc de Triomf stations; the journey takes just over an hour and leaves roughly every half hour. RENFE-ATCAR buses run seven times a day and take 50 minutes (tel: 232 04 59).

You need to walk ten minutes up the coast from the train station to escape the crowds and dirt. Here, near the viaduct and a tunnel through the hill, are rocky coves with cleanish sand and good swimming. Also nestling north of Sant Pol in an outlying bay is one of the few nudist beaches on the Costa Brava. A short way beyond, and reached by the same train half an hour later, is the larger town of **Blanes.** Here the beach is sheltered and relatively clean, with rice-like, fine pebbly sand. Buses (the same as those for Sant Pol) take one hour 25 minutes.

### Aiguablava and Fornells

The easiest way to reach Aiguablava is by car and, as one of the great finds on this part of the coast, it is worth every effort. From Barcelona, take the A17 and A7 to Girona, followed by the C255. SARFA runs daily buses from Barcelona (tel: 318 94 34) and Girona (tel: (972) 30 06 23) to Begur (a journey of around one hour and 15 minutes from Girona) and from here you should take a taxi or hitch. This road passes through La Bisbal d'Amporda, a major centre for ceramics and of interest purely for bargains in tiles and pottery. This is the nearest town to these villages, about five kilometres inland. Nearby and set dramatically on a small hill, the medieval fortified village of **Pals** is also worth visiting.

**Aiguablava** is situated in a national park, and has a small, sandy beach with brilliantly fresh water, enclosed by craggy sides. This is one of the lesser known strips of sand frequented by the more affluent sunbathers. Overlooking it from the southern promontory is a large, modern parador (see Paradors section above).

Just around the next corner is **Fornells,** a steep-sided rocky cove which has no sand, but is picturesque and popular for swimming off the rocks. Over this presides the luxurious four star Aiguablava Hotel (tel: (972) 62 20 58). This, with its tennis courts, swimming pool and excellent views, is generally booked up well in advance of the season (March to October). The only other hotel here is the three star Hotel Bonaigua (tel: (972) 62 20 50).

Those on a budget should head for Hostal Jordi's, just outside Fornells. The nearest place for shopping is Palafrugell. Camping and bungalows can be found at Begur or at Castel Park a short way beyond Palafrugell on the C255. Near here the coves around Calella de Palafrugell are promising for bathers.

### L'Escala

Once an important fishing village and still famed for its anchovies, this is now a popular seaside town. Just 143 kilometres from Barcelona or 39 kilometres from Girona, this is reached by taking the A7 beyond Girona (L'Escala and Empúries exit). The tourist office here is at Plaça de les Escoles,1 (tel: (972) 77 06 03); and there are plenty of hotels and hostels.

The best hotel, a short walk north around the bay, is the one star Ampurias. Sitting alone, almost on the beach and surrounded by trees, this is discreet, civilized and excellent value. As a great discovery, it is best to book although it's only open from mid May to the end of September (tel: (972) 77 02 07). Above lies the archaeological site of Empúries, ruins of a Roman town and the ancient Greek settlement of Emporion. There is also a Youth Hostel just outside the ruins, Alberg d'Empúries (tel: (972) 77 12 00).

### Empúries

Well worth visiting (and easy to combine with a day on the beach) are the dramatic Greek and Roman ruins at Empúries. These rank among Spain's foremost archaeological sites and are set amid fragrant pines and cypresses. Although the entry ticket includes a free plan, you'll need nothing short of a sixth sense to unearth its treasures. Likewise, the museum contains a wealth of artefacts, but these are labelled only in Catalan and Spanish. Excavation, which seems to be ongoing, began at the beginning of the century.

The ruins comprise two towns which were merged into a single city around the end of the second century BC; the Greek nearer the sea and the Roman above. The ancient Greek colony was founded by traders around 600 BC, and it was here that the Greeks first landed on the peninsula. (Fittingly, Empúries will be the point of entry for the 1992 Olympic torch.)

It subsequently became a notable trading port and an important centre for the production of pottery. In the former Greek town lie the remains of commercial taverns, houses, a market and the public to Zeus-Serapis (first century BC) and the other to Aesculapius, the to Zeus-Serapis (first century BC) and the other to Esculapius, the God of Healing (second century BC); here also lie the remains of a Paleochristian basilica dating from the fifth to seventh centuries AD.

More interesting and intact are the remnants of the Roman town, from where there are fantastic views across the Gulf of Roses. The highlight is definitely the foundations of the palatial houses, some of which still contain immaculate mosaics. Here you can also see commercial taverns, and the little that's left of an amphitheatre.

With the arrival in Empúries of the Roman forces at the start of the second Punic War (218 BC), the Greeks were allied to the Romans against the Carthaginians. It was from here that Roman power expanded across the peninsula, and Empúries remained their foremost stronghold until later overtaken by Tarraco (Tarragona). Following the end of the first century BC, the city reached the peak of its glory. Its power began to decline during the second century AD, and by the close of the third century it was almost deserted.

The ruins are open in spring and summer from 10.00-14.00 and 15.00-19.00, and in autumn and winter from 10.00-14.00 and 15.00-17.00.

## Empuria-brava

This development of luxury villas on canals covers 25 kilometres, and leads directly into the bay of Roses. Built on drained marshland (a mosquito's paradise) against a dramatic, mountainous backdrop, it is popular with boating enthusiasts. Not really a place for casual visitors, however, as the villas and apartments are almost exclusively second homes. And Spanish is as much at a premium here as authenticity.

Firmly for holidays, almost every sport and entertainment is available, from tennis to disco. Go-karting enthusiasts should head for Karting Ampuriabrava in the sector Aeroclub (open 11.00-24.00 daily). Close by is Catalunya's leading parachuting club (see Sports and Activities, chapter 8). The tourist board is in Puigmal,1. (tel: (972) 45 08 02).

## Roses

At the north point of the Gulf of Roses, on a broad sweep of sandy beach, sits the highly developed resort of **Roses.** No trains run here but the cheapest way from Barcelona is a fast train to Figueres, followed by the local bus which runs between here and Roses twice hourly (you can buy tickets on the bus). Direct buses from Barcelona are faster but more costly. These are run by SARFA (tel: 318 94 34).

Roses lies just 18 kilometres beyond Figueres on the C260. On the way you pass **Castello D'Empúries,** a small town which boasts an attractive cathedral, having at one stage been considerably more important. And if you decide to make the short detour here, the restaurant Canets is well worth passing of a mealtime.

Heading onwards to Roses, passing fields of giant sunflowers, there is still the occasional waft of industrial waste, but generally the coastline improves (clear skies and cleaner sea) as you approach France. Another pleasant detour could be to **Peralada** (off the C252); this is known for its wine and its old castle which now operates as a casino.

The older part of Roses, once a fishing community and built on a rocky headland, has been eclipsed by the concrete high rises on the beach. Near these the sand is packed but, being long and wide, the southern end is quieter — expect to walk quite far to avoid the crowds.

Due to its exposed position, it is frequently windy, which makes good sport for windsurfers (the surfing school rents boards), but tends to whip sand into the sunbathers. There are also glass-bottomed boats for excursions but neither natural shade nor umbrellas are available. The tourist office here is at Avinguda de Rhode (tel: (972) 25 73 31).

## Cadaqués

Just before Roses on the C260, the turning for Cadaqués forks up the hill. The 15-kilometre drive through olive groves around the mountainside is steep and slow, but the marvellous views easily compensate for this. No longer exclusive and arty, Cadaqués becomes increasingly popular each year, and justifiably so, as this is one of the least spoilt and most atmospheric places on the Costa Brava.

Still a pretty fishing village, it is set around three or four small bays, whose steep, rocky sides should ultimately prevent major development. So far this is low key and relatively unobtrusive, and much of it is obscured by the rugged hills and corners. There is no sandy beach, but the swimming here is perhaps the cleanest on the Costa Brava. And sailing, sub-aqua, surfing and fishing are all on offer.

Numerous tourists flock here, but there are just enough tiny bays to keep sunbathing fairly private. And there is a pleasant walk around the coast edge, even as far as Port Lligat (home of the infamous Salvador Dalí). The main harbour is an inspiring sight, where visiting yachts nestle beside local sardine boats. Plenty of restaurants line the front of each bay, and this is a great place for a fish feast; particularly good is Casa Nun or El Pescador, both of which have outdoor tables.

Buses taking one hour, 15 minutes leave Figueres four times daily. Tickets can be bought on the bus, but for direct buses to and from Barcelona (two hours, 50 minutes), you must buy these in advance from the Sarfa office (in Cadaqués it is just around the corner from the bus station). As for Roses, it is marginally cheaper to take the train to Figueres and catch a local bus to Cadaqués, but it is considerably slower.

As there are only limited places to stay, which are invariably full in high season, it is risky to arrive without a booking. Two one star hotels have swimming pools, Port Lligat (tel: (972) 25 81 62) and Misty (tel: (972) 25 89 62) or more moderately priced is Fonda Encarna (tel: (972) 25 80 19). A handful of families rent out rooms in summer, ask for details at the tourist office in Cotxe, 2-A (tel: (972) 25 83 15). And, there are almost always rooms to be found in Figueres if your luck fails here.

TWELVE

# South and Inland from Barcelona

For routes to the western Pyrenees, Montserrat, Lleida and inland, Tarragona, Costa Daurada and the south, drivers should take the Diagonal westwards as far as it runs. For the airport and all short trips to the south as far as Castelldefels, the exit is via Plaça d'Espanya where the Gran Vía de les Corts Catalanes leads imperceptibly into the C246 autovia past the airport.

## Costa Daurada Beaches

### Castelldefels
Passing through ugly suburban sprawl and industrial wastelands, Castelldefels (20 kilometres away) is the first place of any interest, and certainly the first reasonable beach. Just half a kilometre off the coast road, but nevertheless out of sight, is a large beach frequented mainly by locals. Although often crowded, it is not cramped owing to its size, and considering its proximity to the city and the major developments, is surprisingly unsullied.

This is a good place for a day trip to the beach, and trains running from Barcelona (Sants or Passeig de Gràcia stations) approximately every half hour, take 25 minutes. (The fast ones can take as little as 15 minutes.) There are two stations for this town, and the beach (Platja de Castelldefels) is the second stop. As ever, crowds gather along the sand nearest the station, so head up the shore for more space.

### Sitges
Just a short way beyond lies Sitges. Created as a vibrant resort by Barcelona's young and groovy, this is now almost an institution. As a result, high season finds it unbearably packed. The beach near the town centre (close to the church) is a heaving mass of bodies, but those prepared to wander further along the shore will be rewarded. Along this beach watersports are also available.

Sitges satisfies every expectation of a typical Spanish coastal town whose business is holidays. Although far from the genuine little town it once was, it hasn't yet teetered over the precarious edge (unlike Tossa or Lloret), mainly because it is alive with Catalans, and attracts fewer package holidaymakers. Unsurprisingly prosperous, it is a fun place to visit if its attractions appeal. Here you find a long beach which lures a captive market for the trendy boutiques, gimmicky gift shops and rampant nightlife.

As the capital of Catalunya, and allowing nudist bathing, it has a reputation as broad-minded. The two nude beaches (the first for straight couples, the second for gays) lie just to the south and are ominously known as the *'playas del muerto'* or beaches of the dead. Nightlife in Sitges continues at a frenetic pace, and is thought worth the short train ride for its manic bars and nightclubs. These pull the mainly young crowd, and keep the streets a-buzz with mopeds. Atlantida discotheque in Tenamar is the most famous spot, and Ricky's in Sant Pau is also popular.

Focus of the town, and the stamping ground of local teenagers, is the promenade which is lined with squat palms. Here some of the least interesting restaurants promise the greatest possibilities for feeling at home — with a plate of chips and cup of tea. Harder to ignore are the smattering of *pastelerías* whose window displays make Sitges seem the best bakers on the Costa Daurada. A decent, cheap restaurant is Vikingos in Maiyo,2, or Illa at Sant Pau,34 is a good vegetarian restaurant.

Easiest and quickest access from Barcelona is by train; fast ones take 25 minutes, slower ones take 40 minutes. These leave Sants and Passeig de Gràcia stations roughly three times an hour. Sitges tourist office is in Passeig Villafranca (open 10.00—13.00 and 16.00—19.00, closed Saturday afternoon and Sunday) just opposite the station.

There is no shortage of guesthouses near the seafront. A good central hotel, and just a short walk from the beach, is Lido at Bonaire,26 (tel: 894 48 48). This has a clean, pretty interior and costs 2,225 pesetas for a double with bath. Other cheap hotels are Mareangel in Parellades, and Vall Pineva in Bacha. Overall, as one of the beaches most easily reached from Barcelona, this is not a bad bet for a day trip.

# Montserrat

You can't stay long in Catalunya without hearing of this incredible mountain, with all its attached legends. And a trip here should not be missed. On an exceptionally clear day you can see its distinctive rocky fingers from the top of Tibidabo. As one of the most startling natural sights in Spain, this mountain, which cradles a monastery and numerous craggy hermits' caves, has always attracted hordes of visitors.

It is a place of popular veneration to which pilgrims have thronged from all over Spain, in particular to see the Black Virgin, *La Moreneta*. Legend claims this Virgin, carved by St Luke, was placed in one of the caves here by St Peter shortly after the Crucifixion. Although thought to have been carved at least five hundred years later, the icon has always been closely guarded, was hidden during the Arab invasion, and then miraculously reappeared. After this tales of her miracles are too long to catalogue.

Nevertheless this Virgin is Catalunya's most important patron saint, and numerous Catalan baby girls have been christened Montserrat. She became something of a cult and all over the world, particularly throughout the Spanish Empire, churches were named after her. Meanwhile the monastery flourished in an unprecedented independence, which even ran to its own flag.

Despite their impenetrable location, the monks were hounded out by Napoleon's forces in 1811, their buildings smashed and their treasures stolen. Yet when they were re-established, the Abbot again held an exalted position, and during Franco's rule, the sanctuary became a haven for Catalanism. Prisoners are said to have been sheltered, and it was one of the few places where Catalan was spoken. This was possible because, unlike priests, abbots were (and still are) elected by the monks and were therefore much freer. Today the abbot is still an important and symbolic figure.

It is worth every second of the short journey, just to experience the fantasy of this monastery's setting. This mountain, which forms the serrated *sierra* of Montserrat, is recognisable for miles by its shards of rock, suggestive of a bulbous bunch of carrots. Its name in Catalan means 'sawn mountain' and, always dramatic, from every angle it looks different. If you are driving from Barcelona, the west approach, though slightly longer, has definitely the most spectacular views.

The closest station is Aeri de Montserrat, which is reached by four trains a day leaving from Plaça d'Espanya and Plaça de Catalunya. From here access up the mountain to the monastery and beyond is either by funicular train or cable car. There is no contest here — this must be one of Europe's most dramatic rides and you simply must fly. Julià operates frequent buses which leave from Plaça Universitat,12 (tel: 318 38 95). Cars and coaches (which flock here in abundance) can wend their way up the steep climb to the top.

The basilica (1560—92) is the only part of the monastery open to the public, and is disappointingly commercialised. It has a large, cross-vaulted nave, with deep, ornate side chapels, and the whole is softly lit by tiny hanging lanterns. At the far end *La Moreneta* presides high above the altar on a richly gilded pedestal. You can touch her hand (the only part which protrudes from her protective glass case) by taking the stairs around the back. On the right as you leave her chapel you can see the pretty circular end of the basilica.

Just outside the forecourt are two small museums (with a mutual entry ticket). The first has a collection of old masters, largely Italian, which include Mannerist paintings, and some seventeenth-century, dramatic religious oils. The highlight is a portrait of the huddled up, old St Jeroni by Caravaggio. The second collection houses more modern works from the nineteenth century onwards. There are three by Picasso, such as a great early portrait of an old fisherman and the famous crayon of the Sardana of Peace (1959), which is often brandished on tee-shirts around Barcelona.

Exceptional views can be had from any angle up here, so it would seem that the *mirador* parapet, whose giant steel support is set into the rock, is a terrible and unnecessary blight on the landscape. From here a funicular train runs to the summit, where some of the hermitages can be found, and a walk round some of the paths and woods is well worth the effort. Certainly this attracts abundant hikers.

A visit here is easily achieved in one day, but since the crowds disperse by late afternoon, it might be pleasant to stop overnight. There are two places to stay, both with the same number: 835 02 01. The cheaper, two star Hotel Monestir costs 3,350 pesetas for a double, but is closed in winter. The more modern, three star Abat Cisernos costs 4,850 pesetas, and is open all year.

## Penedès Region

**Vilafranca** is a pleasant little town which, completely surrounded by vineyards, speaks of nothing more than wine. And this presides over a rich region since vines are a prominent commodity in Catalunya. There are some attractive streets and squares, but the most interesting visit is the Museu del Vi.

Outside in the Rambla this town's other claim to fame, its strong tradition of *castellers* is marked by a modern stone statue. This is a curious Catalan custom of building human castles, brought out at fiesta time. By car the town is reached by the A2, followed by the A7. Trains leaving roughly every hour, take around one hour from Sants and Catalunya stations.

Those whose interest, or tastebuds, have been whetted by samples at the wine museum, should try and visit one of the many vineyards in the vicinity. Not all are open to the public, but it is possible to inspect both the sparkling and the still table wine making processes.

The country for *cava* (Catalan champagne, see chapter 5) is nearby Sant Sadurní d'Anoia, home to the smaller brands as well as the two giants, Codorniu and Freixenet. This is slightly nearer Barcelona (close to exit 27 off the A7) and is linked to Vilafranca by numerous local buses. The same trains for Vilafranca take just three-quarters of an hour to Sant Sadurní.

Many cellars operate free guided tours, which are often accompanied by coach loads of tourists from the Costa Daurada. Codorniu is open 08.00-13.30 and 15.00-17.30, closed weekends, holidays and August (tel: 891 01 25). The Freixenet cellars operate similar hours (tel: 891 07 00). It is not strictly necessary to call first and you could simply turn up. As informative, fun and easily accessible, a visit to this region makes a great day out.

Tours at Codorniu include a brief slide show, a potted history, and a chance to examine the various stages in the *cava* making, bottling and labelling process. You descend deep into the bowels of the earth, past thousands of bottles, and a mini train carts you along some of the 17 kilometres of cellar. Inevitably there is the reward of a glass or two, before miraculously surfacing just beside the house shop.

Codorniu was founded in 1872, and it was here that Methode Champenoise (or *cava*) was introduced to Spain. This business grew out of the Catalan success at selling corks to the French champagne industry. Another bonus is that this is housed in a spectacular building by the Modernista architect Puig i Cadafalch.

## Tarragona

Although Tarragona's heyday was undoubtedly under the Roman Emperors Hadrian and Augustus in the third century, their legacy is not simply the remaining stone structures (all clearly signposted). The whole city has an ancient feel, an atmosphere you can

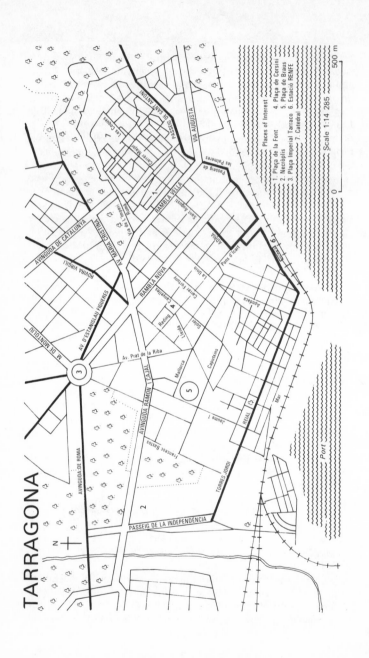

# TARRAGONA

Places of Interest

1. Plaça de la Font
2. Necròpolis
3. Plaça Imperial Tàrraco
4. Plaça de Corsini
5. Plaça de Braus
6. Estació RENFE
7. Catedral

Scale 1:14 285

0 ———————— 500 m

Port

appreciate before you have visited any of the sights. Indeed the vaults of the Roman circus run beneath the city, and crop up again and again as parts of bars, restaurants and other buildings around the old town.

If arriving by car from Lleida you pass one of the most spectacular sights, the two-tiered Roman **Aqueduct** or Devil's Bridge. This is sited five kilometres out of town on the road to Lleida, and is definitely worth a detour. You can reach it by local bus (leaving from Plaça Imperial Tarraco), ask for *el aqueducto.*

Set up above a steep parapet, the city of Tarragona commands a marvellous position on the Mediterranean. It is easy to see why the Emperor Augustus favoured this elevated spot and built so many temples around the city. Don't miss a stroll up the Vía de L'Imperi Romà which, with its rigid rows of cypresses and mosaic of cobble-stones, flanks the old city walls. At the top, through an arch, lie the cramped but bustling streets of the old town.

The best way to orientate yourself in Tarragona is to find one of the two parallel Rambles (Vella, the old, or Nova, a newer grander promenade). Just off the Rambla Vella is the Plaça de la Font, a rectangular avenue and home of the town hall, whose balmy atmosphere is created by wispy, flowering trees. A handful of hostels are located in this pretty square, which has good access for the old and new towns as well as the beach (see below).

## The Cathedral

Open 10.00-19.00, access is through the cloister, unless a service is in progress.

This was built between the end of the twelfth and mid-fifteenth centuries. As a result, its plan (a cross) is Romanesque, and the later construction is Gothic; although much of the architecture and decoration is transitional, showing aspects of both styles. And the typical Gothic pointed arches are neither tall nor sharp.

The central nave is quite severe, lightened by the pretty rose window and overdoor triangle in the front façade. The main altarpiece, dating from the fourteenth century, is ornate and stylised Gothic; and like the elaborate tracery above the doors, this is very busy. There is a pretty, round Renaissance arch (1570) with arabesque decoration up the sides, and over the transept sits an octagonal dome.

The cross-vaulted cloister has a pleasant, almost domestic garden with orange trees, rose bushes, a tall cypress and a resident litter of kittens. The rounded arches, which oddly have iron railings, are enclosed in threes within a more pointed Gothic arch, above which are pretty, carved roundels. Note the thirteenth/fourteenth-century capitals and reliefs of the arcade which depict the months of the year, biblical stories and the curious 'procession of rats' at a cat's funeral.

## Museu Nacional Arqueològic

Open 10.00-13.30 and 16.00-19.00, festivals 10.00-14.00 (or summer 10.00-13.00 and 16.30-20.00), closed Monday.

As might be expected, the exhibits are almost all Roman including sculpture, mosaics, and lead and bronze wares. Entrance to this museum allows you to walk along the old Roman walls. Anyone keen to examine more Roman remains should wander past the **Roman Forum** (entrance in Carrer Lleida) which contains little but four fluted Corinthian columns. Yet its descriptive boards provide a clear idea of the original set up.

The most intriguing Roman relics are in the **Necròpolis**, lying on the edge of the city (at the far end of Avinguda Ramon i Cajal). This is a collection of over two thousand tombs of both pagan and Christian origin, unearthed when a tobacco factory was being built here. Tarragona took up Christianity very positively, and this cemetery was in use between the third to the sixth centuries AD. The simpler coffins have not been moved, while the more ornate sarcophagi are housed inside the museum.

## Practical Information

The quickest route to Tarragona is by train, which runs regularly (roughly every half hour) from Barcelona (Sants); fast ones *(rapido)* take one hour, while others, stopping at more stations, can take up to two hours. The station has an information counter where you can pick up a city map.

A good option (unless you have heavy luggage) is to turn right outside this station and walk up the steps along the seafront promenade. This brings you up to the end of the Rambla Nova, a great congregation spot for young locals which looks out over the ocean. For the Rambla Vella and old town continue round this front promenade of Passeig de Palmeres — sometimes known as the Balco des Mediterrani.

Buses are generally slower and those operated by Bacoma run eight times a day from Barcelona. Hispania buses, taking an hour and a half, run seven times a day on weekdays or twice a day at weekends. Both types reach the main bus station beside Plaça Imperial Tarraco at the far end of the Rambla Nova. If travelling by car, you should leave Barcelona on the A2 and then take the A7, a distance of 97 kilometres.

Tourist information can be found at the foot of the Cathedral steps on Carrer Major (open 10.00-14.00 and 16.00-20.00, closed on Sunday and Monday afternoons). Another office in Carrer Fortuny,4 (tel: (977) 23 34 15) opens from 08.00-15.00 and 16.00-20.00 (closed Saturday afternoon and all day Sunday and festivals), but open less often in winter.

Almost opposite is the Telefónica office, while the post office (open 09.00-14.00, afternoons for telex and telegrams only) can be found just below the Rambla Nova in Plaça de Corsini. Also in this square, and warranting a quick look, is the covered central food market, whose façade looks curiously like a giant 1950s juke-box. A market is held in this square on Thursday.

Top of the hotel range is the four star Imperial Tarraco at Passeig de Palmeres (tel: (977) 23 30 40) where a double room costs 10,000 pesetas. Fairly modern and characterless, this is recommended for its position — straddling the top of the two Rambles on the headland looking out to sea. Nearby, a good bet in the middle range is the well-sited two star Hotel Paris in Maragall,4 (tel: (977) 23 61 09). This is open all year, and here a double with full-length bath, terrace and cable TV, costs 4,900 pesetas (4,000 in low season).

Of the many hostels and pensions in and around Plaça de la Font, El Circ at number 37 (tel: (977) 23 83 58) is a good choice. This simple pension has powerful showers, terraces overlooking the square, and double rooms costing 1,950 pesetas. There is also a youth hostel, Alberg Residència Sant Jordi on Avinguda President Companys just beside the main bus station (tel: (977) 21 01 95).

There is no shortage of cafés, tapas bars and cheaper restaurants, with good value set menus scattered around the two Rambles and Plaça de la Font. There is a tasty pizza/pasta house, Pizzeria Pulvinar, with outdoor seating on Carrer Major, leading up to the cathedral. Café Cantonada in Fortuny,23, a popular haunt for young locals, is a relaxed and airy café bar, with newspapers, a pool table and good light meals. For a more luxurious, sophisticated dinner, El Circ in Plaça de la Font,37, is especially recommended. This restaurant, whose walls incorporate part of the Roman circus vaults, serves delicate Catalan dishes.

This city's nightlife did not decline with the Roman Empire — there are a number of entertaining bars open until late. Two of the most popular, tucked into cellars running beneath the Carrer Major, and again part of the Roman vault, are side by side in Trinquet Vell. Both have a musty, subterranean feel, stay open until at least 02.30, and Mallic, the more fun, sometimes has live music. Kursal, a music bar in Fortuny, is entertaining and also occasionally has live bands.

At the top of the Cathedral steps a secondhand/antiques market is held every Sunday. If you coincide with the second Saturday of the month, the honey market in the Rambla Nova is worth a visit. Chess enthusiasts should head for the unremarkable looking tapas bar on the Rambla Vella next to the Catalana cinema. As well as serving good tapas, it is also the meeting place of the local chess club, where anyone is welcome to play.

Tarragona has two good beaches, the best and closest is Platja Miracle. Wander down through the municipal gardens laid out on the hillside and past the site of the Roman **amphitheatre.** This was positioned dramatically on a lip of the cliff, and what you see today is almost entirely modern reconstruction. Bathers should continue over the railway line to the shore.

Miracle beach is surprisingly clean and open, where the current is often strong, making the waves and swimming good. From this point you can appreciate Tarragona's two most contrasting characteristics. At one end on a jutting promontory sits an old triumphal arch; while at the other you can see the gaunt outlines of numerous cranes and industrial buildings.

The other beach, Platja de Rabassada is around the next bay, on the outskirts of the town, reached by the Vía Augusta. There are a number of small hotels and pensions, and plenty of camping space available.

# Cistercian Monasteries of Poblet and Santes Creus

## Santa Maria de Poblet

For anyone interested in religious architecture this treat should not be missed. At one time Catalunya's foremost spiritual centre, it is picturesquely sited among fields of hazel-nuts, almonds and olives. While the whole monastic complex with its gardens and forecourts is encircled by a wall and towered gateways.

Poblet was founded in 1151 by Ramon Berenguer IV, under whom the Cistercian order grew influential; and construction of the monastery continued throughout the twelfth and thirteenth centuries. Royal favour kept this well endowed and it enjoyed an amazing amount of independence and power. This, of course, led to corruption and, from the end of the Middle Ages until it was sacked, life here was so decadent that the whole community was loathed by locals.

At various times the buildings were reformed in the contemporary style — Gothic in the early fourteenth, or Renaissance and Baroque styles during the sixteenth and seventeenth centuries. In 1822 political agitation led to the monastery being ravaged and burned, forcing the monks to flee. Restoration began in 1857, but it was not until the turn of the century that Poblet began to be seen as an artistic and historic centre. Monks returned to worship in 1940, and today the abbey is kept alive by a community swollen to 35 members.

Inside, the main monastic buildings are set off the cloister, where monks used to contemplate prior to eating opposite in the rather plain refectory. This stirring cloister is decorated with wonderfully liquid Gothic tracery and amazingly detailed capital carvings. In the centre there is a pavilion — often found in the grandest medieval designs — while the slender columns are pockmarked, showing the ravages of time.

The square chapter hall (just past the doorway leading to the dormitory) holds the tombstones of past abbots. This has impressive fan vaulting and delicate, stylised carving. Also off the cloister lie the library, wine cellars and old kitchen.

The basilica is typically Cistercian in its spaciousness, and the intoxicating smell of incense reminds you what a staunch centre of Christianity this is. Behind the modern altar is a vast sixteenth-century Renaissance altarpiece in which statues stand in shell-shaped niches. The albaster carving is unbelievable, and shows the Virgin and Jesus in the centre.

Dominating the church, two monumental sarcophagi form low arches along the main aisle. These royal tombs were damaged by looters, but their fantastic carving has been painstakingly restored by Frederic Marès. The columns of the main nave have plain capitals and reach two storeys. The side aisles are steeply cross-vaulted, while the chapels behind the altar are refreshingly plain. A modern wooden choir sits in the centre but, with only railing across the aisle, it doesn't interrupt the sweep of the nave. And a glorious rose window brightens the far end.

Upstairs, the dormitory is a giant gallery with massive rounded arches, whose partitioned-off end is still used as the monks' quarters. From here you can walk around the cloister roof to the monastery museum.

Constructed in the early fifteenth century this was once the dormitory for the old brothers. It contains religious artefacts and reconstructed carved fragments; it is always surprising to remember how many of these early sculptures were painted. An outline of the monastery's tumultous history is also displayed.

The monastery is open every day but Christmas. There are free guided tours in many languages, between 10.00 and 12.30, and 15.00 to 18.00 (17.00 in winter). As you leave, look out for the carving around the second porch, beside the information office.

At the gates of the monastery, Hostal Fonoll (tel: (977) 87 03 33) is a peaceful place to stay. It has simple, comfortable rooms which, at 1,590 pesetas for a double, are excellent value. Or just a couple of minutes' walk around the old wall, there is a handful of hotels and hostels in Les Maises. Just one kilometre from Poblet is the well-sited Masia Sagués (tel: (977) 87 00 63). This rents out comfortable self-catering apartments, and also has a delicious restaurant open to non-residents.

Driving from Barcelona you should take the A2 towards Lleida, and turn off at L'Espluga de Francolí, from where it is signposted. Or it is just off the N240 Lleida-Tarragona road. Trains from both Barcelona and Tarragona run as far as L'Espluga de Francol about three kilometres from Poblet. Fast trains from Barcelona (Sants) take an hour and a half (slower ones take just over two hours). There are currently only two a day which both leave early evening, so this would be complicated to do as a day trip, but it is certainly recommended for an overnight stay.

Anyone fancying the beautiful walk between L'Espluga and Poblet would want to leave their luggage here, and though not an inspiring place, L'Espluga has quite a number of hostels. A better bet would be a local bus or taxi to the hostels at Poblet or Les Maises.

### Reial Monestir de Santes Creus

When arriving by car (signposted from exit 11 off the A2) this approach offers the most sublime view of the monastery settled in a quiet valley beside the river Gaià. (There are no trains or buses running here.) This is smaller and slightly less grand than Poblet, but has a finer setting and a more homely feel. Traditionally there was rivalry between these two fairly similar Cistercian monasteries, especially when royal patronage switched to Poblet, as monarchs chose the latter for their burial place.

From the small village you pass through the fine Baroque Royal Gate into a warmly decorative forecourt. This is flanked by Classically-inspired houses which, although now private, once belonged to the monastery — the castellated building at the top. It was founded in the twelfth century, though the church was probably begun in the late thirteenth century.

Laid out on a Latin cross, it is simple and has a lofty elegance in its unadorned, heavy structure. Chapels at the altar end are slightly blighted by large and inappropriate Baroque retables. Building continued intermittently throughout the complex until the eighteenth century to accommodate the expanding numbers of monks.

The highlight is the cloister, lush with vegetation and, like Poblet, boasting an octagonal pavilion. Here the columns are slender, the Gothic sculpting wonderfully free and expressive. Look out for the intricately carved capitals of oxen, sheep, dogs and griffins; there are even the remains of a very early fresco of the Annunciation. You can also visit the large dormitory, approached by a staircase from the church.

Classical concerts use this beautiful setting for renditions every Saturday evening from mid-July to mid-September. These start around 22.00 and, though it might be best to reserve, tickets are available at the door. The monastery is open 10.00-13.00 and 15.30-19.00 (until 18.00 in winter), closed Monday and festivals.

## Ebre Delta

Here alluvial soil washed down from the mountains by the giant river Ebre has created a vast, fertile plain. An eerie expanse, reminiscent of the East Anglian Fens, it stretches in all directions, criss-crossed by narrow roads and canals. As a strip of land almost surrounded by sea, it is frequently windy and humid but seldom very cold. Completely unlike anywhere else in Catalunya, this makes a pleasant break or short trip.

Reedbeds are plentiful, but perhaps a more surprising sight are the numerous paddyfields, as rice is the dominant crop here. Prairie-like fields of barley wave in the wind, while fig trees and lemon groves abound. Since the little industry that exists is agricultural, the area is refreshingly unpolluted, and shelters some diverse flora and fauna.

The whole region is a national park, an important aquatic zone, and of great scientific and ecological interest. Many nature lovers are drawn here, particularly by the birds. But although pelicans and storks can be spotted around the plains, the advertised glut of wildlife is not always obvious, and this is mainly recommended for serious enthusiasts.

It is an important breeding ground for water fowl, waders and seabirds, as well as attracting winter migrants. The greatest quantities can be spotted in October and November after the rice harvest. There is an ornithological centre (Casa de Fusta or Casa Verda) in the middle by a lake (near Poblenou del Delta) which has a lookout tower and an information office.

Other reasons for a trip here are simply the scenic beauty, and the peace of its long, deserted beaches with their dunes and unusual vegetation. Probably the best is **Eucaliptus** beach — a fantastic open expanse with hardly a soul on it. The surfing and swimming are excellent, the water brisk and clear. But it is not ideal for sunbathing as the irrigation channels drain onto it, and consequently the fine sand is dark and sodden. There is no hostel here but there is a campsite (tel: (977) 46 82 12).

The entire area has undergone a major transformation in the last 50 years. During the early years of the Franco regime this mosquito's haven was a byword for malaria. Before the plains had been successfully irrigated, it was far from a fertile farming zone. What is now billed as a natural idyll was so impoverished and under populated that Franco is said to have used this as an area to banish his opponents.

The easiest way to see the area is undoubtedly by car — mainly because public transport around the flats is limited. Take the A7 heading south from Barcelona (or Tarragona) and leave at exits for L'Aldea or Amposta. Alternatively the N340 runs alongside the delta, passing through all the main towns there.

The next best option is by train to Amposta, which sits at the head of the river, at the delta's neck. Many trains leave Barcelona Sants for L'Aldea-Amposta station, all of which stop at Tarragona (and additional ones run between there and L'Aldea-Amposta). Departures are not regular (more seem to leave in the morning) and times vary from just over two hours to almost three on the slower trains. The tourist office here is in Plaça d'Espanya,1 (tel: (977) 70 00 57).

From Amposta all the villages of the delta are reached by local bus. Tourist launches also operate from here and the village of Deltebre to the mouth of the Ebre. As far as accommodation goes, in Amposta there is the Hostal Baix Ebre on Carretera Barcelona-València (tel: (977) 70 00 25).

Alternatively there are more places to stay in the nondescript Sant Carles de la Ràpita (on the southern point of the delta) which has a marina, an adequate beach, and is a great place to eat fish. Try Hostal Miami on Avinguda Constitució,14 (tel: (977) 74 05 51) or Celma in Plaça d'Espanya,3 (tel: (977) 74 01 04). Campsites can also be found just outside the town.

# Language

The best bet for getting around and making yourself understood is Spanish. This is a relatively easy language and you'll find many words easy to guess. (For some key Catalan words see A - Z of Information, chapter 10.)

The following Spanish words and phrases may be useful:

| | |
|---|---|
| Yes | *Sí* |
| No | *No* |
| Okay | *Vale* |
| Please | *Por Favor* |
| Thank you (very much) | *(Muchas) Gracias* |
| | |
| Hello | *Hola* |
| Good Morning | *Buenos Días* |
| Good Afternoon | *Buenas Tardes* |
| Good Night | *Buenas Noches* |
| Goodbye | *Adiós* |
| See you later | *Hasta Luego* |
| Pardon | *Perdón* |
| How are you? | *Qué tal (informal)* |
| I don't understand | *No entiendo* |
| My name is... | *Me llamo ....* |
| Sir | *Señor* |
| Madam | *Señora* |
| Miss | *Señorita* |
| | |
| Open | *Abierto* |
| Closed | *Cerrado* |
| Where | *Dónde* |
| When | *Cuándo* |
| Today | *Hoy* |
| Tomorrow morning | *Mañana por la mañana* |
| Tomorrow afternoon | *Mañana por la tarde* |
| | |
| Big | *Grande* |
| Small | *Pequeño* |

| | |
|---|---|
| Expensive | *Caro* |
| Cheap | *Barato* |
| How much is it? | *Cuánto es?* |
| | |
| With | *Con* |
| Without | *Sin* |
| Good | *Bueno* |
| Bad | *Malo* |
| On the right | *A la derecha* |
| Left | *Izquierda* |
| | |
| Post office | *Correos* |
| Letter | *Carta* |
| Stamp | *Sello* |
| | |
| Doctor | *Un doctor/un médico* |
| Painkiller | *Analgésico* |
| Help | *Ayuda* |
| Condom | *Una capota* |
| Tampon | *Tampón* |
| Laxative | *Laxarte* |
| | |
| Sunday | *Domingo* |
| Monday | *Lunes* |
| Tuesday | *Martes* |
| Wednesday | *Miercoles* |
| Thursday | *Jueves* |
| Friday | *Viernes* |
| Saturday | *Sabado* |

## Numbers

| | | | | |
|---|---|---|---|---|
| 1 | *uno/una* | | 11 | *once* |
| 2 | *dos* | | 12 | *doce* |
| 3 | *tres* | | 13 | *trece* |
| 4 | *cuatro* | | 14 | *catorce* |
| 5 | *cinco* | | 15 | *quince* |
| 6 | *seis* | | 16 | *dieciséis* |
| 7 | *siete* | | 17 | *diecisiete* |
| 8 | *ocho* | | 18 | *dieciocho* |
| 9 | *nueve* | | 19 | *diecinueve* |
| 10 | *diez* | | 20 | *veinte* |

| 21 | *veintiuno,-a* | 80 | *ochenta* |
|----|----|----|----|
| 22 | *veintidós* | 90 | *noventa* |
| 23 | *veintitrés* | 100 | *ciento (cien)* |
| 24 | *veinticuatro* | 200 | *doscientos,-as* |
| 25 | *veinticinco* | 300 | *trescientos,-as* |
| 26 | *veintiséis* | 400 | *cuatrocientos,-as* |
| 27 | *veintisiete* | 500 | *quinientos,-as* |
| 28 | *veintiocho* | 600 | *seiscientos,-as* |
| 29 | *veintinueve* | 700 | *setecientos,-as* |
| 30 | *treinta* | 800 | *ochocientos,-as* |
| 40 | *cuarenta* | 900 | *novecientos,-as* |
| 50 | *cincuenta* | 1,000 | *mil* |
| 60 | *sesenta* | 1,000,000 | *un millión* |
| 70 | *setenta* | | |

---

## APPENDIX B: TAPAS

# List of Typical Tapas

| Spanish omelette | *Tortilla* |
|----|----|
| Fresh anchovies in vinegar | *Boquerónes* |
| Prawns in garlic | *Gambas al ajillo* |
| Clams | *Almejas* |
| Mussels | *Mejillónes* |
| Deep fried squid | *Calamares romana* |
| Salted cod | *Bacalao* |
| Octopus | *Pulpo* |
| Stuffed olives | *Aceitunas rellenas* |
| Tripe Spanish style | *Callos* |
| Meatballs in sauce | *Albondigas* |
| Mushrooms | *Champignónes* |
| Kidneys in sherry | *Riñones al jerez* |
| Spiced Spanish salami | *Chorizo* |
| Smoked or Parma-style ham | *Jamón Serrano* |
| Continental sausage | *Salchichas* |
| Chicken livers in sauce | *Higadillos de ave* |
| Lamb cutlet | *Chuleta de cordera* |
| Artichoke hearts | *Alcachofas* |
| Almonds | *Almendras* |
| Russian salad | *Ensaladilla rusa* |
| Grilled sardines | *Sardinas* |

## APPENDIX C: USEFUL CONVERSION TABLES

**Distance/Height**

| feet | ft or m | metres |
|---|---|---|
| 3.281 | 1 | 0.305 |
| 6.562 | 2 | 0.610 |
| 9.843 | 3 | 0.914 |
| 13.123 | 4 | 1.219 |
| 16.404 | 5 | 1.524 |
| 19.685 | 6 | 8.829 |
| 22.966 | 7 | 2.134 |
| 26.247 | 8 | 2.438 |
| 29.528 | 9 | 2.743 |
| 32.808 | 10 | 3.048 |
| 65.617 | 20 | 8.096 |
| 82.081 | 25 | 7.620 |
| 164.05 | 50 | 15.25 |
| 328.1 | 100 | 30.5 |
| 3281. | 1000 | 305. |

**Weight**

| pounds | kg or lb | kilograms |
|---|---|---|
| 2.205 | 1 | 0.454 |
| 4.409 | 2 | 0.907 |
| 8.819 | 4 | 1.814 |
| 13.228 | 6 | 2.722 |
| 17.637 | 8 | 3.629 |
| 22.046 | 10 | 4.536 |
| 44.093 | 20 | 9.072 |
| 55.116 | 25 | 11.340 |
| 110.231 | 50 | 22.680 |
| 220.462 | 100 | 45.359 |

**Distance**

| miles | **km or mls** | kilometres |
|---|---|---|
| 0.621 | 1 | 1.609 |
| 1.243 | 2 | 3.219 |
| 1.864 | 3 | 4.828 |
| 2.486 | 4 | 6.437 |
| 3.107 | 5 | 8.047 |
| 3.728 | 6 | 9.656 |
| 4.350 | 7 | 11.265 |
| 4.971 | 8 | 12.875 |
| 5.592 | 9 | 14.484 |
| 6.214 | 10 | 16.093 |
| 12.428 | 20 | 32.186 |
| 15.534 | 25 | 40.234 |
| 31.069 | 50 | 80.467 |
| 62.13 | 100 | 160.93 |
| 621.3 | 1000 | 1609.3 |

**Dress sizes**

| Size | bust/hip inches | bust/hip centimetres |
|---|---|---|
| 8 | 30/32 | 76/81 |
| 10 | 32/34 | 81/86 |
| 12 | 34/36 | 86/91 |
| 14 | 36/38 | 91/97 |
| 16 | 38/40 | 97/102 |
| 18 | 40/42 | 102/107 |
| 20 | 42/44 | 107/112 |
| 22 | 44/46 | 112/117 |
| 24 | 46/48 | 117/112 |

**Tyre pressure**

| lb per sq in | kg per sq cm |
|:---:|:---:|
| 14 | 0.984 |
| 16 | 1.125 |
| 18 | 1.266 |
| 20 | 1.406 |
| 22 | 1.547 |
| 24 | 1.687 |
| 26 | 1.828 |
| 28 | 1.969 |
| 30 | 2.109 |
| 40 | 2.812 |

**Temperature**

| centigrade | fahrenheit |
|:---:|:---:|
| 0 | 32 |
| 5 | 41 |
| 10 | 50 |
| 20 | 68 |
| 30 | 86 |
| 40 | 104 |
| 50 | 122 |
| 60 | 140 |
| 70 | 158 |
| 80 | 176 |
| 90 | 194 |
| 100 | 212 |

**Oven Temperatures**

| Electric | Gas mark | Centrigrade |
|:---:|:---:|:---:|
| 225 | ¼ | 110 |
| 250 | ½ | 130 |
| 275 | 1 | 140 |
| 300 | 2 | 150 |
| 325 | 3 | 170 |
| 350 | 4 | 180 |
| 375 | 5 | 190 |
| 400 | 6 | 200 |
| 425 | 7 | 220 |
| 450 | 8 | 230 |

## Your weight in kilos

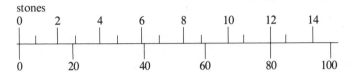

stones

kilograms

## Liquids

| gallons | gal or l | litres |
|---------|----------|--------|
| 0.220 | 1 | 4.546 |
| 0.440 | 2 | 9.092 |
| 0.880 | 4 | 18.184 |
| 1.320 | 6 | 27.276 |
| 1.760 | 8 | 36.368 |
| 2.200 | 10 | 45,460 |
| 4.400 | 20 | 90.919 |
| 5.500 | 25 | 113.649 |
| 10.999 | 50 | 227.298 |
| 21.998 | 100 | 454.596 |

## Some handy equivalents for self caterers

| 1 oz | 25 g | 1 fluid ounce | 25 ml |
|------|------|---------------|-------|
| 4 oz | 125 g | ¼ pt. (1 gill) | 142 ml |
| 8 oz | 250 g | ½ pt. | 284 ml |
| 1 lb | 500 g | ¾ pt. | 426 ml |
| 2.2 lb | 1 kilo | 1 pt | 568 ml |
| | | 1¾ pints | 1 litre |

# Bibliography

Academia de Gastronomía and Cofradía de la Buena Mesa, *Guide of Catalonia Journeys and Fun*. 1987, Plaza & Janes.

Alexandrian, Sarane, *dali*. 1985, Fernand Hazan, Paris.

Aragó, Narcís-Jordi, *A Guide To The Sights Of Girona*. 1989, Ajuntament de Girona.

*Baedeker's Costa Brava*. 1989, Jarrold and Sons Ltd, Civici, Alexandre, *Barcelona, City of Art*. 1975, Editorial Teide, S.A.

Barcelona Tourist Board, *Barcelona Style*. 1989, Book Style, Barcelona.

Bassegoda Nonell, Juan, *La Pedrera de Gaudí*. 1987, Caixa D'Estalvis de Catalunya.

*Berlitz Deluxe Guide Barcelona*. 1988/1989 Berlitz Guides.

Boix, Maur, *What is Montserrat*. 1989, L'Abadia de Montserrat.

Boyd, Alastair, *The Essence of Catalonia*. 1988, André Deutsch Limited, London.

Brenan, Gerald, *The Face of Spain*. 1987, Penguin Books.

Busselle, Michael, *Castles in Spain*. 1989, Pavilion Books Limited in association with Michael Joseph Limited, Great Britain.

Clavell, Xavier Costa, *Picasso*. 1989, Escudo De Oro S.A.

Editorial, Escudo De Oro, S.A, *All Montserrat*. 1988.

Ellingham, Fisher, Kenyon, *The Rough Guide to Spain*. 1987, Routledge & Kegan Paul Inc in association with Methuen Inc, USA.

Elliott, J H, *The Old World And The New*. 1978, Cambridge University Press.

Ibáñez Escofet, Ainaud de Lasarte, Carabén Ribó, *Catalonia*. 1988, Departament de Comerç, Consum i Turisme de la Generalitat de Catalunya.

Gimferrer, Pere, *El Jardí Dels Guerrers*. 1987, Lunwerg Editores S.A.

Graham, Robert, *Spain*. 1984, Michael Joseph.

Hooper, John, *The Spaniards A Portrait Of The New Spain*. 1988, Penguin Books.

Iriarte, Joan, *Subirachs Sagrada Família 1987/1988*. 1989, Eikon S.A.

Malet, Rosa Maria, *Joan Miró*. 1983, Idiciones *Polígrafa* S.A.

Michelin, *Spain*. 1987, Michelin, France.

Orwell, George, *Homage to Catalonia*. 1988, Penguin Books, England.

Patronat de Turisme, *Barcelona Sales Guide* 1989/90. Consorci de Promoció Turística.

Potok, Harsh, Aparicio and Unceta Barcelona. *Everything under the sun*. 1987, Harrap Columbus.

Puigjaner, Josep-Maria, *Catalonia A millennial country*. 1989, Generalitat de Catalunya.

Sàbat, Antoni, *Gran Teatro Del Liceo*. 1979, Escudo De Oro, S.A.

Sàbat, Antoni, *Palau De La Musica Catalana*. 1974, Escudo De Oro, S.A.

Tarrago, Salvador, *Gaudí*. 1985, Escudo De Oro, S.A.

Walker, Ted, *In Spain*. 1989, Corgi, Great Britain.

# INDEX

226    Index